53 Years Of Passion
Love And Dedication
Of German Shorthaired Pointers

R Leick

53 Years Of Passion Love And Dedication
Of German Shorthaired Pointers

Ruby Field

authorHOUSE®

AuthorHouse™ UK Ltd.
1663 Liberty Drive
Bloomington, IN 47403 USA
www.authorhouse.co.uk
Phone: 0800.197.4150

Published by AuthorHouse   07/07/2014

ISBN: 978-1-4918-9408-8 (sc)
ISBN: 978-1-4918-9406-4 (hc)
ISBN: 978-1-4918-9409-5 (e)

Deepthatch GSP's

About Us

The Deepthatch Kennel originated from Dina of Kieve (left-click to enlarge picture) and Windlehill Breeding. The Windlehill affix belonged to Mrs Bibby (Ruby's Aunt).

Over the years there have been eight Dual Champions in England. These following dogs all link back to the successful Windlehill Kennel and the bitch, Dina of Kieve.

- Dual Champion Inchmarlo Griff Graff of Prarau
- Dual Champion Matham Dark Claret of Trolanda
- Dual Champion Swifthouse Tufty
- Dual Champion Geramers Shannon
- Dual Champion Geramers Victress of Swifthouse
- Dual Champion Stairfoot Sobrig
- Dual Champion Keldy White Knight
- Dual Champion Swifthouse Blethchington

Mrs Bibby was like a mother to us, and because of her we had our own GSP in 1963, which was Weekend Mist. A son of Mist was mated to a bitch who brought back some of the Windlehill, Baronet and Dinah lines into the pedigree. This produced Jason of St Andrews (Field Trial and Show Winner). Then came Deepthatch Cinnamon, Deepthatch Driftwood and Deepthatch Doublet.

To become an English Field Trial Champion you have to qualify through from Novice, all age, and then win 2 Open Stakes.

In the USA a Master Hunter Certificate is the highest award to be won in Hunting Tests. This is the nearest award to a British Field Trial Champion. They are run in a brace on Quail and Chukka, and have to pass 6 times under different judges in aspects of hunting, pointing, trainability, retrieving and honouring each other when on point and retrieving birds. They must be steady whilst on point and retrieving. A Junior Hunter is the first award, followed by Master Hunter.

Our son Karl has been involved with the dogs since a youngster, and as he grew up was very successful. He is pictured having achieved shooting left and right on Woodcocks. To become a member of the Woodcock club you achievement must be witnessed by 2 other people. This is sent off to Shooting Times and you become a member. Karl became a member at just 13 years old. He shoots over the dogs with Jim and as a youngster handled a Driftwood Daughter in Junior Handling Classes. Karl worked hard through college and university for many years to become an electrical engineer with his own business, which enables him to continue with his shooting. He has qualified for the English Fitase team, who just recently won the Gold medal at the International Fitase Competition in Norfolk.

Nowadays we continue to work our dogs, as well as showing them throughout the year. Our newest addition Deepthatch Lexi won her first Working Test at 15months and won the puppy class at Crufts 2006. You can see more pictures of dogs past and present on the Photos Page.

Deepthatch GSP's

Welcome to Deepthatch Dual Purpose German Shorthaired Pointers

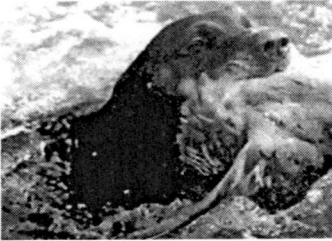

We have owned GSP's since 1954 and still take part in shows, Working Tests and Field Trials. Our Dogs are full of GSP type, brains, beauty and temperament, which are second to none. All our dogs have clear heart and eye tests.

We have both judged around the world and over the years the breed has filled our hearts with special things.

We produce dual purpose dogs and have bred and proved it, owning and training generations to win at Crufts and in field trials and tests.

We hope you enjoy your visit to our site and look forward to hearing from you soon. Above photo by Nick Ridley

Jim and Ruby Field

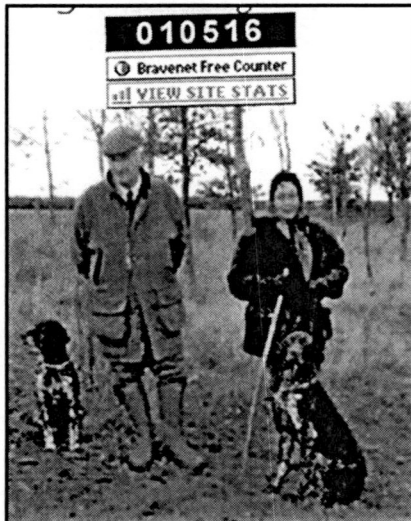

Deepthatch German Shorthaired Pointers

DINAH OF KIEVE

Under the Duals that are from Dinah

With Pups 1954. DECENDENTS FROM DINA OF KIEVE, ALSO ADAM
OF WINDELHILL MATED ARODESEL WREN SENT TO NZ TO MR
JACK DAWSON PRODUCED ALL THE VORSTERHUND DOGS FIELD
AND SHOW EARLY 1960.S SKYLARK GISSELLE BUSHWACKER AND
MELLODEE AND THERE OFF SPRING PRODUCED FIELD AND SHOW
CHAMPIONS THEY ARE BEHIND MANY BREEDERS IN NZ AND
AUSTRALIAN SADLY JACK DAWSON DIED A FEW YEARS BACK

Subject: birth of puppies

Date: Thursday, 21 February 2013, 20:51

about 10 DAYS OLD GSP OPENS THERE EYES////

Subject: birth of PUPPIES

Date: Friday, 14 December 2012, 16:45

WHEN PUPPIES ARE COMING HELP MUM AND WHEN PUPPY BEEN BORN HELP MUM IF SHE IS STUGGLING CUT THE CORD

FOR HER WITHCLEAN STERILE BABY SCISSORS. DRY PUP AND PUT TO MUMS TEAT FOR A DRINK MAYBE 10 MINUITES

LATER ANOTHER PUPPY BEING BORN SAME APPLIES TO EACH PUPPY THEN TAKE FIRST BORN WEIGH AND SEE IF DOG

OR BITCH HAVE A SMALL BOX NEAR MUM WITH HOT WATER BOTTLE COVERED WITH A TOWEL. OR SMALL PIECE OF VET BED PUT PUPPS ON THIS WHILE ANOTHERS BEING BORN. PUT PLENTY OLD TOWELS AT THE BOTTOM OF MUM AS LOTS

OF FLUID AND AFTER BIRTH COMES WITH BIRTH OF PUPPY THEY ARE USUALLY BORN HEAD FIRST BREAK THE BIRTH SACK

CLEAN THERE MOUTH AND HOLD UPSIDE DOWN MOVE PUP FROM SIDE TO SIDE TO CLEAR AIRWAVES AND LUNGS

WHEN MUMS FINISHED MAKE HER CLEAN BED PUT ALL PUPPS TO HER TO FEED MAKE SURE THEY ARE ALL SUCKING WELL

GIVE MUM SOME WATER AND MILK WITH SOME GLUCOSE IN MAKE SURE SHE IS HAPPY WITH PUPS AND THEY ARE CONTENTED

THEN NEXT DAY MAKE SURE THEY ARE GOING TO TOILET FINE AND ALL IS WELL AND MUM DONT LIE ON THEM AT THREE DAYS

OLD YOU TAKE TO VET HAVE TAILS DOCKED DEW CLAWS REMOVED WHEN PUPS ARE GETTING STRONGER AND MOVING

ABOUT WEIGH THEM CHECK TO SEE THERE PROGRESS PUT ANOTHER DOG BED SIDE OF THEM SO MUM CAN REST

IN THERE BUT KEEP HER EYE ON THE PUPS ABOUT 10 DAYS OLD THERE EYES OPEN AND THEY EXPLORE AND PLAY WITH EACH OTHER.

AT ABOUT THREE WEEKS OLD I MAKE SOME READY BREAK LET THEM EXPLORE IT DIP. MY FINGER IN IT AND LET EACH PUP LICK IT

THIS WILL LEARN THEM TO LAP UP. AFTER I INTRODUCED THIS MADE SURE THEY HAVE DIGESTED IT ALRIGHT I INTRODUCE SOME SCRAMBLED. EGGS. STILL HAVING SOME MILK FROM MUM MADE READY BREAK WITH FRESH MILK OR GOATS MILK AND A LITTLE GLUCOSE

AFTER ANOTHER WEEK I MASH SOME SARDINES AND THEN SOME PILCHARDS IN TOMATO SAUCE THEY SOON LAP UP.

THOSE ARE BRAIN FOOD/// ALTERNATIVELY THEY HAVE ALL THESE FOODS THEN I COOK CHICKEN MAKE BROTH WITH IT

AND ROYAL CANIN STARTER FOOD MEAL. AND MINCED BEEF AT ABOUT SIX WEEKS OLD I LET MUM SLEEP BY HER SELF

BUT SHE CAN SEE PUPS AND GET TO THEM IF SHE WISHES PUPS HAVE SNOWSILK BED KENNEL ALL WASHABLE AND

VET BED TO LIE AND SLEEP ON AND A HEAT LAMP OVER THEM. IF NOT WARM ENOUGH WHEN I TAKE TO VETS FOR TAILS DEW CLAWS OR MICRO CHIP I TAKE A SMALL BOX WITH HOT WATER BOTTLE IN COVERED WITH A TOWEL OR VET BED.

TO KEEP PUPS WARM THEY SHOULD BE AROUND 60 FARENITE THEY ARE EXPLORING AROUND THEM BY THIS AGE AROUND THE GARDEN ETCALL ENCLOSED IN. THEY PLAY EAT AND GO TO SLEEP.

I ENCOURAGE THEM TO RETRIEVE FURRY ANIMALS /. THROW SOME CUBED CHEESE TO SEE THERE NOSES AND THEY LOVE CHEESE //

IF NICE WEATHER PUT THERE FOOD DOWN ON GRASS PUT THEM ALL AROUND IT TO EAT THIS WILL ENCOURAGE THEM TO GO TO TOILET ON GRASS REPEAT THIS UNTILL THEY GO TO THERE NEW HOMES.

Name of Dog Ch. Inchmarlo Raphoe
Sire Karl Breeder Mr. I.E.T. Sladden
Dam Ch. Inchmarlo Cora Owner/s Mr. I.E.T. Sladden
Date of Birth 6.3.71

Saltus v.d. Forst Brickwedde

Name of Dog Ch. Ferrier Jaegar
Sire Ch. Nevern Jasper Breeder Lord Ferrier
Dam Bramble of Windlehill Owner/s Mr. M. Meredith Hardy
Date of Birth 1.5.58

arko vom heidfeld

Major General Palmer who became the Club's first Vice-President in those early days is still a member and a Vice-President.

This 'At Home' was followed by a Test Trial and Rally at Ashvale on 26th September, 1953, at which there were four categories for the 27 dogs entered. Results:—Dog, Bitch and Puppy Conformation, Dog, Blitz of Longsutton; Bitch, Lt. Col. Reynold's Inge of Bengarth; Puppy, Sqdn. Ldr. (now Air Vice-Marshal) D.W. Atkinson's Nevern Jasper. Handler's Control, Blitz of Longsutton, Test Trial, Blitz of Longsutton tied with Arko v. Heidfeld

It was in 1953 that Mr. & Mrs. Sterne made a tour from their home in Longsutton to as far north as Scotland, covering 1,680 miles in 13 days and seeing 18 dogs plus an assortment of owners—one of whom thought he had an English Pointer and could not understand where the other half of the dog's tail had got to! (in 1962 a man registered his Weimeraner as a German Shorthaired Pointer and wondered why the other German Shorthaired Pointers had spots) Arising out of the many questions asked about the training, conformation and breeding of German Shorthaired Pointer the first number of 'The German Shorthaired Pointer—Retriever News' was published in January 1954, and continued to be published three times a year until the autumn of 1958. This publication was followed by News Letters and from 1961 to 1972 a Year Book. The production of the year book had become too costly, so once again News Sheets were produced to keep members informed about the breed On the 4th September, 1954 the first Club Field Trial was held at Brandsby Hall, Yorks. There were 21 entries Results:—Test Trial: 1st Nevern Jasper 2nd Blitz of Longsutton; 3rd Max of Phillimore; Reserve Nevern Aurora.

Name of Dog Ch. Springfarm Sandpiper
Sire Ch. Nevern Jasper Breeder Mrs. Johnson
Dam Niccola of Stockhill Owner/s Miss Curtis (now Mrs. Pruce)
Date of Birth 12.4.56

Afra v.d. Brille

Name of Dog Sh. Ch. Adrem Venus
Sire Sh.Ch. Jason of Caesaromagus Breeder Mrs. J. Thackery
Dam Keephatch Pearl Owner/s Mrs. J. Thackery
Date of Birth 15.1.68

Subject: wins c la game fair basc international weekend

Date: Saturday, 6 April 2013, 16:27

we continue to show and work our gsps working test field trials as to date membership in the old days 1956 was 1 pound 10 shillings that was insurance included the first to be registared was hektor 1 born 1872 berlin 1880 first time i entered the ring exhibitig my shorthair was in sixties at handsworth park everyone those days were vetted with vet efore you entered the show//// here are some exhibits at show in open dog top was miss wards

ch patrick of malahide next heeleys max of berolina 3rd was messigner with fritz of prara next ian sladden with griff

graf of prara then myself r field with week end mist then mrs danniels with sh ch danpoint artillery. that was first solid liver gsp i had seen.

the next picture isgraham lakin with shch midlander mark anthony myselfr.field with week end mist then ian sladdenand griff graff of prara the judge was dr. gordon from usa. while i was judging gsps at paignton show

some german judges there doing golen retrievers took apicture of my line up and put in the german blatter this was sent to me and translated in english by anne spoors thankfully.

Deutsch-Kurzhaar in England

Dr. Christoph Engelhardt, 1. Vorsitzender des Deutschen Retriever Clubs e.V., war im Juli vergangenen Jahres auf einer der größten englischen Zuchtschauen in Exeter. Hier sein kurzer Bericht (s. auch Foto), den er den "Kurzhaar-Blättern" freundlicherweise zur Verfügung stellte.

Subject: socialising and feed for pups

Date: Wednesday, 23 January 2013 19:40

IS EXAMENED FOR MOTH DENTITION D'MALES HAVE TWO TESTICLES DOWN IN SCOTRUM OR YOU CAN FEEL 2 JUST ABOUT TO ENTER THE SCOTRUM NEVER FEED DRIED FOOD ON ITS OWN ALWAYS PUT YOGOURT OR SARDINES DOG TIN FOOD. SOME MEAT AND VEG// AS FEED ALONE CAN GIVE THEM BLOAT//// HARD FOR PUPS TO DIGEST ON HEART KIDNEY AND DIGESTIVE SYSTEM/// THEN WHEN NICE WEATHER TAKE YOUR PUP TO WATER A GOOD ENTRY . . . HELPS HAVING AN ADULT WHO LIKES AND ENTERS. WATER FREELY PUT PUPS DUMMY ON ALONG CORD SIT YOUR PUP PLAY WITH HER WITH THE DUMMY THEN THROW IN WATER SEND HER TO FETCH DONT WORRY AT THIS STAGE STEADINESS AND DELIVERING TO HAND KEEP SENDING THE DUMMY AND CORD A LITTLE FURTHER EACH TIME TO GET PUP SWIMMING AND ENJOYING IT IF YOUR DOGS NOT STEDY ON RETRIEVING PUT ON ALONG LINE YOU AT THE CONTROL AT END SEND PUP FOR RETRIEVE IF ITS NOT STEADY GOES TO RETRIEVE. BEFOREYOU SAID PULL IT BACK AND PUT BACK IN THERE POSITION AND REPEAT THE RETRIEVE AGAIN

Subject: birth of puppies

Date: Friday, 18 January 2013, 12:53

MAKE NOISE OVER THE PUPS LOOK AT THEM TO MAKE EYE CONTACT WITH YOU MAKE THEM STAND BE HANDLED TO STAND TAKE PICTURE. AT ABOUT 4 WEEKS OLD TEACH THEM TO RETRIEVE AND FETCH A FLUFFY TOY LIKE A PLAYFULL GAME/ HAVE EACH ONE ON SOFT LEATHER LEAD TO GET THEM USED TO SOMETHING AROUND THERE NECK. WALK WITH

THEM AND BACK IN GARDEN THEY ARE WORMED WITH DRONITAL SOLUTION AT 3 AND 5 AND 7 WEEKS OLD.
I
I GIVE EVERT 2 WEEKS AS ANY EGGS THERE IF THEY HAVE WORMS LUCKLY I HAVE NEVER SEEN THEM HAVE WORMS

PUPPS GOING TO THERE NEW HOMES THEY ALL HAVE A NEW PIECE OF VET BED DRONITAL SOLUTION WORMING LIQID AN
AND ROYAL CANIN STARTER FOOD TIN SARDINES AND DOG FOOD AND DIET SHEET.

learning yor dog right left and back

sit your dog in front of you about 3yards away making the dog keep
eye contact with you place adummy to the right hand side of dog . . .
come back in front of the dog making sure dog keps eye contact
with you and put your right hand up in the air make sure dog has
eye contact with you then just point your right hand to retrieve. dog
retrieves come back to handler . . . make sitting position again in
front of you and place retrieve to the left come back to be in front of
your dog make sure dog has eye contact with you . . . put left hand
in the air make sure dog looks at you pause for awhile then point
your hand to the left for dog to retrieve .back to you . . . making
the dog sit in front of you dog keping eye contact on you turn dog
around to let it see you place to the back of dog . . . turn to face
you . . . and send dog . . . saying get back fetch ad dog returns to yu
with retrieve praise your dog and stroke down its front and praise
it . . . .

teach your dog to retrieving fur for first time . . .

show your dog rabbit let it smell and investige rabbit you holding in
your hand the whole time . . . sit your dog and say stay and walk
away to place rabbit for dog to retrieve go back to dog and send
your dog to tetrievethe rabbit . . .to you no problem . . .//

Weekend Monsieur

2 awards in Field Trials at Ford. Won first Weimeraner Field
Trial. Produced 2 RCC Winners. Took 2 firsts at Crufts. RCC at
Bournemouth, BOB at Leeds and was the first GSP to win AV
Working Test (no classes for HPR's in those days)

Deepthatch German Shorthaired Pointers

Deepthatch GSP's Photographs

Nouvelle Lexi

Reserve CC Winner at SWKA under Judge Mary Small. August 2006

2nd Official Puppy Test Working Trial

1st Post Graduate Bitch GSP Champ Show 2006

2nd in Special puppy at Crufts 2005 under Maureen Nixon

HANDLER OF THE YEAR MR FIELD WITH TROPHY FOR HANDLER OF THE YEAR

Monday, 13 May, 2013 21:00

From: "RUBY FIELD"

//////

Subject: wins c la game fair basc international weekend

Date: Saturday, 6 April 2013, 16:27

we continue to show and work our gsps working test field trialsas to date membership in the old days 1956 was 1pound 10 shillings that was insurance included the first to be registared was hektor 1 born 1872 berlin 1880
first time i entered the ring exhibitig my shorthair was in sixties at handsworth park everyone those days were vetted with vet efore you entered the show//// here are some exhibits at show in open dog top was miss wards

ch patrick of malahide next heeleys max of berolina 3rd was messigner with fritz of prara next ian slddeb with griff

graf of prara then myself r field with week end mist then mrs danniels with sh ch danpoint artillery.that was first solid liver gsp i had seen.

the next picture isgraham lakin with shch midlander mark anthony myselfr.field with week end mist then ian slddenand griff graff of prara the judge was dr. gordon from usa. while i was judging gsps at paignton show

some german judges there doing golen retrievers took apicture of my line up and put in the german blatter this was sent to me and translated in english by anne spoors thankfully.

1966 German Pointer at Handsworth Park

FIELD TRIALS

HERE ARE SOME PICTURES OF FIELD TRIAL AT HAMBLEDON JIM GOT GROUND FOR GSP CLUB TWICE AND GSPA CLUB LEFT TO RIGHT RICHARD KUBANJUDGE JIM FIELD JUDGE DAVID LAYTON WITH MIDLANDER SIRUS HAMBLEDON AGAIN AGUN. AUBREY GREVVILE WILLIAMS JUDGE JIM FIELD JUDGE AGAIN LEFT TO RIGHT JERRY KEW WITH INCHMARLO DARK DAMSEL GOING TO RUN HIS DOG JUDGE AUBREY GREVILLE WILLIAMS GIVING JERRY INSTRUCTIONS OF HIS BEET TO RUN HIS DOG JUDGE JIM FIELD IN UK YOU FIELD TRIAL AND WORKING TEST SINGLY IN USA ABRACE TWO DOGS///

Crufts in DOG WORLD

—by SIMON PARSONS—

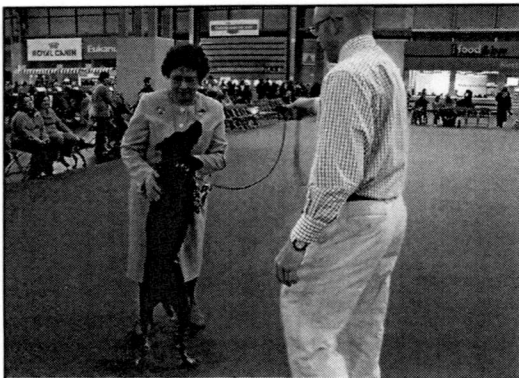

Deepthatch Nouvelle Lexi
myself and Greg Hoffester at Crufts 2010
last picture of Lexi

IT MIGHT amuse readers, and bring back happy memories for some, to look back over the years and see how DOG WORLD has covered the Crufts show over the decades.

Let's start in 1929, "the 42nd year of Cruft's, the largest dog show in the world, this year's event bigger than ever—1,492 dogs benched in the Royal Agricultural Hall, London." Note the apostrophe and note the number of dogs—who would have believed it would increase nearly 15 fold in 70 years? And there was, of course, no qualifier then.

The 'world record entry', incidentally, was 9,862—few dogs would be entered, as they are now, in just a single class. After all, there was prize money on offer, and Charles Cruft boasted that he paid more than anyone else.

The logistical difficulties of covering the show must have been enormous, for it was held on a Wednesday and Thursday and then, as now, the paper was dated Friday!

Nevertheless they managed to report fully the first day and, succeeding in getting copies available on the second day of the show at 3.30pm, an astonishing feat considering the paper was printed in Bradford, and one it would be hard to match today even with modern technology.

There was a report on Mr Cruft's invitation lunch where one of the toasts was 'The Press' (somehow I can't see the Kennel Club following suit in that respect). Apparently our own editor, Phyllis Robson "paid a tribute to Mr Cruft, who was a wise man, in that he knew the value of publicity and believed in extensive advertising, which made him very dear to the hearts of the press."

In spite of the tight deadlines, almost every breed had a critique in that week's paper, none of them, though, written by the judge, all by a ringsider appointed by the paper. I see there were classes for 'King Charles Spaniels (old type)'—Cavaliers in other words, headed by that pillar of the breed, Miss Mostyn-Walker's Ann's Son, who "in the judge's opinion was the only one that approximated to type."

There were no photos from the show, though several of the judges plus Mr and Mrs Cruft, but large pictures were given of the competitors at Wood Green and Palmers Green members' show, and of Messrs Spratt's Patent Ltd's dinner at the Great Central Hotel.

The paper itself, as today, was full of breed notes (well over a page for Alsatians), show reports, comment, ads and regional news, and a full page of 'answers to correspondents' on such questions as "Do you think a Bull Terrier would be a suitable breed for me to take to Fiji?", "You say orange juice is good for a dog who has any skin trouble. What quantity should I give my young Sealyham?" and "What is the proper size, or weight, of a Whippet?"

Robert Leighton wrote 'Notes for Novices', Mrs Robson 'Chat of the week', James Saunders gave advice for novice Dalmatian owners and J W H Beynon extolled the Japanese Chin. In 'Notabilities and their Dogs' Mrs Robson featured an opera great, Dame Clara Butt, and her husband Kennerley Rumford.

A bit of class was added to the paper with the inset of two sepia lithographs, of the Irish Setter, Ch Menaifron Pat O'Moy, and particolour Pekingese, Cha-Ming Winkle Boi.

In the following week's paper were the second day reports and news from the trade stands, but only three photos actually taken at the show, one of them a head study of a new breed, the 'Ivicine', on show at Crufts. The big mobile ears give it away as, of course, the Ibizan Hound.

The paper's leader column gave itself a pat on the back, as well it might, and explained how the staff of the proprietors, Watmough's of Idle, had succeeded in this amazing feat of production.

★   ★   ★

TEN YEARS on, and Cruft's, following Charles' death after 53 years in harness, was run by his widow, Emma. Once again it was a Wednesday-Thursday show, but this time DOG WORLD obviously waited until the whole event was over for there was a full list of CC winners, and several pictures from the show including Mrs M Sadleir arriving with a team of five Bloodhounds.

DOG WORLD's format was little different from 1929; and the fuss we make today about Crufts was scarcely in evidence—no direct mention of it until the thirty-fifth page! An interesting feature was "The dog of yesterday and to-day—progress or decline?" in which experts such as Baroness Burton, Marion Keyte-Perry and Major J Y Baldwin discussed the state of their breed. Mr Saunders gave us "More about the employer and the kennel help problem" and Mrs Robson, who managed to edit the paper throughout the war years while staying in America, was already across the Atlantic and telling readers about her Florida vacation and her deep sea fishing!

Meantime, DOG WORLD was balloting "the whole of dogdom" on "Do you want only judges' critiques on your dogs?", a significant question as most of the Crufts reports were still from ringsiders.

Unlike today there were pages and pages of classified advertisements—16 pages for puppies and stud dogs of the various breeds plus many 'situations vacant and wanted': "Gentlewoman wants country post in kennel of small dogs where own two Miniature Pekes allowed (perfect manners and quiet), experienced kennel work, car driving, good needlewoman, capable and quick working in all things," or "Mrs E G Oliver, Bedale Hall, Bedale, Yorkshire, personally recommends her kennelman, E A Hone (married, no family), to anyone requiring a thoroughly competent man; genuine dog lover; leaving owing to dispersal of kennels through death." There's a sad story there regarding the end of the great kennel of Hellingly Mastiffs following the mysterious death of Mr Oliver.

★   ★   ★

THERE WAS no Crufts in 1949 so let's go ahead a year. By now the show was run by the Kennel Club and DOG WORLD, at a cost of 5d (about 2p), was in a smaller more tabloid format. Still no front page picture of the BIS, indeed just a normal page of

BIS at Crufts ten years ago was 'Cassie', Brenda White's Bearded Collie, Ch Potterdale Classic of Moonhill. This year Brenda is one of the breed judges. photo Dalton

news, dog man's diary and a breeder's ad (in this case Donald Becker's Schnauzers), plus an item headed "Britain's Greatest Dog Show". It reads: "This is the special Cruft's show report number of the DOG WORLD. It records in word and picture one of the greatest of all shows. Judges, reporters, photographers, artists and our own editorial and printing staff, have worked together to produce this special number for dog breeders all over the world.

"In addition to readers at home, thousands of dog lovers in America will learn about Cruft's show from a special 56 page American edition of this issue.

"This week's DOG WORLD is largely devoted to the dogs which won at Cruft's. Next week in addition to some 'close up' camera studies of some of the show's big winners, we shall deal with **the dogs which did not win.** At a show of such magnitude there are many exhibits among the losers which are, nevertheless, of very high quality. There are young dogs which have to take secondary honours for no other reason than their youth. It is with such exhibits that we shall deal next week.

"This issue of the DOG WORLD marks a new high level in its circulation. Week by week more dog lovers in this country, and abroad, are becoming readers. We ask pardon for again urging everyone to place now a firm order with the newsagent for the DOG WORLD weekly."

Indeed in the following week's paper Walter Worfolk listed some of the dogs who appealed to him but who didn't win on the day. Can you imagine that today?

You had to wade through 20 pages of classifieds and news before discovering who had won BIS—Mr Lloyd's Witch, featured elsewhere in this supplement. Fred May's charming caricatures of some of the judges and personalities added a bit of fun. Most breeds had a report published in that week's issue, the big difference being that most (though not all) were now actually written by the judge. Each report was accompanied by an ad from a well-known exhibitor (not necessarily a Crufts winner).

Pictures, again, from the show were few, two pages' worth, including Raymond

Headlines from the DOG WORLD report on Crufts 1939, the first one held after the death of Charles Cruft, hence the poetic tribute.

Oppenheimer in plus fours judging Bull Terriers.

★ ★ ★

ON TO 1959 and, even though our pre-show supplement did not yet exist, much of the issue on sale at the show was devoted to Crufts-related articles—"Crufts—how it all began" in Warner Hill's *Bench & Field* column, "Charles Cruft would cry at today's 'wasted' space" by outspoken editor Leo C Wilson—really he was referring to the much-improved layout of the show—apparently old Mr Cruft had been rather stingy with ring and bench size.

"Can Cruft's model itself on America's Westminster?" asked Nigel Aubrey Jones, somewhat prophetically as a few years later Crufts did have to introduce the dreaded qualifier. "Give obedience a fairer crack of the whip," pleaded E Sandon Moss.

In the Crufts report issue itself, the front page was almost entirely devoted to a paid advertisement (featuring Mrs Anthony Blake's Smooth Fox Terrier, Ch Watteau Chorister), with the BIS winner on page 3: "Two US offers for Cruft's BIS rejected". This was the Welsh, Ch Sandstorm Saracen. There were many more photos (including the first ever Beardie CC winners, Britt and Beauty Queen of Bothkennar), and a 32-page supplement with Crufts news and show reports, plus 'Rambling Around Olympia' by Ralph Blake.

One caption read: "Few exhibitors can claim to have won their first-ever CC at Cruft's but this feat was accomplished by Miss B Osborne last Friday when her Greyhound, Treetops Ringdove, went through to BOB under Mr Leo C Wilson." The glamorous young owner is better known today as Barbara Wilton-Clark.

Then: "Cruft's investment in giving Mr J E Trigg his expenses so that he could bring his Japanese Akita, Panyau, to the show paid good dividends in the large amount of space devoted by the national press to the dog and, indirectly, to the show." How times change! Panyau, pictured with his sailor owner, looks much more like a Shiba in both size and type.

★ ★ ★

BY 1969, DOG WORLD, now based in Ashford, Kent, was back to its full size. In addition to the results issue, we now had the pre-show supplement out a week before the show, full, as is this one, of ads and information about the show.

Its main article was an interview by Dennis McCarthy with KC secretary Charles Binney in which they discussed "Criticism, democracy, judges, committees, power and shows."

"Crufts needs a stiffer qualifier," said Les Atkinson, and this was the time of the 'export drive'. At that time Ministry of Agriculture staff were present at the show to issue the necessary certificates to dogs who had been sold on the day. Sir Dudley Forwood was in charge of the overseas visitors lounge.

The last 'full' champion gundog to win BIS at Crufts was Collette and Mary Tuite's Irish Setter, Ch Astley's Portia of Rua, in 1981. Mary is one of the breed's judges this year.

photo Garwood

As for the show itself, it was the year the Queen visited, and also the year of the blizzards. The paper was full of horror stories of exhibitors' journeys to and from the show.

★   ★   ★

IN 1979 there were rumours the show, the first at Earls Court, would be cancelled, due to problems at the preceding Boat Show. "Cheer up: The show's on" we wrote the week before. Our pre-show supplement was effectively combined with what we now call *The Best of British Dogs* as the results of the 1978 Top Dog league, compiled by Bryan Mitchell, were listed.

The Feb 16 issue featured the BIS winning Kerry Blue, Ch Callaghan of Leander, on the front, and editor Ferelith Somerfield recorded the reactions to the new venue. As now, each group's success stories were featured separately, though not in such detail—who compiled the reports was not mentioned but, at my first Crufts for DW, I can remember helping the team of Feffie, Bryan, Maureen Long and Tom Horner, plus an even newer arrival, Kerry Williamson, who had an especially exciting Crufts winning her first ever CC.

We asked readers to say what they thought of the new venue, and in the following week's paper recorded the answer: "Move it to the NEC", voted 479 out of 546 who replied.

★ ★ ★

BUT TEN years on Crufts was still at Earls Court (though the move eventually came in 1991). Our issue on sale at the show featured *'Dynasty'*—a pictorial spread of the remarkable Renwick family which spawned, among many other distinguished dog people, that year's BIS judge, Lionel Hamilton Renwick.

Best of British Dogs featured Top Dogs and Stud Dogs (no Brood Bitches yet, though), and the report issue was in a similar format to that we use today. On the front, now in full colour, was the BIS ('Cassie' and Brenda White, 'the bookmakers' choice' according to Mrs Somerfield). Inside were the usual reports on all the aspects of the show, unknown in Mr Cruft's day—obedience, agility, juniors and so on. Pictures galore (though it was a pity we were unable to feature group judge Ann Wynyard's sensational purple dress in full colour), and results for every breed.

Crufts, and DOG WORLD, have come a long way.

★ ★ ★

AND SO to 1999—and at this year's show Chrissy Smith and I will compile the general news, Glen Dymock will cover the gundog group, Sally Pointon pastoral, Pam Blay working, Rose Massey toys, David Craig hounds, Michael Sarjeant terriers, Trudy Short utility, Bruce and Bronwyn Bartley obedience, Peter Lewis agility and flyball, and Averil Cawthera-Purdy juniors. See you there!

Crufts 1969—the year of the blizzard and the year the Queen visited, the only time the reigning monarch has done so, though Kennel Club president Prince Michael of Kent regularly attends, and the Princess Royal did so last year. Here the Queen and judge Fred Parsons admire a group of Clumbers: from left, Mr and Mrs Henson's Theme of Fatpastures, Mr Rostron's Alansmere Snow Gleam, Mrs Buchanan's Frastan Oberon, Mr and Mrs Stanley's Frastan Helen Of Beauty and Mrs Furness' Raycroft Sultan and Solo. Sultan was the reserve dog CC behind Alansmere Snow Man, owned by Mrs Kirkpatrick (now Gillies-Compton)—Snow Man and Snow Gleam were bred by Alan Hall and John Evans who have won BIS at Crufts with a Cavalier—Alan is judging Clumbers this year. photo Central Press

winningfield and crufts

From: "RUBY FIELD"

well here we are jim field mark spearing winning working and show jim with lovesong winning 50th anniversary basc team and jimfield with miss daisy winning for england in the international///

Spearmark Dual Purpose GSPs

Kentisworth Kissingberry
Sire: Deepthatch Jonquil
Dam: Kentisworth Chianti
Winner of Liz Ashton Trophy
& Shooting Times Trophy

Spearmark Archener
Sire: Sh Ch Isara Kurzhaar
Bootlegger
Dam: Kentisworth Kissinberry
Top winning GSP at field
trials this season
Mother & Daughter 1st
& 2nd in one trial

~ 2nd Open Stake ~ 3rd
All-Aged Stake ~
~ 2nd All Aged-Stake ~
~ Won at Championship
shows & Crufts ~

~ 1st Kennel Club Novice Trial
~ GSPA All-Aged Stake ~
~ 1st Italian Spinone All-Aged ~ 1st
Hampshire Gundog All-Aged ~
~ Mary Championship show
wins & 2nd at Crufts ~

Mark Spearing
Tel: 07843 278764   mark.gspmad@btinternet.com

Deepthatch Dual Purpose GSPs

The original Windhill Kennel (Bloodlines going back to Dinah of Kieve)
Wishing you all a good year in 2005—working,
showing, working tests or just having fun
The breed has filled our hearts with special things
throughout the world and doggy friends
Ruby & Jim Field—7 Farriers Road, Middle Barton, Chipping Norton,
Oxford. OX7 7FU—01869 347538

Deepthatch Jonquil
Sire: Ch & FT Ch Stairfoot Sobrig
Dam: Pardaillan Image
of Deepthatch (2CC)

wins include:
Best Veteran & Best Field Trial
Windsor Gundog—1997

Placed 2nd and 3rd Crufts 1997

Many field Trials to his credit

Super temperament
and a joy to live with

Deepthatch Dual Purpose GSPs

The original Windhill Kennel (Bloodlines going back to Dinah of Kieve)

Wishing you all a good year in 2005—working,
showing, working tests or just having fun
The breed has filled our hearts with special things
throughout the world and doggy friends

Ruby & Jim Field—7 Farriers Road, Middle Barton,
Chipping Norton, Oxford, OX7 7EU—01869 347538

Deepthatch Daisy won a class
of 30 entries with 4 full
Champions in it at Crufts

She has won ELEVEN
Working Awards,
7 I myself handled her to win,
then this year Jim handled
her to win:
1st in Novice with 28 entries

1st and 2nd in Graduate

then wins the Open
beating Lovesong in 2nd place

Then her first Field Trial run
wins.

Deepthatch Miss Daisy
Sire: Kentisworth Amigo
Dam: Deepthatch Lucinda

Heart Tested Clear

Deepthatch Dual Purpose GSPs

The original Windhill Kennel (Bloodlines going back to Dinah of Kieve)

Wishing you all a good year in 2005—working,
showing, working tests or just having fun
The breed has filled our hearts with special things
throughout the world and doggy friends

Ruby & Jim Field—7 Farriers Road, Middle Barton,
Chipping Norton, Oxford, OX7 7FU—01869 347538

Deepthatch Miss Daisy
Has won at Championship Shows and Best of Breed at Open Shows

Deepthatch Dual Purpose GSPs

The original Windhill Kennel (Bloodlines going back to Dinah of Kieve)

Wishing you all a good year in 2005—working,
showing, working tests or just having fun
The breed has filled our hearts with special things
throughout the world and doggy friends

Ruby & Jim Field—7 Farriers Road, Middle Barton,
Chipping Norton, Oxford, OX7 7FU—01869 347538

Deepthatch Lovesong
Sire: Redmires Rocket to Stardom
Dam: Deepthatch Jubilee
Heart Tested Clear

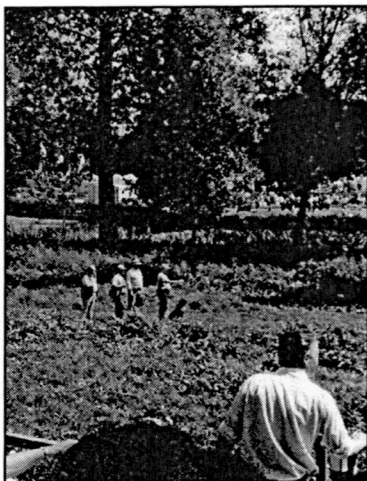

Chosen again for a team at Game Fair
with 3 retrievers. Nothing is practised,
you only meet the other handlers of the
team on the day, early morning. Then at
each test you are given the commands.
Here on the right is Lovesong with
handler Jim Field being directed for a
retrieve from lake. Never puts a foot
wrong, terribly good for breed before
50,000 spectators. Picture taken by a
friend in the stand who has known Jim
for many years.

Lovesong is very much adored by us, has over 40 Working Test and Field
Trial awards, plus many 1st prizes at Championship Shows—2nd at Crufts

deepthatch lovesong retrieving a pidgeon

Ballyheige

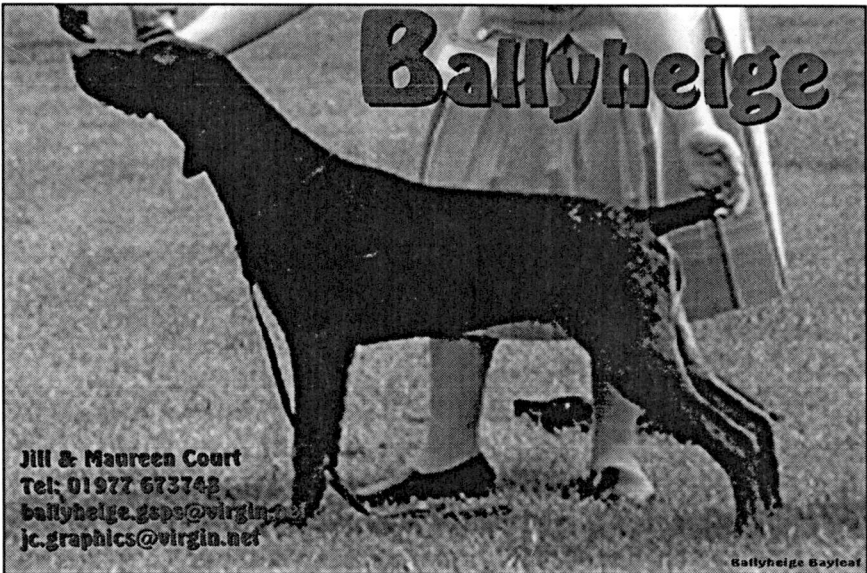

Jill & Maureen Court
Tel: 01977 673748
Bellyheige.gsps@virgin.net
jc.graphics@virgin.net

Deepthatch Dual Purpose GSPs

The original Windlehill Kennel (Bloodliness going back to Dinah of Kieve)

Ruby & Jim Field—7 Farriers Road, Middle Barton,
Chipping Norton, Oxford. OX7 7EU
Telephone: 01869 347538
www.deepthatch.co.uk

Deepthatch Nouvelle Lexi
Sire: Kentisworth Dubonet ~ Dam: Deepthatch
Lucinda ~ Eyes Tested Clear

Wins include Working Tests, Graded Excellent on pointing Partridge at Pointing Test, Field Trials, Challenge Certificate and Reserve Challenge Certificate at Championship Shows making her top GSP in field and show. She always gives us her best.

National Gundog Championship Show ~ 1st Limit Bitch & BCC

"Deepthatch Nouvelle Lexi—Elegant, flashy liver and white with a classic old fashioned head. Correct, slightly domed skull and lovely dark eyes. Excelled in lay of shoulder and short, straight back. Good depth of chest and plenty of substance withour courseness. Correct tailset. Forechest well developed with elbows close to the body, straight legs and tight feet, correct hind angulation and close fitting skin with harsh coat. Handler didn't get the best of her but when she was moved by another person she look a million dollars. Delighted to award her the CC". Judge: Barbara Stamp.

Welsh Kennel Club Championship Show ~ RBCC

"Beautiful head with the darkest of eyes and correct mouth. Lovely neck, short coupling, strong back and excellent angulation. Well ribbed short loin and tight feet. Moved with strength and easy ground covering stride. Powerful bitch but very feminine and obviously a bitch.

Field Trial Critique ~ All Aged Stake

"This dog's first run was inn thick cover crop of maize and fat hen where there was a lot of birds running forward and she kept her head but no point was to be had. Remaining very steady to birds that were lifting in numbers in front of her, her second run was in sugar beet, where she worked her beat with a cheek wind, like a true professional covering the ground with style and pace. She came on point to a cock bird which she fushed on command and was steady to shot, unfortunately the bird was missed. She was then asked to make a blind retrieve on a partridge some 80 yards out of her beat and once in the area took scent on a line 30 yards further in the field and made a speedy recovery to hand, at this point a partridge lifted away from her which was shot and fell inhto a ditch, which she marked and made light work retrieving to hand. Water work was very good. Judges: Chris Snelling & Fred Alcock.

PICTURE

THIS TO GO ON BACK OF COVER OF THE BOOK PLEASE PICKING UP AT MR FLEMINGS RUBY JIM FIELD WITH KATHY WYSS AND LOVESONG AND MISS DAISY//

donations for ch show when i was show sect geofry sterne 10
pounds which was alot of money then aubrey greville williams

Monday, 22 April, 2013 17:05

From: "RUBY FIELD"

while I WAS SHOW SECTERARY HAD GENOUROUS
DONATIONS FROM GEOFREY STERNE AUBRY GREVILL
WILLIAMS JOAN HYDE JIM WAS AWARDED HANDLER
OF THE YEAR HALF A POINT FOLLOWING YEAR FOR
HIGHEST MARKS IN FIELD TRIALS OF GSP CLUB JIM WON
50TH ANNIVERARY WORKING TEST SECOUND AT 60TH
ANNIVERSARY CHOSEN FOR TEAM AT CLA GAME FAIR
WITH LOVE SONG MILLENIUMM CHALLENGE 2 MARK
AWAY FROM FIRST PLACE LET DOWN BY LABRADOR
PICKED UP THE WRONG RETRIEVE ALSO WON THE
FOLLOWING YEAR INTERNATIONAL 4TH AND WON
BASC TEAM EVENT AND WON FOR ENGLAND AT THE
INTERNATIONAL WEEKEND WITH MISS DAISY////

Subject: pointing

Date: Friday, 22 February 2013, 17:08

whenOUT WORKING YOUR DOG SUDDENLY COMES ON POINT PRAISE IT AND GET UP CLOSE TO IT AND STROKE ACROSS TOPLINE GIVING CONFIDENCE AND PRAISE. IF YOU ABLE TO GO ON GROUND WHERE THEY HAVE PENS AND RAISE PHEASANT
WHEN THEY ARE FLYING OUT OF PEN. WORK YOUR DOG ON A LOOSE LINE INTO COVER NEAR BY WITH PHEASANT OR PARTRIDGE ITS AVERY GOOD TO TRAIN YOUR GSP TO WORK THROUGH COVER THEY POINT AND THEN YOU HAVE CONTROL TO MAKE THEM SIT AND BE STEADY WHEN THEY FLY UP COVEYS OF THEM OR JUST ONE OR TWO.

Pardallian image of Deepthatch on Point

flushing the bird

Deepthatch Lucinda

Kentishworth Kissingberry
Deepthatch Lovesong at Crufts

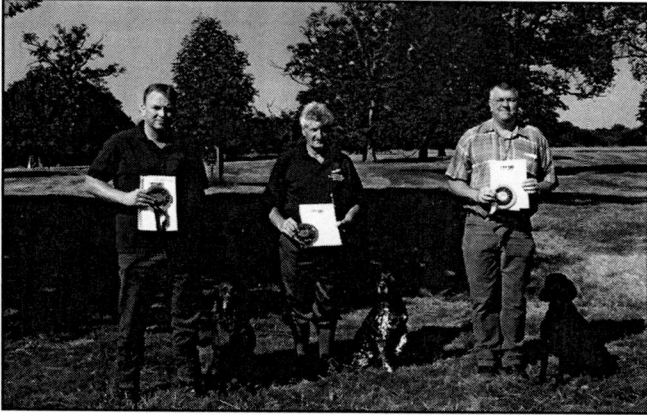

BASC TEAM WORKING TEST WINNERS: Mark Spearing with Kentisworth Kissing Berry, Jim Field and Deepthatch Lovesong, Mr Russell de Cliffors with Birkenwald Carla

50TH ANNIVERSARY OF GSP CLUB
WORKING WEEKEND WINNERS

millenium team for cla game fair at blenium
palace this team was second

English team winners at international 2 day working test

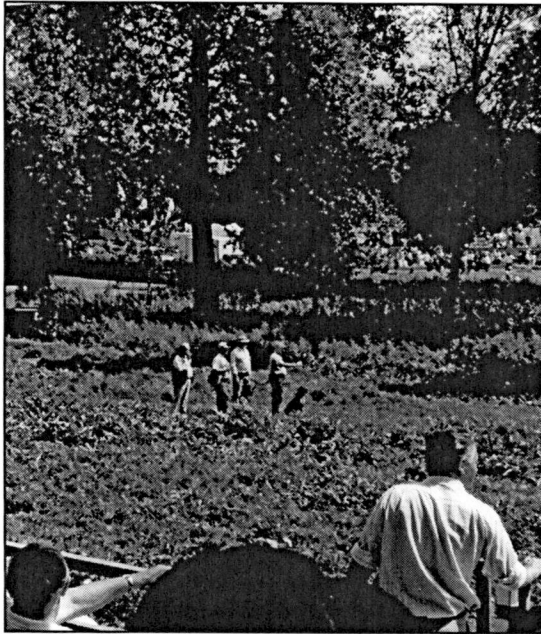

at bleinham palace international jim field with deepthatch
lovesong and two juges ready for along blind water retrieve

pointing deepthatch nouvelle lexi

Subject: pointing

Date: Friday, 22 February 2013, 17:08

whenOUT WORKING YOUR DOG SUDDENLY COMES ON POINT PRAISE IT AND GET UP CLOSE TO IT AND STROKE ACROSS TOPLINE GIVING CONFIDENCE AND PRAISE. IF YOU ABLE TO GO ON GROUND WHERE THEY HAVE PENS AND RAISE PHEASANT
WHEN THEY ARE FLYING OUT OF PEN. WORK YOUR DOG ON A LOOSE LINE INTO COVER NEAR BY WITH PHEASANT OR PARTRIDGE ITS AVERY GOOD TO TRAIN YOUR GSP TO WORK THROUGH COVER THEY POINT AND THEN YOU HAVE CONTROL TO MAKE THEM SIT AND BE STEADY WHEN THEY FLY UP COVEYS OF THEM OR JUST ONE OR TWO.

Crufts

Mrs R Field
7 Farriers Road
Middle Barton
Oxford
OX7 7EU

17th March 2008

Dear Ms. Field,

Crufts 2008

I hope you enjoyed Judging at Crufts this year. With just 27 dogs short of a world record entry and a public attendance of 160,000 this was a great show and your contribution will have added much to that success.

It was clear to me when visiting the show rings each day that everybody, including your Stewards appeared to be having a good time.

With such a high public attendance and dog entry, together with a significant increase in publicity on television, via the internet and other media, Crufts is the number one canine event of its kind world-wide. I hope that you feel yourself part of that success.

I would like to thank you, on behalf of the Crufts Committee for judging and that like me you thought it to be a really memorable occasion.

Yours sincerely,

Eric Smethurst

Chairman—Crufts Committee

judging crufts

my best of breed jeny jennings champion jennaline pegies-grazin.ruby

GUNS AT FIELD TRIAL///

LEFT HAND SIDE RICHARD KUBAN MIDDLE JIM FIELD RIGHT ALL SCHUTSE USA /////

POINTING AND FLUSHING AND STEADINESSS

DOGS POINTING AND BACKING IN USA THEY CALL HONOURING PUPSIN THERES NOW SILK WHELPING AND BABY KENNEL/////

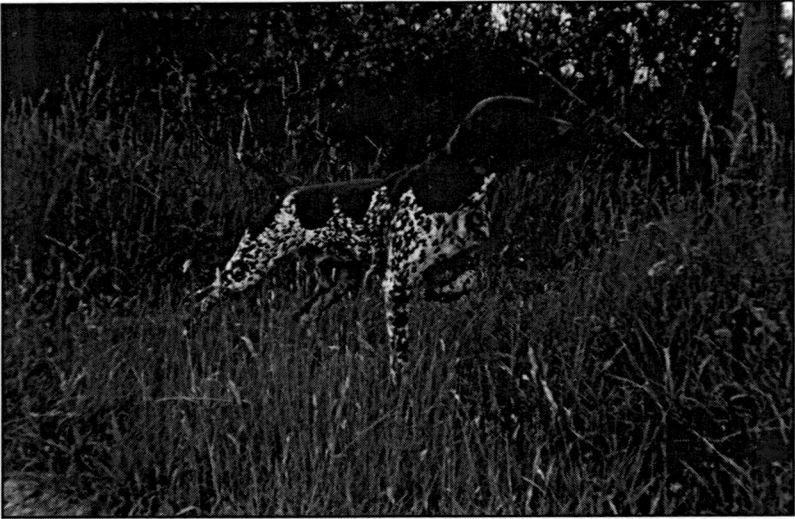

deepthatch montague owned by paul hargeaves

A VISIT TO THE U. K.—DEEPTHATCH GSPs

Mr. and Mrs. J. R. Fields—7 Farriers Road, Middle Barton Chipping Norton, Oxon OX7 7EU, England

Ruby Fields has been active in GSPs for almost 50 years, since the breed was introduced in England, and has judged throughout the world for the past 25 years, as well as serving as Show Secretary for the GSPC of England. James Fields has served on Field Trial Committees for 19 years and has received the highest marks in Field Trials—Handler of the Year—missing it by just 1/2 point two other years.

In the course of doing this article I enjoyed several pleasant conversations with a lovely lady. Mrs. Ruby Fields. Her co-operation and assistance has been invaluable and are greatly appreciated.

"Health and Temperment
A Must for any Breeder" . . . Ruby Fields

Mrs. Ruby Fields "and Friends".

"I have been reading the News since 1966. I will try to give you an insight of how the GSP presents itself in field and show in England. Titles are very hard to win.

As regards making a FT champion; you must win two open stakes and each year we only have a few open stakes. Then you enter only 12 dogs run, 16 in a two day stake, so it is all luck. Dogs are run singly, 2 judges, 4 guns, each trial on foot. Your dog must hunt to find birds, which are wild, and your luck is in if your dog points, flushes the bird and the gun doesn't miss it for your dog to retrieve when told, on the ground allotted your dog. No dogs go over the same ground.

As far as shows go you can expect 200 entries each show. You must win your class, which many times has 26 to 30 in it, then you challenge with all class winners for the C.C. (Challenge Certificate) You must get three C.C.s under different judges for a show title.

Judges must do a written comment on the 1st and 2nd place dogs in each class. It is published in Dog World and Our Dogs weekly dog magazines, sold here and throughout the world.

I have enclosed field trial marks and what we look for. Water work must be completed at each trial and field trial judges have to do critiques just like show judges.

We raise, train and handle our own dogs. I deliver my own pups and mom and pups stay by my bedside the first 2 days. I try to keep pups as much as possible with human contact and everyday noise and they are almost housetrained when they go to their new homes.

I worm bitches before I mate them and I worm pups at four and six weeks. I worm two weeks after in case there are eggs. I have never seen any worms from them but I carry on worming till 10-12 weeks old.

I cook chicken giblets and vegetables and garlic throughout her pregnancy. When the pups are three weeks I introduce oat and rice cereal. Then mashed sardines, then onto minced chicken and vegetables and garlic and parsley. Baby milk and then on to fresh cows milk and whole meal biscuits with their meal.

Our newest little star is Deepthatch Katy who won the GSP Club working test, Italian Spumoni working test and Hungarian Vizsla Club with 100 marks of a possible 100 at 11 months old.

Pardaillan Baron (Deepthatch Driftwood son)

We were the origional Windlehill Kennel, started with Dinah Of Kieve, by my aunt, Mrs. Bibby. Through her divorce we went over to the "Deepthatch" kennel name. Mrs. Bibby died three years ago. I do miss her badly.

Of Dinah of Kieve; Her stock went throughout the world. United States, Canada, Australia and New Zealand. Two bitches, Annabel and Anneliese went to Maryland in 1954.

We were in five countries last year. We were at the Kleeman International Field Trial for four days and were delighted with three dogs being awarded a K S. title. Herr Claus Kieffer had them together on stage before 600 people or more for their awards. He caught hold of their arms, held them in the air and announced father and son from USA. Brought tears to my eyes. What an achievement for handlers and dogs! We were there a week then my husband judged cold game working test for retrievers. On to your country for AKC Hunt Tests where we saw GSPs, GWPs, Vizslas, Brittanys, English Pointers, Gordon and English Setters and Irish Setters, all competing to do the same. What contrast and so lovely to see.

Thank you, Margaret, for all your hard efforts and work for GSP News. Hope you all continue to enjoy your Shorthairs and God bless you all and your country."

Excerpt from Mrs. Field's comments judging at the Birmingham National Dog Show—"I have spent most of my lide with German Short-hairs and was horrified to see so many light eyes, flat skulls and straight necks, giving a terrier breed look. Standard calls for

a dark eye, sufficiently round skull and arched, muscular neck thickening towards shoulders. I could not see any dark ring aroung the light eyes at all in many dogs. Also, the shape of the eye and expressions were not soft. Please, I hope we will all try to work together on correcting these faults that have crept into our breed."
Ruby Fields

Mr. James R. Fields with Handler Of The Year Trophy and Image of Deepthatch

It iv extremely difficult to earn titles in England. Example; there have been just 7 Dual Champions in the history of the breed in England. All 7 of those Dual Champions trace back to the Fields' foundation bitch, Dinah Of Kieve

Success born of dedication and skill.

Start of Field Trial—Guns, dog and man to pick up, steward sEileen Winser Brockett Park and Mr. C. Wilkinson, and judges J. Fields and R. Jurban

Judge's Report

Venue	Cranbourne, Dorset
Stake	Novice
Host(s)	Lord Cranbourne
Steward	Mr. C. Wilkinson
Types of game	Pheasant/Woodcock/Pigeon

Weather/scenting conditions The weather throughout remained overcast but dry. Scenting conditions were good.

Many thanks to both for allowing the use of an excellent ground on which to test a variety of HPR breeds, and to our keeper who, as Steward of the beat, ensured a plentiful supply of game.

The trial was run along a wooded/pasture water course which proved more than adequate for these novice dogs. Towards the end of the day, a number of hedgerows were utilized, together with planted areas of Kale, and it's fair to say dog had game on his/her beat.

Whether due to the season nearing its end, or a general improvement in handling, is difficult to say, but the dogwork for this novice stake was much improved on some earlier trials. It followed then that almost everyone was able to return home having seen something good in their dog's work.

The end of an extremely pleasant day saw four dogs competing for the awards. Unfortunately, although each of these dogs had produced some good work, none had been consistent enough to merit a first place.

Results:
2nd place: Mathams Bias GSP dog
During this dog's first run he used the wind well and showed a good use of nose. However, there were times when he appeared somewhat hesitant, dwelling rather too long on some scents. This detracted a little of his overall performance.

His second run was far more positive. Still working methodically, he had an excellent find on a cock pheasant which he produced well. Unfortunately, the bird was missed by the guns. After it's initial find the dog worked on with a good deal more purpose, culminating in a positive point on a hen bird. Although showing a certain stickiness on point, the bird was nonetheless produced and shot, falling some 40 yards into the woods. The dog was sent for the retrieve and, out of sight from the handler, had to be left to his own devices. After a brief wait, the dog returned with the bird, effectively making light of a difficult retrieve.

Overall, it's first round hesitance denied us the option of awarding a first place

3rd Place: Deepthatch Jonquil GSP dog
A good run in the first round with all the enthusiasm required by a hunting dog, together with good use of the wind, was marred only by the absence of game. His second run proved more productive. Setting off with a pace suited to conditions, he made contact with game and eventually pointed. Unfortunately he never got to grips with this particular bird which flushed some ten yards further out.

The dog worked on into a wooded area where it was clear birds were running. A number of indications were finally followed by a nice point. This bird, when produced, flew over the back gun who was not in the best position for a clean shot. Working on into a more open woodland, the dog produced a good find on a cock bird. Flushed, the bird was shot and fell some 60 yards along the adjoining track, close to the wood. It was certainly a tricky retrieve, and an opportunity for the dog to shine.

However, although the retrieve was made, both dog and handler seemed somewhat out of tune. Despite this hiccup, it should not be long before this dog is pushing a first place.

4th Place: Aschfahl Liberty Belle Wiem bitch

On it's first run, this bitch came onto immediate point. The bird was nicely flushed and flew well out over the left hand gun who took it nicely. Being only a few more yards to cover, the dog was worked on and seemed a little surprised when a second bird flushed in front of it before flying on unscathed. Both dog and handler were taken across the field in the direction of the fall. The bird had fallen into a drainage ditch the other side of a tall mound. Having given the handler instructions, the dog was sent on the retrieve. Out of sight of the handler, but in view of both judges, the bitch made a workmanlike job of the task.

Working alongside a hedgerow, the bitch came onto a hesitant point. When sent in to flush, a hen bird flew out, only to drop straight back down where it then proceeded to run along the hedge. Clearly a bird that had been wounded earlier. The handler was asked to work the dog on and at this point both dog and handler seemed unsure how to handle the situation, with the dog being very hesitant in it's approach. The bird eventually ran out of the hedge and proceeded to run/glide towards some maize cover where it was shot by the forward gun. The dog made a competent retrieve.

The dogs second run was less eventful. Running in heavier woodland it failed to obtain a point although it did make light of a trick retrieve on a cock bird which had fallen into a stream.

We understand this was a first time in field trials for both dog and handler. With this in mind, it shouldn't be too long before they see an improvement on this fourth place.

C of M Rainscote Russian Roulette at Daxpack

It's first run lacked a little in drive although she produced a nice point on a cock pheasant. Positive on the flush, she then carried out a competent retrieve.

Like many of the dogs on the day, she worked far better on her second run and she again had a nice find in some light woodland. This time she was less than positive on her flush. With the guns merely saluting the bird, she left without a retrieve. A little more experience for the dog should go a long way towards seeing it amongst the places.

Mrs. S. Kuban and Mr. M. Bower

Deepthatch Driftwood

Deepthatch Jonquil

Callaways Lady Hamilton

KARL OUR SON SHARED HIS LIFE UNTILL THIS DAY
WITH SHORTHAIRS

"RUBY FIELD"

KARL PLAYING WITH PUPS WHICH WILL INCREASE
THEIR BERNEFITS OF RELATIONSHIP WITH HUMANS
AND DEVELOP NATURALLY WITH THE REST IN LITTER
KARL IN SCOTLAND WITH MONSIER AND CINNAMON
THEN JUNIOR HANDLIING WITH DRIFTWOOD SON///
THEN WON BASC SCHOOLS SHOOTTING COMPETION
THEN ON SHOOT AT HAMBLED ON SHOOTTING A LEFT
AND RIGHT ON WOODCOCK ONLY YOUNG WHICH MAKES
HIM MEMBER OF WOODCOCK CLUB///

Karl and UK shooting team

Karl through his life with gsp and achievements

The German Shorthaired Pointer Club

JUBILEE YEAR

* * * * * * * * * * * * *

President: G.C. STERNE, Esq.

CATALOGUE OF 19-CLASS BREED

FIFTHTEENTH

CHAMPIONSHIP SHOW

BENCHED OPEN   **TO ALL**

(Under Kennel Club Rules and Regulationss)
to be held at
THE DOG CENTRE, STONELEIGH, KENILWORTH, WARWICKS.

JUDGE: I.E.T. SLADDEN

SATURDAY 22nd OCTOBER, 1977

Show Opens: 8.30 hrs. Judging: 9.30 hrs.

SHOW MANAGER: MR. B. BOTTERMAN

GUARANTORS TO THE KENNEL CLUB:

Mrs. R. Field, 7 Farriers Road, Middle Barten, Oxford.
Mr. M. Brander, Wittingehame, Mains, Haddington, Scotland.
Mr. A. Greville Williams, Hurstleigh, Winkfield, Windsor, Berk.
Mr. W. Simpson (Hon. Sec.), Northwold House, Northwold, Thetford, Norfolk.
Mr. A. Church, 69 Whippingham Road, Brighton, Sussex.
Mr. Oates, The Gardens, The Street, Pleshey, Chelmsford, Essex.

HON. VETERINARY SURGEON: J.A.C. Kew, Esq., M.R.C.V.S.

STEWARD: Mr. Sharpe, Mr. Roberts

HON. SHOW SECRETARY: MSRS. R. FIELD
7, FARRIERS ROAD,
MIDDLE BARTON,
OXON.

Tel: STEEPLE ASTON 47245.

CAR PARK FREE BENCHING FREE CATALOGUE—40p
THE GERMAN SHORTHAIRED POINTER CLUB

President: G.C. STERNE

Hon. Secretary: MR. W.K. SIMPSON Field Trial Secretary: MRS. S. KUBAN

Show Secretary: MRS. R.L. FIELD Treasurer: MR. J. OATES

Management Committee

MR. BRANDER MAJOR FORDYCE BURKE
MR. AUBREY GREVILLE WILLIAMS MR. J. KEW
MR. SIMPSON MRS. M. LOWE
MRS. SIMPSON MAJOR WILKINSON
MRS. BOTTERMAN MR. T. ASHTON
MR. A. CHURCH

Field Trial Committee

MR. M.J. FIELD MAJOR WILKINSON
MR. B. BOTTERMAN MRS. L. PETRIE HAY
MR. J. KEW SIR MICHAEL LEIGHTON
MRS. S. KUBAN MR. BRANDER

Show Committee

MR. T. ASHTON MR. N. ELSON
MRS. J. BATES MRS. R.L. FIELD
MRS. P. COLGRAVE MRS. R. GREEN
MR. A. CHURCH MRS. G. SEARLE

THE SHOW COMMITTEE WISH TO EXPRESS GREAT APPRECIATION
TO ALL CONCERNED TO MAKE THIS SHOW POSSIBLE, TO OUR
JUDGE OF THE DAY WHO IS A FIELD TRIAL AND CHAMPHIONSHIP
SHOW JUDGE. SO WE HOPE YOU WILL BE HONOURED WITH HIS
OPINION. TO OUR TWO KIND STEWARDS, MR. ROBERTS AND MR.
SHARPE; ALSO TO THE GENEROSITY OF DONATION FOR ROSETTES.

MR. G. STERNE £10
MR. J. GASMAN £5
MRS. J. DICKINSON £5
MR. T. ASHTON £2
THANKS TO EVERYONE WHO HAS CONTRIBUTED TO THE BOTTLE
AND TIN STAND.
HOPE YOU ALL ENJOY A GOOD DAY.

RUBY LOUISE FIELD
(Show Secretary)

Subject: whistles

Date: Tuesday, 19 March 2013, 20:17

LARGER WHISTLE IS THE REFEREE STOP WHISTLE./// THE SMALLER WHISTLE BUFFALO HORN IS THE WHISTLE FOR TO USE TO CALL BACK AND QUARTER WITH. IF YOU HAVE ABOUT TWO OR THREE GSPS THEY WILL GO ON POINT AND BACK EACH OTHER. THEY CALL HOUNOR IN USA WHEN THEY FIN GAME. THE SEASON FOR SHOOTTING GAME STARTS 12TH AUGUST TO 1ST FEBRUARY YOU MAY SHOOT PIDGEON ALL YEAR ROUND.

DOG HISTORY

LEFT HAND SIDE CH NEVERN JASPER GRAT DOG AND PRODUCER RIGHT HAND SIDE ISGO VON BLITZDORF WITH SOME OF HIS PROGENY CH DESIMA WEEDDANBROOK WEDDA ISGO VON BLITZDORF PRODUCED ABER MAX GORMIRE ADAM SAW HIS GRAVE WHEN AT FIELD TRIAL HELD AT LADY DE HAVILLANDS GROUND LORD DE HAVILLAND WALKED ME TO HIS GRAVE STONE OLD REMUS AS HE CALLED HIM///

AT STUD

NEVERN JASPER

"NEVERN JASPER." Sire: "Saltus von der Forst Brickwedde." Dam: "Nevern Jenny." Born February, 1953. An outstanding combination of working ability and conformation. Winner: Test Trial 1954 and Senior Stake 1955. Best of Breed and K.C. Challenge Certificate winner, Cruft's 1955. Many other awards. Apply: S/Ldr. D. W. Atkinson, Registrar, R.A.F., Hospital, Nocton Hall, Lincs.

AT STUD

ISGO VON BLITZDORF (REMUS)

"Reproduced by courtesy of The Tail-Wagger Magazine"

Weedonbrook Wedda Decima Rindy of Brandsby at four months at nine months at fifteen months "ISGO VON BLITZDORF" ("REMUS"). Class I Registration K.C. Stud Book No. 778 AN. Imported from Germany, Height 24 ½ inches. Weight 65 pounds. Very dark eyes. Sire of Best Puppy and Best of Sex, Cruft's 1955, of Best Puppy and Best of Breed, Brandsby, 1954, of Best Puppy, Leicester, 1955, and of 2nd Novice Dog, Test Trial, 1955. Fee 10 Guineas.
Apply: Mrs. de Havilland Emley Woodhouse, nr. Huddersfield, Yorks. Telephone: Flockton 318.

NEVERN JAGERIN HEIDIE
Litter sister to Nevern Jasper.
A Mating has been arranged between this fine maiden Bitch and Isgo von Blitzdorf. Puppies will be available March/April 1956.
Enquiries to: W. K. Simpson, 31 Nevern Place, London, S.W.5.

Miss A. W. Ward's Sh. Ch. PATRICK OF MALAHIDE
Best of Breed and Gundog Group Winner at Crufts Ch. Show 1968.

Subject: ch patrick of maahide gundog winner crufts 1968

Date: Monday, 8 April 2013, 12:52

enclosed picture///

Subject: members of hpr clubs

Date: Sunday, 7 April 2013, 20:43

we also are members of munsterlander club italin spinnone club kc club dina of kieve pup lord and lady

ferrier had pup which produced ch ferrier jaeger mr macmillan had one and then archbishop of canterbury through adam of windelhill produced many ft champions in new zealand for mr jack dawson voisterhund skylark gisele eve tiger and bushwhacker they were australin and new zealand ft champions

also we competed in dog triathon where you had ateam of four handlers and dogs miss jaffe had vits deepthatch jezabel jim had deepthatch lovesong i had deepthatch jonquiel mr preston had deepthatch jubillee had all water work retriving and clay shootting one shot another had dog every time you shot aclay dummy was thrown and dog had to retrieve it deepthatch team were 3rd good fun////

members of hpr clubs

we also are members of munsterlander club italin spinnone club kc club dina of kieve pup lord and lady

ferrier had pup which produced ch ferrier jaeger mr macmillan had one and then archbishop of canterbury through adam of windelhill produced many ft champions in new zealand for mr jack dawson voisterhund skylark gisele eve tiger and bushwhacker they were australin and new zealand ft champions

also we competed in dog triathon where you had ateam of four handlers and dogs miss jaffe had vits deepthatch jezabel jim had deepthatch lovesong i had deepthatch jonquiel mr preston had deepthatch jubilee had all water work retriving and clay shootting one shot another had dog every time you shot aclay dummy was thrown and dog had to retrieve it deepthatch team were 3rd good fun////

puppies

mrs biby with litter sired by week end mist anddamalyn kerisma not shape colour of there eyes and shape of the skull at that young agedo miss her/// 10 pups sire rocketto stardom dam d. jubillee lasssie lovesong lucinda litter . . . . ///

puppies mrs bibby with alyn kerisma and weekend mist puppies

litter of puppies bt deepthatch jubilee and redmires
rocket to stardom lassie lovesong lucinda litter.ruby.

Tuesday, 14 May, 2013 13:18

JUDGING AT CRUFTS///

WELL BACK IN UK FIELD TRIALS WORKING TEST SHOWS THEN ON TO JUDGE CRUFTS// 282 ENTRIES ///A WORLD RECORD ENTRY // PEOPLE CAME FROM EAST WEST OF USA CANADA HILL AND CHECK REPUBLICK ITALY ROMANIA NZ AUSTRALIA I WAS TAKING TO MY STEWARDS BEFORE JUDGING TELLING THEM WHAT I WAS GOING TO DAY 2 PEOPLE WALKED IN THE RING SAID I AM FROM NZ SHOOK MY HAND AND THE OTHER WAS FROM AUSTRALIA WHAT AWAY TO SEE ALL OUR GSPS IN ONE PLACE//// 2 YEARS AFTER I WAS EXHIBITING GREGG HOFFESTER CAME OVER HIS FIRST TIME AT CRUFTS FROM USA HE RAN LEXI FOR ME I WON FIELD TRIAL CLASS. SADLY A WEEEK LATER SHE WAS KILLED TOP WINNING DOG IN SHOW AND FIELD WE BOTH HAD OUR LIVES SHATTERED ENCLOED PICTURE OF LEXI LAST PICTURES OF HER SENDING PICTURES OF RETRIVING PHEASANT IN THE SNOW AT HER LAST FIELD TRIAL./// ON DISK. NEXT PICTURE OF ALL MY DOGS YEARS A GOAT WINDSOR SHOW///

kentisworth bernie

at windsor show myself jubillee jonguil katy jezebell

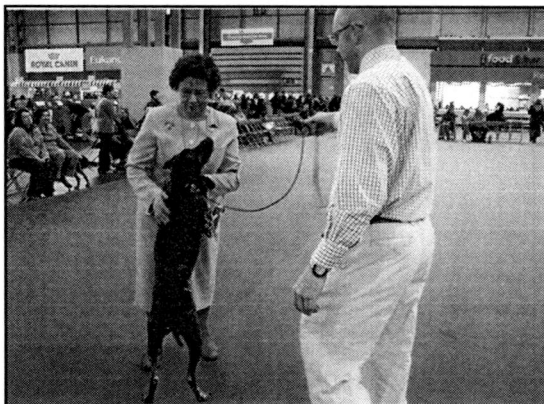

crufts lexi being handed over to me by greg hoffester usa who ran
lexi for me last picture of lexi.

OUR NEWESTADITION//

WITH THE HELP OF KENNEL CLUB AND HEALTH CHEQUE ON MISS DAISY WE HAD PERMISSION TO MATE MISS DAISY AGAIN WHICH GAVE US 6 PUPPIES 2BITCHES 4 DOGS WE HAD ONE OF THE BITCHES AND HERE SHE IS WON HER FIRST FIELD TRIAL THEN 2 ND IN OPEN JIM AWARED BEST HANDLER WITH HER BESIDES WINNING A WORKING TEST WITH 49 DOGS IN HER CATOGRIE/////

Deepthatch Dual Purpose GSPs

The original Windhill Kennel (Bloodlines going back to Dinah of Kieve)
Ruby & Jim Field—7 Farriers Road, Middle Barton,
Chipping Norton, Oxford. OX7 7EU
Telephone: 01869 347538
www.deepthatch.co.uk

Deepthatch Pocana

1st Minor Puppy Bitch, WELKS ~ 1st Puppy Bitch, GSPC
Open Show ~ 1st Puppy Bitch, Southern Counties
1st Puppy Bitch, Paignton ~ 1st Puppy Bitch, National
Gundog ~ 1st Junior Bitch, Midland Counties
Best Puppy, Reserve Best Bitch, 3rd Best Puppy in Show at
Witney & District Open Show ~ Lots of Seconds

1/2 point away from her first Working Test 2nd ~ 3rd
Brittany Working Test ~ 3rd Laverstoke GSP Club
5th Hampshire Gundog Society ~ 5th GLPC Test.

Her mock Field Trial Judge said "She will win her
first Field Trial next season. She shined".
Lets hope our luck and health makes that come true, thanks to all the Judges.

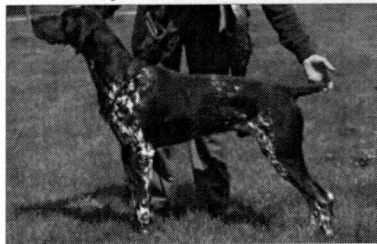

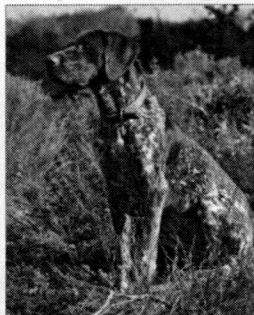
21 open working tests

Subject: socialising and feed for pups

Date: Wednesday, 23 January 2013, 19:40

IS EXAMENED FOR MOTH DENTITION D'MALES HAVE TWO TESTICLES DOWN IN SCOTRUM OR YOU CAN FEEL 2 JUST ABOUT TO ENTER THE SCOTRUM NEVER FEED DRIED FOOD ON ITS OWN ALWAYS PUT YOGOURT OR SARDINES DOG TIN FOOD. SOME MEAT AND VEG// AS FEED ALONE CAN GIVE THEM BLOAT//// HARD FOR PUPS TO DIGEST ON HEART KIDNEY AND DIGESTIVE SYSTEM//// THEN WHEN NICE WEATHER TAKE YOUR PUP TO WATER A GOOD ENTRY . . . HELPS HAVING AN ADULT WHO LIKES AND ENTERS. WATER FREELY PUT PUPS DUMMY ON ALONG CORD SIT YOUR PUP PLAY WITH HER WITH THE DUMMY THEN THROW IN WATER SEND HER TO FETCH DONT WORRY AT THIS STAGE STEADINESS AND DELIVERING TO HAND KEEP SENDING THE DUMMY AND CORD A LITTLE FURTHER EACH TIME TO GET PUP SWIMMING AND ENJOYING IT IF YOUR DOGS NOT STEDY ON RETRIEVING PUT ON ALONG LINE YOU AT THE CONTROL AT END SEND PUP FOR RETRIEVE IF ITS NOT STEADY GOES TO RETRIEVE. BEFORE YOU SAID PULL IT BACK AND PUT BACK IN THERE POSITION AND REPEAT THE RETRIEVE AGAIN

Deepthatch Dual Purpose GSPs

The original Windlehill Kennel (Bloodlines going back to Dinah of Kieve)

**Ruby & Jim Field—7 Farriers Road, Middle Barton,
Chipping Norton, Oxford. OX7 7EU
Telephone: 01869 347538
www.deepthatch.co.uk**

Deepthatch Miss Daisy

Sire: Kentisworth Amigo ~ Dam: Deepthatch
Lucinda ~ Heart & Eyes Tested Clear
2nd at 60th Anniversary Open Test and won Open at Burton Lazars with
a score of 98 out of 100 making Deepthatch dogs top in working
She has won 17 awards in the field and won for England
at the International Weekend for HPRs

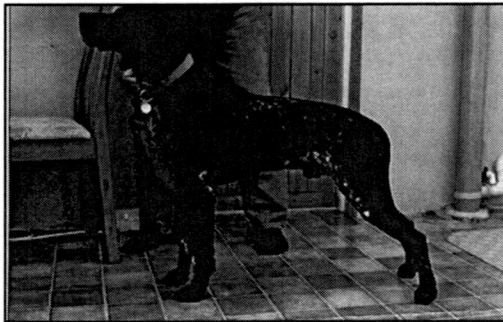

Spearmark Palus Nebularim

Gained Stud Book Number ~ Has won in Limit at
Championship Show and awards at Field Trials
With the blessings of the Kennel Club and my health check, Spearmark Palus
Nebularium was mated to Deepthatch Miss Daisy which produced 6 puppies,
4 of which have won in Championship Shows and awards in Working Tests

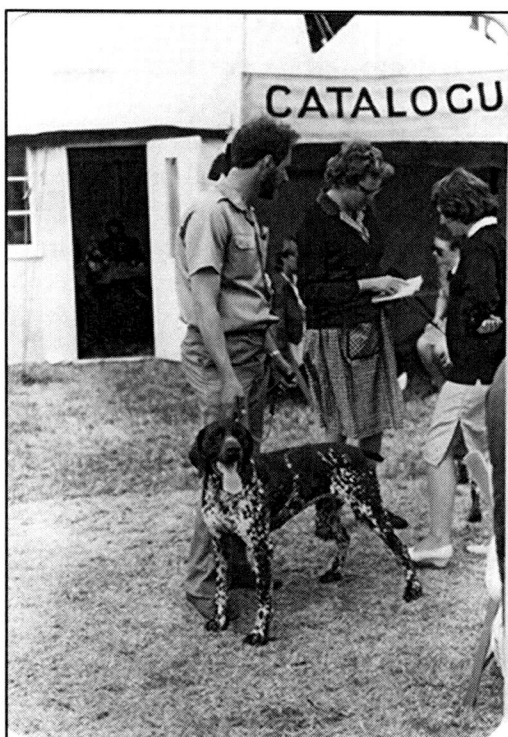

Breed Standard

Last updated September 2007

A Breed Standard is the guideline which describes the ideal characteristics, temperament and appearance of a breed and ensures that the breed is fit for function. Absolute soundness is essential. Breeders and judges should at all times be careful to avoid obvious conditions or exaggerations which would be detrimental in any way to the health, welfare or soundness of this breed. From time to time certain conditions or exaggerations may be considered to have the potential to affect dogs in some breeds adversely, and judges and breeders are requested to refer to the Breed Watch section of the Kennel Club website here http://www.the-kennel-club.org.uk/services/public/breeds/watch for details of any such current issues. If a feature or quality is desirable it should only be present in the right measure. However if a dog possesses a feature, characteristic or colour described as undesirable or highly undesirable it is strongly recommended that it should not be rewarded in the show ring.

General Appearance

Noble, steady dog showing power, endurance and speed, giving the immediate impression of an alert and energetic dog whose movements are well co-ordinated. Of medium size, with a short back standing over plenty of ground. Grace of outline, clean-cut head, long sloping shoulders, deep chest, short back, powerful hindquarters, good bone composition, adequate muscle, well carried tail and taut coat.

Characteristics

Dual purpose Pointer/Retriever, very keen nose, perseverance in searching and initiative in game finding, excellence in field, a naturally keen worker, equally good on land and water.

Temperament

Gentle, affectionate and even-tempered. Alert, biddable and very loyal.

Head and Skull

Clean-cut, neither too light nor too heavy, well proportioned to body. Skull sufficiently broad and slightly round. Nasal bone rising gradually from nose to forehead (this more pronounced in dogs) and never possessing a definite stop, but when viewed from side a well defined stop effect due to position of eyebrows. Lips falling away almost vertically from somewhat protruding nose and continuing in a slight curve to corner of mouth. Lips well developed, not over hung. Jaws powerful and sufficiently long to enable the dog to pick up and carry game. Dish-faced and snipy muzzle undesirable. Nose solid brown or black depending on coat colour. Wide nostrils, well opened and soft.

Eyes

Medium size, soft and intelligent, neither protruding nor too deep-set. Varying in shades of brown to tone with coat. Light eye undesirable. Eyelids should close properly.

Ears

Broad and set high; neither too fleshy nor too thin, with a short, soft coat; hung close to head, no pronounced fold, rounded at tip and reaching almost to corner of mouth when brought forward.

Mouth

Teeth sound and strong. Jaws strong, with a perfect, regular and complete scissor bite, i.e. upper teeth closely overlapping lower teeth and set square to the jaws.

Neck

Moderately long, muscular and slightly arched, thickening towards shoulders. Skin not fitting too loosely.

Forequarters

Shoulders sloping and very muscular, top of shoulder blades close; upper arm bones, between shoulder and elbow, long. Elbows well laid back, neither pointing outwards nor inwards. Forelegs straight and lean, sufficiently muscular and strong, but not coarse-boned. Pasterns slightly sloping.

Body

Chest must appear deep rather than wide but in proportion to rest of body; ribs deep and well sprung, never barrel-shaped nor flat; back ribs reaching well down to tuck-up of loins. Chest measurement immediately behind elbows smaller than about a hand's breadth behind elbows, so that upper arm has freedom of movement. Firm, short back, not arched. Loin wide and slightly arched; croup wide and sufficiently long, neither too heavy nor too sloping starting on a level with back and sloping gradually towards tail. Bones solid and strong. Skin should not fit loosely or fold.

Hindquarters

Hips broad and wide, falling slightly towards tail. Thighs strong and well muscled. Stifles well bent. Hocks square with body and slightly bent, turning neither in nor out. Pasterns nearly upright.

Feet

Compact, close-knit, round to spoon-shaped, well padded, turning neither in nor out. Toes well arched with strong nails.

Tail

Previously customarily docked.

Docked: Starts high and thick growing gradually thinner, customarily docked to medium length by two fifths to half its length. When quiet, tail carried down; when moving, horizontally. Never held high over back or bent.

Undocked: Moderately long, not reaching below hocks. Strong at root, becoming gradually thinner. Carried horizontally or just below line of back.

Gait/Movement

Smooth, lithe gait essential. As gait increases from walk to a faster speed, legs converge beneath body (single tracking). Forelegs reach well ahead, effortlessly covering plenty of ground with each stride and followed by hindlegs, which give forceful propulsion.

Coat

Short, flat and coarse to touch, slightly longer under tail.

Colour

Solid liver, liver and white spotted, liver and white spotted and ticked, liver and white ticked, solid black or black and white same variations (not tri-colour).

Size

Dogs: minimum height 58 cms (23 ins) at withers, maximum height 64 cms (25 ins) at withers. Bitches: minimum height 53 cms (21 ins) at withers, maximum height 59 cms (23 ins) at withers.

Faults

Any departure from the foregoing points should be considered a fault and the seriousness with which the fault should be regarded should be in exact proportion to its degree and its effect upon the health and welfare of the dog and on the dog's ability to perform its traditional work.

Note

Male animals should have two apparently normal testicles fully descended into the scrotum.

P.O.T.Y. 1988
Puppy Of The Year Tournament

P.O.T.Y. 1988 is sponsored by: On The Circuit,
American Express, and British Airways.

Qualifying Rounds:

* November 11 Host Club—Scottsdale Dog Fanciers, Horsemans
  Park, Scottsdale, Arizona 4:00p.m.
  ALL NEW QUALIFYING ROUND
* November 25 Host Club—Golden Valley Kennel Club, Stanislaus
  County Fairgrounds, Turlock, California 7:00p.m.

I certify that I am the actual owner of the dog whose name appears
above. I (we) agree to abide by the rules and regulations of the
P.O.T.Y. tournament. I (we) certify that the dog entered is not a
hazard to other persons or dogs.

General Information: The entry fee for the Puppy Of The Year
Tournament is $6.00 per puppy, per qualifying round. All puppies
must be between 6-12 months of age on the date of the qualifying
round(s) entered. If a puppy has qualified for the final and is over
a year old on that date, he is still eligible to compete. There are no
point qualifications needed to etner P.O.T.Y. AKC and Miscellaneous
breeds are eligible for entry at AKC host clubs. There are no breed
classes, each puppy will be placed into its appropriate group for
judging (Toy, Hound, Working, etc.). There will be four placings per

group, with the first place group winner going on to the Final Puppy Of The Year Tournament. You may enter one or all of the qualifying rounds, however group winners are not eligible to compete after winning a round. In this case if an entry has already been accepted, the fee will be refunded. **Professional handlers may only show dogs they own.**

P.O.T.Y. is run independently of the American Kennel Club and of the Host Clubs involved. Puppy Of The Year is a privately run, sponsored, non-sanctioned event. We do not send written conformation of entries, if you require this please send a stamped self-addressed post card with your entry.

Simi Valley P.O.T.Y.

HERDING GROUP

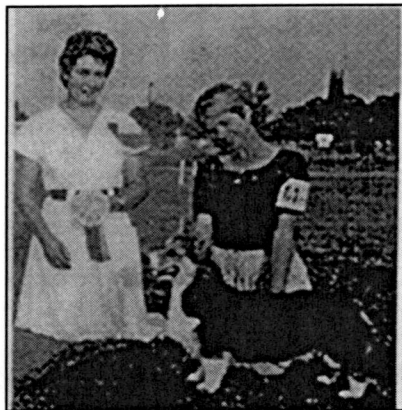

Pembroke Welsh Corgi, ROSEWOOD XPRESS, bred and owned by Liisa La Guire.

Beautiful head and expression. Super coat. Stood square; very balanced young dog who, when moving, showed true drive, balance and power. Did not put a foot wrong. A bright future ahead for this youngster.

Ruby Field, Judge

NON-SPORTING GROUP

Keeshond, VAN d PIERS SHORELINE BREEZE, Owned by Sharon Pierce of Simi Valley.

This was a very hard class to judge as there were so many top quality puppies. However this youngster stood out, particularly on movement.

Lovely coat, head and expression. Very sound overall. And on the move a true pleasure to watch.

Ruby Field, Judge

Beagle, JUST-WRIGHT LIMITED EDITION, owned and bred by Julie Wright. What presence this dog has for one so young. Good head and shoulders. Lovely soft expression. Hindquarters and feet moved with reach, drive and balance. Beautifully marked. Handled to perfection on the day.

Ruby Field, Judge

HOUND GROUP

THE GSP—BREED CHARACTERISTICS

Origins of the breed

The German Shorthaired Pointer was developed in Germany during the 19th century as an all-purpose gundog, sharing a similar ancestry to other HPR (hunt, point, retrieve) breeds from the continent of Europe but being distinct from them.

It is a shortcoated, medium sized dog having an alert and intelligent disposition. Its ability in the shooting field to perform the all-embracing role of game finder, pointer and retriever has won it recognition as the ideal rough shooters dog here in Great Britain. At home on the salt marsh, open moor and woodland/farmland it is truly a versatile gundog.

The GSP has a very highly developed air scenting ability and is an exceptional gamefinder, a staunch pointer readily holding birds for the gun. The GSP is a tireless worker being persistent on the hunt for game whether ranging over open ground or hunting in the cover of woods. They are required to be steady in the field to the flushing of game, shot and fall of game, which they should retrieve tenderly to hand from either land or water.

The tail is customarily docked in working dogs solely to prevent tail injuries whilst working in close cover.

Breed Characteristics

Working Homes

Most responsible breeders look first for working homes, then show homes and lastly pet homes. About 700 German Shorthaired Pointers are registered each year so it is obvious that a great many are going to pet homes. People see some of the gundog breeds leading very quiet sedentary lives and imagine that all gundog breeds are the same, with the same requirements. This is a dangerous generalisation. Some dogs in every breed are going to behave outside the norm for their breed. A German Shorthaired Pointer by it's very breeding for a highly difficult and complex number of expectations, is not going to be a norm within the gundog group. They have been bred to work outside in all weathers, eight hours a day, seven days a week, and some of them are capable of doing just that. They need plenty of varied exercise, they need human love and companionship and they need occupying. They are very like children and are slow to mature, some never do, and their adolescence can be very trying. They are physically strong dogs with strong wills and need consistent handling from the cradle to the grave. Discipline with a capital D and Training with a capital T often stifles the initiative and can produce hard headed dogs. Many are like a piece of elastic, the harder you pull your end the further away the other end becomes.

One of a German Shorthaired Pointers most endearing traits is his love of his people and unless brought up from a very small puppy to kennelling, prefer to live as one of the family. They are remarkable for their companionship traits and do not thrive away from people. Many dogs come into rescue for just this reason. If you have to chastise a German Shorthaired Pointer the "more in sorrow than anger" approach usually works best. They should never be allowed to exercise without supervision. A good home does not need acres of land for him to roam. Nor is it possible to share a picture book garden with one, unless you can fence off a fairly large piece of it for him to enthusiastically turn into the mountains of the moon. They love to dig and their faeces need collecting regularly. If shut outside or inside for long periods on their own they can become very noisy and destructive. They can also use their considerable enterprise and initiative to escape in order to find the company, exercise and interest that they need.

Before taking one on be very sure that all members of your family are equally keen. Are you young, strong and patient? Do you love long walks? Live within easy reach of the countryside or a large park? This is not the breed for the elderly, no matter how active, and young children can get knocked about by a young thoughtless dog. They have an average life expectancy of 10 to 12 years so unless you can see your future stretching before you without overseas postings, or having to change your accommodation into places where pets are not allowed, don't have one. It will break both yours and the dogs heart to part and they are not the easiest breed to re-home.

A properly reared German Shorthaired Pointer is one of the greatest joys in this life and if they are not in the other then I don't want to go.

The Ideal Hind Angulation

submitted by Ruby Fields

This article follows the theme of angulation in relation to the hind limb. It is the stifle or knee joint that is of interest and I recall a very determined German vet asking the vet at the Curragh, in Ireland, for a precise definition of a "good turn of stifle" on the stallions we were looking at. These were the best the Irish National Stud had to offer and the Irish vet looked skywards in exasperation and just replied, "Heaven knows" with his wonderfully rich accent. The German vet was none the wiser however and still wanted to know the measurements that went to make the perfect turn of stifle.

While this is an amusing tale that illustrates two aspects of assessing angulation (the art and the science) it is not very helpful to aspiring judges (nor to the German vet). So I will try and tell you how to assess a "turn of stifle" and hopefully Heaven will agree with my assessment.

Compromise

The anatomy is clear and as the diagram shows, stifle angulation is made up from the relationship of two principle bones, the femur and the tibia. The angulation we want to measure is between a line drawn from the hip to the center of the stifle joint and from here to the center of the hock. This is depicted approximately by the line X-X. I say "approximately" because we need to compromise a bit based on the landmarks we can use reliably to help us. There are also some distractions that can lead the unwary to assess angulation wrongly.

With practice, the hip joint can be accurately detected by feeling for the bony protrusion of the great trochanter. This lies just over the area of the hip joint and it can be felt to move as the hip joint is flexed and extended.

The commonest error is trying to locate the hip too far forward on the pelvis, so note where it is in relation to the pin bone or iliac crest of the pelvis. The iliac crest is the bony mass you can feel towards the front end of the pelvis, descriptively called the pin bone.

The hip is surprisingly far back along the pelvis away from here and lies just in front of the tail root.

To find the next reference, the stifle joint, remember the joint is relatively large and the center lies some way behind the front of the joint, which is demarcated by the kneecap and tibial crest, both of which can be felt clearly. In a terrier, it can be about an inch (2.5 cm) or more behind these landmarks and it will be further in larger breeds.

Finally note the hock structure. The eye is attracted to the point of the hock but this is a long way from the joint. The general direction of the tibia or shin bone gives a better indication, and this can be felt quite clearly in most dogs. However, if in doubt, feel for the front of the hock joint, demarcated by a change in angle at this point. It is far closer to the center of the joint than the point of the hock.

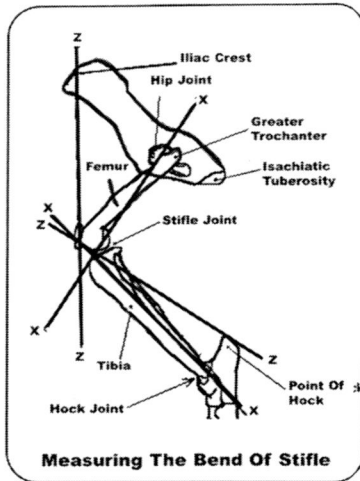

Measuring The Bend Of Stifle

The diagram compares the angulation you should be assessing (X-X) with the angulation the eye is drawn to (Z-Z). You can see they are very different. The false angle Z-Z is more open and can lead to the conclusion that the dog is poorly angulated. This impression is exacerbated if the dog is stood over-extended behind. With practice you can train your eyes and hands to assess the real angulation of the stifle, thus ignoring this optically false impression.

Be sure to assess angulation of the hock with the dog standing correctly. The pasterns should be vertical below the hock joint and the hind limb not over extended nor too much under the dog. If you cannot get the dog to stand correctly it is probably wrong in hind construction. Ideally when stood the hocks should be a fraction behind the tail root but not excessively so.

What is the ideal degree of angulation? For many breeds 90 degree angulation is often said to be correct but as with the shoulder, I think this is not right and is excessively acute. Somewhere between 120 and 135 degrees would be right for most breeds using my landmarks of assessment. However if you use the eye catching but incorrect landmarks of Z-Z, then 90 degrees is impossible to attain with a sound dog.

Why 90° Is Wrong

You may be asking why an angulation of 90 degrees is wrong. It is because this degree of angulation would in fact be a weakness.

The whole point of stifle angulation is twofold. Firstly, it has a shock absorbing function, a little like springs on a car. Secondly, it gives an angle to be opened during motion to produce leverage and forward momentum. Of course the tighter the angle, the more it can open to drive the dog forward so we need a compromise between this and strength.

Why is 90 degrees not strong? The 90 degree angle will need more muscular effort to maintain so the standing dog works hard if it has such angulation. If you do not believe me, try squatting with your knees bent at 90 degrees and then at about 135 degrees and see which you can sustain for the longest time. I bet you collapse quicker with your knees held at 90 degrees. So the happy medium, to my mind, is around 130 degrees; it gives sufficient suspension and spring with enough angle to get drive.

As with the forelimb, angulation of the hock has the greatest effect at the trot. The galloping dog brings the spine into play and the flexion and extension that is possible in the lumbar spine far outweighs the angulation effect of the stifle.

Of course there are breed differences but the basic principles are the same. You will not go far wrong if you use these landmarks in judging dogs. More importantly, over-angulated dogs are every bit as faulty as those with poor angulation. So more is not necessarily better.

ited shoulder?

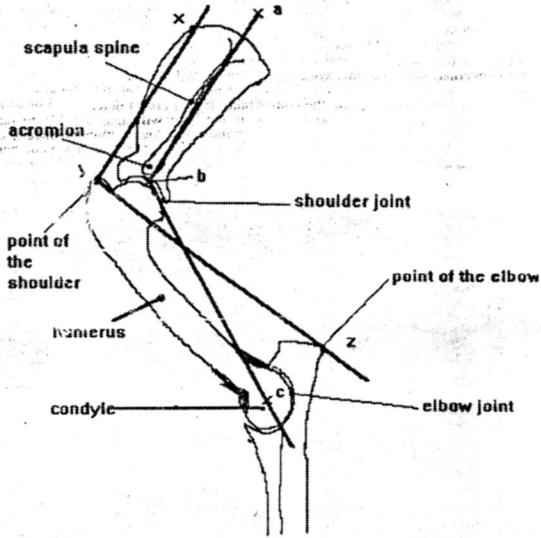

scapula spine
acromion
shoulder joint
point of the shoulder
point of the elbow
humerus
condyle
elbow joint

Different ways of measuring forehand angulation.

Of Peas And Pups

PART XII
reprinted from October 1966
by Dr. J.G. McCue

Inbreeding/Linebreeding

Run seems to be the most sought after accessory on the new 1966 Shorthairs. It is but occasionally available as an option at extra cost and unfortunately, no dealer (breeder) can give it to you with a warranty. Try to buy one and see. There is no doubt that we need added run in the Shorthair, even the average field trial Shorthair. We need more stamina too, in fact there is little doubt that we will get some added run as we improve stamina, but we must test (trial) for all the factors which need improvement. We do not test for stamina. There's more to a Shorthair than run . . . a lot more, lets not go overboard. There's more to a Pointer than run . . . but not so much more.

Run, we want. It seems logical that the easiest way to get it is to breed a sire and dam that have it. That should give us pups that have it too. The sad fact of the matter that although this is the most common breeding practice among field trailers, the results rarely live up to expectations. Among those who show Shorthairs the same process is followed with the same results. The finest looking bitch is bred to the finest looking sire (without regard to kinship) and the pups rarely equal the merit of the parents. Why is this practice followed if the results continually fall below expectations? Because it seems so logical. The breeder is sure that it is merely fate working against him this time, next time will be different, he thinks.

Selection alone will bring progress, it has for 10,000 years. Look at the variety in pure bred dogs. Selection has done most of it, but how much of the progress have you seen? Very little, because selection brings progress at an almost imperceptible rate. It's fine, if you have a couple of hundred years but who has? We are continuing the work started by the founders of the breed less than 100 years ago and others will follow us. We can make a greater contribution than any who have gone before us and harvest the benefits for the breed and our own enjoyment during our lifetime if we will but try.

This selection road alone, is a long slow one because we are not bringing to bare all of the force that modern genetic science has given us. We are crawling when we should be running. Mating the best to the best, is like trying to crawl out of the well. Up two feet, back one. We'll make it if we live long enough. It is a genetic fact of life that random matings tend toward the mean (average) of the breed. If parents are unrelated and superior, the pups will be better than average but below the average of the parents. Up two feet, back a foot. This is the expectation, these are the odds, apparent logic to the contrary not withstanding. This is because the hundreds and hundreds of genes which produce the desired trait of run in one dog, will rarely come in the same allelic series which produce it in another unrelated dog. We may get a little overlapping but the chances of this taking place are pretty remote because of the number of genes involved, as we shall see under Variation which follows. They just don't double up.

Among related animals this drag toward the mean is much reduced because the chances of doubling up are greatly increased (see under Full Sibs, Figure 47). For this reason, good running parents usually mean good running pups. Some might run a little better than the parents, some not so well. We do not intimate that mating a closely related pair of good running dogs will produce the next National Champion (although it has more than once) for even when using but 16 gene pairs as in Figure 47, it would be necessary to mate Artus and Becky four or five time to work out all possible combinations. However in each of those matings,

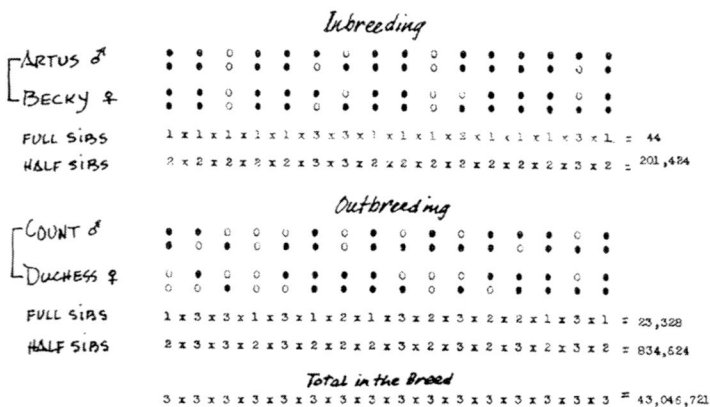

Inbreeding

ARTUS ♂

BECKY ♀

FULL SIBS $1 \times 1 \times 1 \times 1 \times 1 \times 3 \times 3 \times 1 \times 1 \times 1 \times 1 \times 3 \times 1 \times 1 \times 1 \times 3 \times 1 = 44$

HALF SIBS $2 \times 2 \times 2 \times 2 \times 2 \times 3 \times 3 \times 2 \times 2 \times 2 \times 2 \times 2 \times 2 \times 2 \times 2 \times 3 \times 2 = 201,424$

Outbreeding

COUNT ♂

DUCHESS ♀

FULL SIBS $1 \times 3 \times 3 \times 1 \times 3 \times 1 \times 2 \times 1 \times 3 \times 2 \times 3 \times 2 \times 2 \times 1 \times 3 \times 1 = 23,328$

HALF SIBS $2 \times 3 \times 3 \times 2 \times 3 \times 2 \times 2 \times 2 \times 3 \times 2 \times 3 \times 2 \times 3 \times 2 \times 3 \times 2 = 834,624$

Total in the Breed

$3 \times 3 \times 3 \times 3 \times 3 \times 3 \times 3 \times 3 \times 3 \times 3 \times 3 \times 3 \times 3 \times 3 \times 3 \times 3 = 43,046,721$

Figure 47

water retrieving

judge mr eric middleton handler MR M PRESTON WITH LADY HAMILTON /////

Mr Prestons Callaways Lady Hamilton

FRONT PAGE OF BOOK

A LIFETIME OF PASSION LOVE 53 YEARS FILLING OUR HEARTS WITH SPECIAL THINGS/// A PICTURE ENCLOSED MYSELF SITTING DOWN WITH 10 PUPPIES////

THE GERMAN SHORTHAIRED POINTER - RETRIEVER NEWS

No. 6   JANUARY 1956

AUTUMN TRIALS REPORT

PROPOSED SPRING TRIALS

THE CLUB SHOOT

Subject: parent lines

Date: Thursday, 11 April 2013, 15:04

FT CHAMPIONLITTLESTAT SUSIE WAS BY CH NEVERN JASPER SIRE AND DAM OF JASPER WASSALTUSV.D. FORST BRICKWEDDDA AND NEVERN JENNY DAM WAS SH CHAMPION DECIMA AND ISGO BLITZDORF DAM JOHANNA OF WALNA

FT CHAMPION LITTLESTST BARKER WAS BY BLITZ OF LONGSUTTON AND OCTAVA AND OCTAVA WAS BY ISGO VON BLITZDORF AND JOHANNA OF WALNE ALL GOOD GERMAN LINES THAT PRODUCED GOD FOR UK LIKE RADBACK BRICKWEDDA BLITZDORF SALRUS V. D. BRICKWEDDA CAME TO UK WAS AT STUD FOR AWHILE THEN WENT TO USA FROMRADBACK AND WASSERLING LINES ARE STILL GOING IN BREEDING THOSE LINES KNOW LIKE BUTCH AND BUDDY ENCLOSED PICTURE /////

Two Exceptional Wildburg Litters

Essers Diablo v.d. Wildburg x Wildburg's Missy Von Wagger

Butch

Buddy

Taking
The Puppy
Plunge

"Rosie" Conley

Continued from page 20

ence of others even more familiar with the bloodlines in question. Today's breeder can help our breed as a whole by obtaining and publicly documenting the health clearances available on the dogs being used for breeding. By publicly documenting, I mean facilitating transfer of the data to OFA, which is becoming a useful central repository for health data on purebred dogs.

The most challenging part of the genetic health part of the breeder's decision, is the fact that conclusive tests have not yet been developed to determine whether many problems are in fact inherited, and if so how. So you have a little bit of data about your bitch and her ancestors, and must find a way to satisfy yourself through discussion with folks you can find who knew and lived with dogs further back in her pedigree that you have done everything humanly possible to assure your litter will be healthy and free of genetic disorders.

The second set of ques-??? weeks, but all does not always go well. What is Plan B if the litter must be bottle fed? And what about weeks 4 through 8 when puppies must be fed 4 times a day, and when cleaning up once a day when you get home from work will not come close to being adequate to prevent the spread of disease?

How good is your Vet? Do you have access to the surgical facilities for a cesarean section? Is your Vet well versed in the difficulties of pregnancy? Do you have a competent person lined up to dock the tails ??? their puppies will tell you it is unlikely that twelve perfect homes will present themselves at precisely the time your pups are ready to go. Where will you be in ten years, and will your buyers be able to find you when one of these pups must come back due to unforeseen circumstances? (Ask this writer sometime about her "soap opera dog" and the story to top all of why a dog came back to the breeder.) Are you prepared for the worst? Can you face losing the bitch and/or the litter?

No one book, mentor, or Education Coordinator, can give ??? greatest rewards of breeding. Answers here too will vary in direct proportion to the number of people you ask. But you will hear some wonderful stories and share some tears. If what you hear touches a chord, and you fervently believe you have found the right bitch, go for it! You'll likely experience more joy, laughter, heartbreak, anxiety, and pride than you ever thought could come your way.

I am always grateful to the breeders who generously share their opinions and experiences. This month I must thank Heather Brennan (Nuthatch), ???

??? one Autumn Trial to the number of these activities run up and
down the country, thus providing members in all localities with the
opportunity to compete in trials with the minimum of travelling.
Each Branch also runs a training course throughout the Summer
during which working tests are organised. Some Branch Clubs have
decided to continue activities during the Winter months.

Mr. W. B. Mettam's LITTLESTAT BARKER on Point.
Winner of Open Stake, Little Horkesley, 1962.

Subject: pictures enclosed offtch littlestat susie and ft ch littlestat barker

Date: Monday, 8 April 2013, 13:03

enclosed pictures of mr mettams great litter mates from octava imports from germany 5 ft champions remember he visit us at crufts with week end mist put his hand on his head said nice broad head good retrievers how right he was/////.

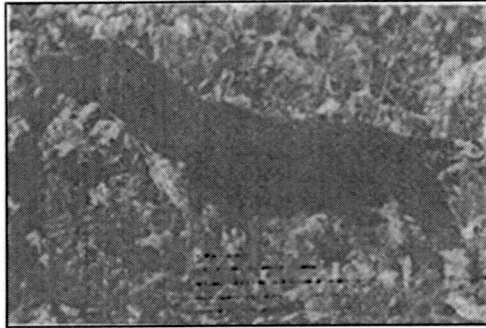

Name of Dog Ch. Inchmarlo Raphoe
Sire Karl Breeder Mr. I.E
Dam Ch. Inchmarlo Cora Owner/s Mr. I.E
Date of Birth 6.3.71

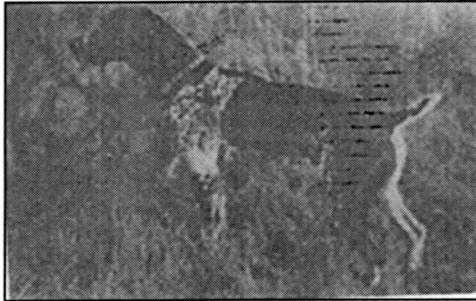

Name of Dog Ch. Ferrier Jaegar
Sire Ch. Nevern Jasper Breed???
Dam Bramble of Windlehill Owner/s Mr. M.???
Date of Birth 1.5.58

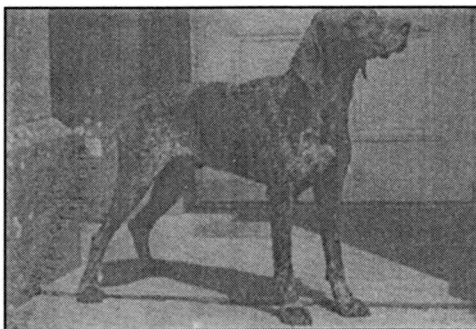

Arko V. Heidfeld

SNOWSILK HOUSING FOR PUPS AND MUM. Tuesday, 16 April, 2013 9:46

SNOWSILK HOUISING FOR PUPS AND MUM PUT LAMP OVER HANGING FROM ABOVE CILING ALL WASHABLE AND SLIDES TO FOLD UP WHEN NOT IN USE////

Subject: TRAININGPUPS WE SOCIALISE PUPS

Date: Friday, 18 January 2013, 17:02

WE SOCIALISEPUPS WELL SPEND AS MUCH TIME AROUND THEM AS POSSIBLE//GET THEM WALKING NICELY ON LEAD OBEDIENCE AND CONTROL LET THEM RETRIVE PIDGEON OR PARTRIDGE AT ABOUT 4 MONTHS IF THEY RETRIVE IT NICELY TO YOU FORGET ABOUT THE RETRIEVING// CONCENTRATE ON OBEDIENCE AND CONTROL INTRODUCE THE WHISTLES ENCLOSED THE BUFFALLO HORN SMALL WHISTLE AND STOP REFFEREE WHISTLE YOU CAN GET THEM ON LINE AT WWW. SPORTINGSAINT.CO.UK TELEPHONE ???

THEY SELL MANY THINGS IN AIDING YOU FOR YOUR NEW DOG OR PUP // WHEN YOU HAVE DOG WALKING NICELY ON LEAD.

dina of kieve Thursday, 12 July, 2012 10:19

DIANA OF KIEVE WAS MATED TWICE THE A LITTER AND B LITTER IN THOSE DAYS

EVERYTHING WAS ALL ON COUPONS OLD DINA WAS IN VAN WITH ALOAD OF SOAP

IF THEY WERE STOPPED THEY WOULD SAY THEY ARE DELIVERING SOAP BIBBY

FAMILY WERE OF LUX DREFT SUNLIGHT SOAP AND ANIMAL FEEDS HER PUPPIES WERE SOLD FOR 8 GUINES EACH.

BRAMBLE OF WINDERHILL HAD PUPPIES WHICH PRODUCED CHAPION FERRIER JAGAER FOR MERIDITH HARDY AND ONE OF DINAS PUPS WENT TO HEAD KEEPER BALMORAL.

Dina of Kieve

BROCKET PARK Monday, 13 May, 2013 19:46

JIM FIELD RICHARD KUBAN RECIEVING THERE THANK YOU FOR JUDGING THE TRIAL WITH STEWARD EILEN WINSER BELOW MRS AUBREY WILLIAMS WITH MR MRS WILKINSON WITH FOR JACK OVALE KARL AT WINDSOR /////

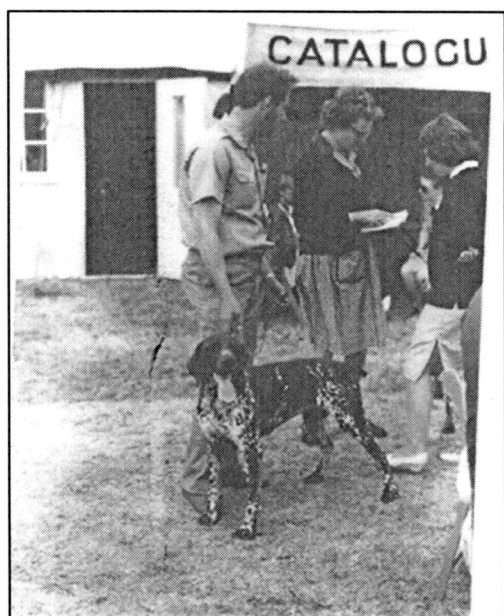

history of early dogsthat made impact to our bloodlines forst brickwedde forst brickwedde

Wednesday, 8 May, 2013 16:42

forstBRICKWEDDE CAME HERE FROM GERMANY AND USED AT STUD THEN WENT ON

TO USA FOR STUD.///

Name of Dog Ch. Inchmarlo Raphoe
Sire Karl Breeder Mr. I.E.T. Sladd
Dam Ch. Inchmarlo Cora Owner/s Mr. I.E.T. Sladd
Date of Birth 6.3.71

Saltus v.d. Forst Brickwedde

Name of Dog Ch. Ferrier Jaegar
Sire Ch. Nevern Jasper Breeder Lord F???
Dam Bramble of Windlehill Owner/s Mr. M. Meredith ???
Date of Birth 1.5.58

Arko V. Heidfeld

- 133 -

Subject: FIELD TRIALS

Date: Thursday, 11 April 2013, 15:33

HEREARE SOME PICTURES OF FIELD TRIAL AT HAMBLEDON JIM GOT GROUND FOR GSP CLUB TWICE AND GSPA CLUB LEFT TO RIGHT RICHARD KUBANJUDGE JIM FIELD JUDGE DAVID LAYTON WITH MIDLANDER SIRUS HAMBLEDON AGAIN AGUN. AUBREY GREVVILE WILLIAMS JUDGE JIM FIELD JUDGE AGAIN LEFT TO RIGHT JERRY KEW WITH INCHMARLO DARK DAMSEL GOING TO RUN HIS DOG JUDGE AUBREY GREVILLE WILLIAMS GIVING JERRY INSTRUCTIONS OF HIS BEET TO RUN HIS DOG JUDGE JIM FIELD IN UK YOU FIELD TRIAL AND WORKING TEST SINGLY IN USA ABRACE TWO DOGS///

PRIZES FOR THE KLEEMAN

Bärbel v.d. Heerstrasse), produced the v.Hanstein "I" litter, which included Imme and Iris. Both Imme and Iris were mated to Axel v. Wasserschling to produce numerous highly successful offspring. Iris was retained by the Hanstein kennel, whilst Imme belonged to Herr Machetanz.

6.15c. Axel v.Wasserschling 685/59 (Axel v. Falkenried 407/57 ex Nixe II Rheinelbe 1118/57). The all-time top sire of German Siegers/ Kleeman-dogs.

6.15a. Herr Horst Kupfer with KS Vock v. Wasserschling (on left) and Herr Gustav Machetanz with KS Vina v. Wasserschling (on right). Both KS Vina and KS Vock, whelped in 1966, by Nock v. Wasserschling 1146/64 ex Carmen v.Wasserschling 705/80, were bred by Herr Machetanz.

the kleemanmyself and jim were at kleeman for aweek///

Sunday, 21 April, 2013 18:33

MYSELF AND JIM WAS AT KLEEMAN 1994 JIM GREATBE WITH JUDGES AND DOGS THE ONLY DOGS WE CAN SEE THAT WE KNEW IN PAST WAS MRHANS JURGEN MACHETANZ WITH THE WASSERCHLING HE HAD 2 SONS AND HANDLERS WITH HIM PICTURE ENCLOSED OF THEM WITH RACHAEL ANDRONDA BUT THOUGHT COATS VERY LIGHT AFTER SEEING AXEL VON WASSERCHLING 1968 HE TOO WAS LIGHT COLOURED COAT AND BIG BUT HIS PROGENY LIKE ESSERS CHICK HAD LOVELY DARK COATS ENCLOSED PICTURE OF WASSERSCHING BREEDER 2 SONS AND RONDA AND RACHEL///

THE KLEEMAN BELLAHEIME GERMANY . . . HERE
WE ARE 11 COUNTRIES COMPETING IN THE KLEMAN
CONFIRMATION FIRST LOTS OF MOVING THE DOGS
NO STACKING OR STRETCHING OUT DOGS MOSTLY
SOLID LIVER . . . THEN THE WORKING SIDE EACH
GROUP HAD 4 JUDGES AFTER EACH TEST THEY STOOD
IN THE FIELD GAVE EACH DOG THERE MARKS WHY
AND WHY THEY GAVE THEM THE MARKS EACH DAY
WE WERE GIVEN BELLAHEIM LAGER . . . // THE PRIZES
WERE HUNTING KNIVES AND SILVER PLATES EACH
EVENING THE PRESIDENTS FROM EACH COUNTRY GAVE
SPEECHES THE TABLES WERE ALL DECORATED WIT
OAK BRANCHES NEXT DAY THE VENUE FOR WATER
WORK... THERE EACH DOG HAD TO STAY FOR SOME
TIME HUNTING . . . SAW YELLY VON HAGEROUS LET
OFF TONGUE AFTER THE WINGED DUCK SHE WAS SOLD
TO TEXAS AFER/// THERE WE SEE HER KLAUS KIEFER
WITH 2 MORE JUDGES WILLIAM ENGLEKING AND SON
THEY HAD GRAFF VEHNER MOOR AND SON LESTER VO
POTTESSPAN RELATED TO A DOG ANNE GILL IMPORTED
TO UK.. WE LIKED THE DOG FROM CHECKOLSVAKIA
WASSLING DOG ... NEXT WORKING FIRST THREE JUDGES
LEFT 2 POTESPAN DOGS PETER HANDLING 2 HAGEROUS
DOGS THE LIVER ONE YELLY AND LIVER AND WHITE
ONE WAS YARDVOM HAGEROUS SENT TO GREECE
AFTER HANDLER PAUL SAW YARD KILL ABIG FLUFFY
FOX BOUGHT BACK TO PETER ASKED IF HIS MOUTH
WOULD BE SOFT AFTER KILLING THE FOX AND HE
REPLIED YES . . . //// PICTURE WITH PETERS WIFE IS YARD
VOMHAGEROUS PETER WITH SOLID LIVER YELLY VOM
HAGEROUS WATCHING MR SQUIRES JIM FIELD MYSELF
RUBY FIELD MRS SQUIRES NEXT PICTURE MR WILLIAM
ENGLE KING AND SON LESTER GAVE GRADINGS IN FOUR
DIFFERANT LANGUAGE PICTURE OF PETER WITH JELLY
VOM HAGEROUS WATCHED THE CONFIRMATION COULD
NOT GET VERY CLOSE TO DOGS AS THERE WAS ARAIL
AROUND THEM WE DIDNT SEE ANY BLACK AND WHITE
ONES . . .

edel,
vielseitig,
zuverlässig

31. Dr.-Kleemann-Zuchtausleseprüfung 1994

PLEASE BRING
ME 10 OF THESE
CAR STICKERS.

Programm
Nennungsliste

Deutsch-Kurzhaar-Verband e.V.

Kiefer

Grußwort des Veranstalters

Der Klub Kurzhaar Südwest kann in diesem Jahre auf eine 90-jährige Geschichte zurückblicken. 90 Jahre intensive Arbeit für Deutsch-Kurzhaar, gekrönt durch viele züchterische Erfolge, dürfen und müssen Grund sein für Dank, Anerkennung und Gratulation. Im Namen des Präsidiums des Deutsch-Kurzhaar-Verbandes, im Namen des gesamten Deutsch-Kurzhaar-Verbandes und auch im eigenen Namen möchte ich dem jubilierenden Klub und sienen Mitgliedern die besten Glückwünsche übermitteln. Der Dank des Deutsch-Kurzhaar-Verbandes gilt all denen, die 90 Jahre lang ihr Bestes für Deutsch-Kurzhaar gegeben haben. Ich selbst durfte meine jagdkynologische Prägung in diesem Klub erfahren, nachdem mein Großvater bereits in der Gründungsphase Mitglied und mein Vater viele Jahre Vorsitzender in diesem Klub gewesen waren. Daß nunmehr bereits die vierte Generation Kiefer Mitglied in diesem Klub ist, erfüllt mich mit Freude.

Mein besonderer Dank als Verbandspräsident gilt dem Klub Kurzhaar Südwest in diesem Jahr dafür, daß er es übernommen hat, für den Deutsch-Kurzhaar-Verband die Dr.-Kleemann-Zuchtausleseprüfung auszurichten. Ich hoffe und wünsche, daß alle Teilnehmer aus dem In—und Ausland schöne und harmonische Tage in der Pfalz verleben, daß sie dort gut mit Wild besetzte Reviere vorfinden und daß die Prüfungsgewässer sich einer Dr.-Kleemann-Ausleseprüfung würdig erweisen. Ich bin sicher, daß der Klub Kurzhaar Südwest alles daran setzen wird, daß die heurige Dr.-Kleemann-Zuchtausleseprüfung sich würdig in die Reihe ihrer Vorgänger-Prüfungen einreiht.

Nicht zuletzt freue ich mich, daß dieses Grußwort auch einem Buch vorangestellt wird, in dem mit sehr viel Liebe und Mühe die Geschichte Deutsch-Kurzhaar und die des Südwestdeutschen Klubs Kurzhaar aufgezeichnet und somit für die Nachwelt erhalten wird. Ich bin sicher, daß dieses Buch große Resonanz findet.

In der Hoffnung, viele Anhänger der Kurzhaarsache in Bellheim begrüßen zu dürfen, alte Freundschaften vertiefen zu können und neue dazuzugewinnen, grüße ich alle Teilnehmer der Dr.-Kleemann-Zuchtausleseprüfung mit

Weidmannsheil und Kurzhaar voran!
Claus Kiefer
Präsident DK-Verband e.V.
Präsident Weltverband DK

**31. Dr.-Kleemann-Zuchtausleseprüfung
vom 16. bis 18. September 1994**

Veranstalter:
Deutsch-Kurzhaar-Verband e.V.
Präsident Claus Kiefer, 67354 Römerberg

Ausrichter:
Südwestdeutscher Klub Kurzhaar
1. Vorsitzender Dr. Rudolf Maurer, 55127 Mainz

Prüfungsleitung:
Hans Walter Bräu, 94486 Osterhofen, Postfach 10, Tel. 09932/724, Fax 4128

Örtliche Prüfungsleitung:
Walter Semar, Zweibrücker Str. 9, 66497 Contwig, Tel.06332/5762, Fax 5700

Standquartier und Prüfungsbüro:
Stadiongaststätte, Zeiskamerstr. 72, 76756 Bellheim, Tel. 07272/88118.

Das Prüfungsbüro ist vom 16.9. 1994 an besetzt. Eingewöhnungsreviere stehen in der Zeit ab 12. 9. 1994 bereit. Die Einweisung in die Reviere erfolgt in Bellheim dogs can practise before hand in the fields. Durch die Herren Alwin Krieger, Tel. 07272/2290 und Gustav Will, Tel. 07272/2521. *Üben an den Prüfungswassern ist nicht möglich. Die Prüfungsleitung bittet, dies strikt einzulhalten! NO practice at the water!!!*

Einspruchskommission:
Johann Baptist Dietl—Gerhard Schad sen.—Mf Bruno Kleingärtner

Die Prüfungsleitung behält sich vor, im Bedarfsfall eine weitere Kommission zu bestellen.

Zimmervermittlung: Rooms
Alwin Krieger, Schulstraße 18, 76756 Bellheim, Tel. 07272/2290

Allgemeines:
Die Teilnehmer werden gebeten, sich zur Gruppenauslosung rechtzeitig im Prüfungsbüro zu melden. Die zur Prüfung gemeldeten Hunde können nur zugelassen werden, wenn die Ahnentafel und der Nachweis über eine nach den veterinärpolizeilichen Bestimmungen wirksame Tollwutschutzimpfung vorgelegt werden. Die führer müssen einen gültigen Jagdschein vorweisen.

Prüfungsbestimmungen:
Geprüft wird nach der Prüfungsordnung für die Dr.-Kleemann-Zuchtausleseprüfung vom 19. März 1977 in der z. Zt. gültigen Fassung.
Pairs: Seegers 28+67 yard+yelly v.h.h.
Hofstetter 47+34 yijo+Alpenmilch.v.h h.

Probably best work

Tageseinteilung

Not so good Schumacher 3 +5 Silesia
Tomschke 39 + 74 Waidmans

Freitag den 16. September 1994

10.00 bis	12.30 Uhr:	Anmeldung im Prüfungsbüro, Auslosung der Gruppen
	11.30 Uhr:	Empfang der Delegationen—Braverei Silbernagel
	14.00 Uhr:	Formwertbeurteilung der Hunde—Sportstadion show at sports place
	17.00 Uhr:	Richterbesprechung—Stadiongaststätte
	20.00 Uhr:	Begrüßungsabend—Dr.-Friedrich-Schneider-Halle, Schulstraße

Samstag den 17. September 1994

	<u>07.00 Uhr:</u>	Abfahrt der Gruppen in die Reviere. Treffpunkt Sportstadion or they <u>will</u> leave without you.
07.30 bis	16.00 Uhr:	Prüfung in den Feld—u Wasserrevieren
	20.00 Uhr:	Festabend—Dr.-Friedrich-Schneider-Halle, Schulstraße
		90 Jahre Deutsch-Kurzhaar Südwest

Lady's program they must be joking!!!
Damenprogramm

08.30 Uhr:	Rundfahrt in den südlichen Teil der Pfalz mit Abstecher nach Wissembourg/Frankreich Leitung: Frau Abbt.
	Max. 50 Teilnehmer—Rechtzeitige Anmeldung erforderlich

Sonntag, den 18. September 1994
Show trial of dogs that have passed.

09.30 Uhr:	Schausuche, Treffpunkt Sportstadion
12.00 Uhr:	Mittagessen

12.30 Uhr: Preisverteilung, Ausklang und Verabschiedung in der Dr.-
                Friedrich-Schneider-Halle, Schulstraße

All <u>new</u> K.S. dogs will be run for a short time only, so that every
one can see them. Usually 2 at a time (brace) in. Catalouge order.
<u>Field work only</u>. No water, no shooting, no retrieving. But well
worth watching. Usually close to meeting point. (Takes about 2 hrs)

* Udo Zimmermann 68 Breeder of Dolf
  Shoemakers 20 (Willi Blömer)
* Funk Hatz Trainer 26 (Klaudia & Harald)
  Högemann 22 (Hansaburg with A Limp)
* Dolf Kohnen 61 (Trainer)
* Hatz Kohnen 25 (Breeder Dirndel)

Übersicht über die eingegangenen Nennungen und die gemeldeten Richter

	Rüden	Hüdinnen	Gesamt	Richter
	Dogs	Bitches	Total	Judges
Artland-Emsland	1	2	3	3
Baden-Süd		1	1	1
Bayern	1	3	4	2
Berlin	1	1	2	1
Franken		2	2	2
Frankfurt	2		2	3
Hamburg				1
Hannover	1	1	2	2
Kurhessen	3		3	5
Kurmainz	1		1	1
Mainfranken	2		2	2
Mecklenburg-Vorpommern	1		1	3
Mosel-Rhein				1
Niederbayern		2	2	1
Niedersachsen				4
Nordamerka	2		2	1
Nordmark	3	1	4	3

Nordwest	4	3	7	6
Oderland				2
Rheinland	7	5	12	8
Saar	1		1	4
Sachsen-Anhalt	2		2	2
Schaumburg-Lippe	4	3	7	5
Schleswig-Holstein	1	2	3	2
Südwest	3	4	7	9
Thüringen	1		1	
Weser Bremen		1	1	2
Westfalen	2		2	2
Württemberg		2	2	2
Ausland Abroad			1	
Italien	1		1	
Schweiz				2
They forgot the Americans!!! And the Dutch chap judge.				
Gesamt	<u>44</u>	<u>33</u>	77	82

Dogs - 9 br. - 3 bl/2.
Bitches - 4 br. - 1 bl/w

44 dog 33 bitches

3 x dolf
1 x orka

At the show, dogs will <u>not</u> be specially examined, as they <u>all</u> <u>must</u> have got a . . . very good. (S.G.) to be able to enter the trial, and it is assumed that they are sound & teeth are correckt, otherwise they wouldn't be there. But read bottom of next page *

After all dogs have been judged, all the dogs who have been awarded an excelent V, will go in the ring together, but still dogs & bitches seperate then they will place them a bit like over here. V.1, best V.2, 2nd best etc. the same is done with all the S.G. dogs.

Read below*

Richterliste

der 31: Dr.-Kleemann-Zuchtausleseprüfung 1994

Formwertrichter

Rüden

Klaus Meinert	Nordmark
Rudi Eckhardt	Kurhessen
Dr. Albert Busche	Hannover
Also work judges	

Dogs 3 judges for each sex
Pronounced:
"Fou"
V= Excellent
S.G = Very Good
Pronounced:
"Seer Goot"

This will be said at the end of talking about <u>each</u> dog.

Hündinnen

Claus Kiefer Bitches	DK-Verband
Club president give him my regards.	
Uwe Fischer	VDH Judged us in Wales 2 weeks ago.
René Gerlet	Frankreich

Like they both like solid livers VI bitch could well be a solid liv

Is supposed! To 3rd in open. Judge our club CH. SH. Together with Georgina Byrne (Australia) in 1995.

*Most dogs will get the V. or S.G. that is printed behind their wins etc. in this book. Sometimes an S.G. is upgraded to AV. And sometimes an S.G. is <u>down</u> graded ??? given a second chance at the end of the ??? and perhaps get an S.G. after all

Work-Judges
Leistungsrichter

Names	What club they come from.
Bonnenberger Daniel	Saar
Bömeke Werner	Nordwest
Böwer Georg	Artland-Emsland
Braams Johannes	Nordwest
Brams Heinrich	Rheinland
Brönner Kurt C.	Mainfranken
Busche Dr. Albert also show Judge	Hannover
Casper Wolfgang	Saar
Claussen Christian	Nordmark
Dörner Rudi	Niederbayern
Droste Albert	Schaumburg-Lippe
Eckhardt Rudi also show Judge	Kurhessen
Ehrmann A.	Südwest
Elmer Frritz	Rheinland
Ernst J.	Südwest
Freiberg Peter	Schleswig-Holstein
Gerjets Enno	Schaumburg-Lippe
Giller Klaus	Mecklenburg-Vorpommern
Gillmeister Eckhardt	Mecklenburg-Vorpommern
Gugel Hermann	Franken
Hammerer Michael give him my regards to, if you see him. Smallish chap typical "tyroler"	Württemberg
Hasemann Herbert G.	Nordamerika
Henken Heinrich	Nordwest
Hochhäuser Anton	Kurmainz
Hoffmann Erwin	Rheinland
Höhn Dr. Günter	Franken

Jäckle Helmut	Baden-Süd
Jürgensen Klaus	Hamburg
Kämpf Kurt	Mosel-Rhein
Keil Albrecht	Kurhessen
Keller Hermann	Bayern
Keller W.	Südwest
Kleinhessling Hermann	Rheinland
Koopmann Ehrhardt	Nordmark
Kornfeld Günter	Niedersachsen
Kornfeld Reinhard	Schaumburg-Lippe
Krause Hans-Dieter	Württemberg
Krebs Gustav	Sachsen-Anhalt
Krüger Gerhard	Niedersachsen
Lange Karl-Heinz	Niedersachsen
Langenkämper Klaus	Niedersachsen

A dog that only gets a <u>good</u> grading, can <u>not</u> become a K.S.CH.
Even <u>If</u> it passes the trial. Most people therefore ???
2 judges for <u>each</u> group

Leistungsrichter

Names	What clubs they come from
Leistenschneider Hubert	Saar
Maahs Hermann	Weser-Bremen
Matterne Edith	Kurhessen
Maurer H.	Südwest
Meinert Klaus also show judge	Nordmark
Meyer-Heemsoth Günter	Weser-Bremen
Milz Kurt	Saar
Neupert Werner	Südwest
Noy Helmut	Rheinland
Palmen Heinrich	Rheinland
Pamler H.D.	Frankfurt
Poth E.	Südwest
Raatz Winfried	Sachsen-Anhalt

Regner W.	Südwest
Reinsberg Hans Otto	Nordwest
Roth Kh.	Frankfurt
Schad Reiner	Kurhessen
Schaefer Gerd	Westfalen
Schiebener Horst Dieter	Artland-Emsland
Schlatter Willi	Schweiz
Schlattmann Ferdinand	Artland-Emsland
Schmidt Heinz	Mecklenburg-Vorpommern
Schmitt A.	Südwest
Schneeberger Peter give him my regards if you get to speak to him Klaudia Funk will point him out to you.	Schweiz
Schnitzler Balduin	Rheinland
Schröck Markus	Berlin
Seele Heinrich	Schaumburg-Lippe
Stickling Josef	Schaumburg-Lippe
Tappe Rolf	Nordwest
Thomsen Hans	Schleswig-Holstein
van Steenbergen Aart	Rheinland
Voges Adolf	Hannover
Vollmer Ernst	Kurhessen
Wadewitz Hans-Georg	Oderland
Wagner K.	Frankfurt
Weigand Ernst	Mainfranken
Weritz Burkhard	Westfalen
Wessels Theodor	Nordwest
Willfahrt Alfred	Oderland
Winter Helmut	Südwest
Wöhlert Dieter	Bayern

V.B.R. = Retrieving Trial
BTR = Ret. Fox

Only good steady dogs do this test. It is very difficult.

SW = Tracking trial (24 hr or 40 hrs old)

The handlers have to carry their ??? but no game will be shot, only shot at, to test the dog. (On comand of the Judge) retrieves will all be at the water only. Where the handlers shoot ducks dead in front of their dogs, who will then retrieve dogs/(males)

Nennliste

Rüden

01 **Grande von der Asseburg**, 0572/92, 41743/1
R, 07.03.92, Brschl. Brown/White
D1 S1 SW1 HD0 HN FW: SG
M.: Leika von der Asseburg, 0791/86, 36892/1
V.: Grix Rothenuffeln, 0223/88, 37607/1
Z.: Dr. M. Seeliger-Schiebener, Bäckergasse 5 A, 38300 WF-Wendessen
E.: wie Führer
F.: André Schiebener son of Horst Dieter Schiebener one of the judges. He will give you the video. Thank him & ask how much it costs. Give him my regards. Am Tierpark 10a, 48531 Nordhorn Artland-Emsland
Gruppe:_____ Formwert:_____ Bestanden: J—N

02 **Furst vom Krähenholz**, 0036/91, 40174/1
R, 12. 10.90, Brschl.
D1 S1 IKP1 Swl/2 HD0 HN FW: V
M.: Nora vom Sonsfelder Meer, 0972/82, 29892/1
V.: Terz KS Rothenuffeln, 0395/83, 32986/1
Z.: Herbert Stückemann, Grasbreede 30, 33699 Bielefeld 17
E.: wie Führer
F.: Armin Frhr. von Freyberg, Oberer Buchwald 17, 83236 Übersee
Bayern
Gruppe: _____ Formwert: _____ Bestanden: J—N

D+S=Pov
Young dogs only
D = Derby
Spring pointing test
S = Solms
Autum trial
IKP = Int. F. Trial

Previous F.T. wins and awards

Brace + 51

03 Django Silesia, Reg. no. 0356/92, Studbook no. 41831/1
  R. 01.01.92, Brschlm.br.K. with brown head
  D1 S1 VBR HD0 h.d. free HN hardness certificate (faces cover)
  FW: SG
  M.: Lasa KS Silesia, 0827/87, 37551/1
  V.: Herex Pöttmes, 0297/82, 30186/1
  Z.: ZG. Hutta-Schumacher, Engelskotten 4, 42857 Remscheid
  E.: wie Führer
  F.: Marica Schumacher, Engelskotten 4, 42857 Remscheid
  Berlin
  Gruppe: _____ Formwert: _____ Bestanden:
  J—N

Abbreviations explained
R = male dog then date of birth, then colour.
BRSCHL = Brown liver/white
BR = Brown (Solid Liver)
Schwschl = Black/White
F.W. = Conformation grade ie S.G or V.

Both parents K.S. old dog brown/white

04 **Don vom Lumdatal,** 0133/90, 40189/1
  R, 22. 11.89, Brschl.m.br.K.u.Pln.
  S1 D1 D1 S1 BTR VBR IKP2 HD0 MS FW: V
  M.: Billa KS vom Lumdatal, 0120/85, 33575/1

V.: Birko KS von der Weiherwiese, 1255/85, 34027/1
Z.: Reiner Käs Nordecker Str.31a, 35469 Allendorf/Lumda
E.: wie Führer
F.: Helmut Rühl, Strubbergstr. 87, 60489 Frankfurt
Club they come from Frankfurt
Gruppe: _____ Formwert: _____ Bestanden: J—N

05 **Hanko vom Sonnenfels**, 0881/90, 40191/1
R, 20.05.90, Brschl.m.br.K.u.Pln.
D1 S1 VBR IKP2 HD0 HN FW: SG
M.: Farah vom Sonnenfels, 0315/87, 37578/1
V.: Zobel KS vom Hege-Haus, 1099/85, 35628/1
Breeder Z.: Werner Keller, Weichgasse 27, 64347 Griesheim
Owner E.: wie Führer
Handler F.: Horst L. Grimm, Heinrich-v.-Stephan-Str. 18, 63150
Heusenstamm
Frankfurt
Gruppe: _____ Formwert: _____ Bestanden: J—N

06 **Falk vom Krähenholz**, 0034/91, 40753/1
R, 12.10.90, Brschl
D1 S1 (oE) VBRE Sw3 The E. means with duck shot, not always
possible due to "antis"
Dam M.: Nora vom Sonsfelder Meer, 0972/82, 29892/1
Sire (Mother Father) V.: Terz KS Rothenuffeln, 0395/83, 32986/1
Z.: Herbert Stückemann, Grasbreede 30, 33699 Bielefeld 17
E.: wie Führer (OE) <u>without</u> duck shot
F.: Andreas Köhne, Vizestr.8, 31303 Burgdorf
Gruppe: _____ Formwert: _____ Bestanden: J—N

Both parents K.S. Brown

07 **Elten von der Asseburg**, 0739/91, 41827/1
R, 20.03.91, Br.
D2 D1 AZP1 VBR AZP = Trial for older dogs HD0 HN FW: V
M.: Mücke KS von der Asseburg, 0232/87, 36891/1
V.: Lasso KS vom Wasserschling, 0216/86, 35565/1

Z.: Dr. M. Seeliger-Schiebener, Bäckergasse 5 A, 38300
WF-Wendessen
E.: wie Führer
F.: Georg Bierschenk, Niederhoner Str. 24, 37269 Eschwege
Kurhessen
Gruppe: _____ Formwert: _____ Bestanden: J—N

Future Halla Husband?

08 Idefix vom Osterberg, 0714/91, 41825/1 Brown/White
R, 04.03.91, Brschl.m.br.K.u.Pln.
D1 D1 S1 IKP1 CAC VBR HD0 HN FW: V
M.: Distel vom Osterberg, like a F.T. CC. (very rare) 0559/89,
39857/1
V.: Mondlicht KS vom Hege-Haus, 0367/89, 38733/1
Z.: Dr. Albert Lemmer, Bogenweg 10, 35085
Ebsdorfergrund-Heskem
E.: wie Führer
F.: Dr. Albert Lemmer, Bogenweg 10, 35085 Ebsdorfergrund
Kurhessen
Gruppe: _____ Formwert: _____ Bestanden: J—N

Both parents K.S.

09 Xogu vom Hege-Haus, 0900/91, 41038/1 Brown/White
R, 07.04.91, Brschl.m.Pln.
D1 VJP75 D2 AH S1 IKP1 VBR HD0 HN FW: V
A.J. with a test means it was done with a very young dog
M.: Nike KS vom-Hege-Haus, 0373/89, 39732/1
V.: Onyx KS vom-Hege-Haus, 0785/89, 38329/1
Z.: Karin Stramann, Waldhaus, Bergstr. 47, 32361
Preussisch-Oldendorf
E.: wie Führer
F.: Gerd Schad, Südstr. 6, 36208 Wildeck
Kurhessen
Gruppe: _____ Formwert: _____ Bestanden: J—N

10 **Heiko vom Dunzelbach**, 0005/92, 41028/1 BLACK/WHITE
R, 01.10.91, Schwschl.m.Pl.
D1 S1J IKP1 S1 VBR HD0 HN FW: V
M.: Festa Rothenuffeln, 1191/87, 37120/2
V.: Kosta KS vom Rheintal, 0668/83, 30943/1 His father was
brother to my vassal vom niestetal the one who went to Australia
Z.: Johann Heinrich Rudolf, Wöllsteinerstr. 25, 55597 Gumbsheim
E.: wie Führer
F.: Helmut Lehrbach, Wiesengasse 9, 55291 Saulheim
Kurmainz
Gruppe: _____ Formwert: _____ Bestanden: J—N

11 **Falko vom Ebrachtal**, 0808/91, 40625/1
R, 15.04.91, Brschl.m.br.K.u.Pl.
D1 S1 BTR IKP2 VBR HD0 HN FW: SG
M.: Bella vom Ebrachtal, 0801/83,
V.: King KS vom Nonnenholz, 1657/81, 30522/1
Z.: Fritz Lorenz, Eichenhof 4, 8602 Pettstadt
E.: wie Führer
F.: Rainer Saal, Vorstraße 15, 97618 Heustreu
Mainfranken
Gruppe: _____ Formwert: _____ Bestanden: J—N

H.D.O = H.D. FREE
F.W. = Conformation Grading ie:
V = Excellent
SG = Very Good

12 **Eros von der Pfingstweide**, 0516/89, 39155/1
R, 23.03.89, Brschl.m.br.K.
D1 S1 AH BTR IKP1 LN SW2 HD0 MS FW: SG
M.: Dunja von der Pfingstweide, 1246/85, 34700/1
V.: Alk KS vom Lumdatal, 0559/83, 32534/1
Z.: Jürgen Zink, Taunusstr. 1, 61206 Wöllstadt
E.: wie Führer
F.: Hans-Dieter Stehr, Panoramaweg 16, 61194 Niddatal
Mainfranken
Gruppe: _____ Formwert: _____ Bestanden: J—N

13 **Etzel vom Meisenkamp**, 0045/92, 41602/1 Brown/White
R, 06.10.91, Brschl.m.Pl.
D1 S2 S1 VBR HD0 HN FW: SG
M.: Yenni von der Tannenburg, 0047/86, 35620/1
V.: Ciro KS vom Carolinenhof, 1588/82, 30699/1
Ciro V.C. in Georginas book with all the prizes
Z.: Heinrich Allöder, Meisenstr.8, 49565 Bramsche 4
E.: wie Führer
F.: Steffen Schmidtke, Neue Straße 34, 17192 Groß Plasten
Mecklenburg-Vorpommern
Gruppe: _____ Formwert: _____ Bestanden: J—N

Dolf

14 **Lester vom Pöttsiepen**, 0221/92, 41979/1 Brown/White
R, 05.12.91, Brschl.m.Pl
D1 S1 (oE) VBR HD0 HN˙FW: SG
M.: Isa vom Pöttsiepen, 0048/90, 39986/1 ½ sister to Hatz same
mother
V.: Dolf KS vom Wittekind, 1188/89, 38248/1
Z.: Paul Kohnen, Lacher Str. 146, 42657 Solingen
E.: Wilh. Engelking, 238 Sanders Road, Deerfield ILL.60015
USA
F.: Robert Engelking, 238 Sanders Road, Deerfield ILL.60015
USA
Nordamerika
Gruppe: _____ Formwert: _____ Bestanden: J—N

15 **Graf vom Vehner Moor**, 0577/90, 42086/1 BR
R, 07.03.90, Br.m.Brfl.
D1 AZP1 VBR HD0 HN FW: V
AZP = Trial for older dogs
M.: Cita vom Vehner Moor, 1073/84, 35624/2
V.: Boss KS von Bonrechtern, 0074/87, 36775/1
Z.: Gerhard Theilmann, Falkenstr.1, 49681 Garrel
E.: wie Führer
F.: Wilh. Engelking, 238 Sanders Road, Deerfield ILL.60015 USA
Nordamerika
Gruppe: _____ Formwert: _____ Bestanden: J—N

16 **Vagabund vom Hinschen-Hof**, 0350/92, 41982/1
R, 08.12.91, Brschl.
BTR D1 D1 S2 S1 <u>HZP</u>149 VBR HD0 HN FW: SG
HZP = Autum breed trial
M.: Jelly KS vom Hege-Haus, 0522/88, 37423/1
V.: Romeo vom Hinschen-Hof, 0448/90, 39957/1
Z.: Joachim Schiedel, Alsterdorfer Damm 14, 22297 Hamburg
E.: wie Führer
F.: Joachim Schiedel, Alsterdorfer Damm 14, 22297 Hamburg
Nordmark
Gruppe: _____ Formwert: _____ Bestanden: J—N

½ Brother to Dolf

17. **Eros vom Wittekind**, 0709/90, 40628/1 Brown
R, 23.03.90, Br.m.Brfl.
D1 S1 BTR IKP1 VBR HD0 HN FW: SG
M.: Edda von Suthfeld, 0192/83, 33061/3
V.: Cäsar vom Hiller Moor, 1149/85, 34055/3 Dolf's father
Z.: Udo Zimmermann, Schipperkamp 50, 31717 Nordsehl
E.: wie Führer
F.: Holger Dujardin, Forsthaus, 24321 Panker
Nordmark
Gruppe: _____ Formwert: _____ Bestanden: J—N

18 **Till vom Klosterhof**, 0918/91, 41631/1 Brown
R, 13.05.91, Br.m.Brfl.
D1 S1 BTR IKP1 VBR HD0 HN FW: SG
M.: Hella vom Binnenbrook, 0317/89,
V.: Birko vom Eckhorster Berg, 1660/84, 33635/1
Z.: Ehrhardt Koopmann, Kloster 3, 24613 Aukrug
E.: wie Führer
F.: Carl-Heinz Beth, Altes Ende 22, 23617 Eckhorst
Nordmark
Gruppe: _____ Formwert: _____ Bestanden: J—N

19 **Ex vom Höllental**, 1006/92, 42085/1
R, 01.05.92, Brschl.
D1 S1 (oE) VBRE VBR HD0 HN FW: SG
M.: Centa vom Höllental, 0208/89, 38256/1
V.: Donnerwetter vom Wittekind, 1190/89,
Z.: Werner Weidlein, Vorderer Kindleinsweg 6, 9742420
Schweinfurt
E.: wie Führer
F.: Josef Schulte-Wülwer, Neubörger Str. 21, 26909 Neubörger
Nordwest
Gruppe: _____ Formwert: _____ Bestanden: J—N

Dolf

20 **Vax von der Wulfenau**, 1034/91, 42081/1 Brown/White
R, 31.05.91, Brschl.m.br.K.u.Pln.
D1 S1 (oE) VBRE IKP1 VBR HD0 HN FW: V
M.: Sonja von der Wulfenau, 1186/88, Daughter of my Quinta
V.: Dolf KS vom Wittekind, 1188/89, 38248/1
Z.: <u>Willi Blömer,</u> Wulfenau 54, 49413 Dinklage nice old chap
give him my love if he is there. Usually wears long green loden
mantel
E.: wie Führer
F.: Herm.-Josef Schomakers, Im Timpen 21, 26903 Surwold
Nordwest
Gruppe: _____ Formwert: _____ Bestanden: J—N

21 **Weisser vom Hege-Haus**, 0438/91, 40240/1 White!
R, 20.01.91, Weiß m.br.Abz.
D1 VJP72 HZP181 S1 (oE) IKP1 BTR VBR HD0 HN FW: SG
M.: llex vom Hege-Haus, 0310/88, 38863/1
V.: Hannibal vom Hege-Haus, 0257/87, 37422/1
Z.: Karin Stramann, Waldhaus, Bergstr. 47, 32361
Preussisch-Oldendorf
E.: wie Führer
F.: Holger Hensel, Bauerschaft Düstrup 16, 49086 Osnabrück
Nordwest
Gruppe: _____ Formwert: _____ Bestanden: J—N
Both parents K.S. young dog

22 Wasov von der Hansaburg, 0391/92, 41977/1 <u>Black/White</u>
R, 22.01.92, Schwschl,
D1 S1 (oE) VBR BTR HD0 HN FW SG
M.: Una KS von der Hansaburg, 0195/89, 38794/1
V.: Veltin KS von der Hansaburg, 1088/90, 39944/1
Z.: Hubertus Högemann, Kirchstr.8, 26169 Friesoythe tallish
chap (with a limp)
E.: wie Führer
<u>F.: Hubertus Högemann</u>, Kirchstr.8, 26169 Friesoythe
Nordwest
Gruppe: _____ Formwert: _____ Bestanden: J—N

23 Astor von der Ziegelheide, 0607/91, 40919/1
R, 08.03.91, Brschl.m.br.K.u.Pln.
D1 HZP (oE) 134 S1 (oE) VBRE BTR IKP2 VBR HD0 HN FW:
V
M.: Milva vom Wasserschling, 0855/86, 35570/1
V.: Lasso KS vom Wasserschling, 0216/86, 35565/1
Z.: Helmut Willmes, In der Ziegelheide 19, 46397 Bocholt
E.: wie Führer
F.: Helmut Willmes, In der Ziegelheide 19, 46397 Bocholt
Rheinland
Gruppe: _____ Formwert: _____ Bestanden: J—N

24 Sisto vom Wasserschling, 0986/91, 40921/1
R, 06.06.91, Brschl.
D1 S1 (oE) VBRE BTR <u>SW2</u> JKP1 HD0 HN FW: V
M.: Peppy vom Wasserschling, 0762/88, 37690/1
V.: Lasso KS vom Wasserschling, 0216/86, 35565/1
Z.: Hans-Jürgen Machetanz, Gautinger Str. 34, 82131 Stockdorf
E.: wie Führer
F.: Henk van Haren, Pr.Irenestraat 42, NL-6566 BR Millingen
a.d. Rijn
Rheinland
Gruppe: _____ Formwert: _____ Bestanden: J—N

ES = Europe <u>Ch.</u> CACIB = CC
Both parents K.S.

25 **Ilex vom Pöttsiepen**, 0043/90, 39176/1 <u>Black/White</u>
R, 16.10.89, Schwschl.m.Pln.
Dl Dl Sl VBR BTR IKP1 CACIB ES HD0 MS FW: V
M.: Diana KS vom Pöttsiepen, 0715/82, 30791/1 Hatz's mother
V.: Blanc KS vom Hege-Haus, 1559/85, 34492/1
Z.: Paul Kohnen, Lacher Str. 146, 42657 Solingen
E.: wie Führer
F.: Paul Kohnen, wish him luck from me, Hat'z breeder Lacher
Str. 146, 42657 Solingen (Dirndel husband big champ)
Rheinland
Gruppe: _____ Formwert: _____ Bestanden: J—N

Both parents K.S.

26 **Kristan vom Pöttsiepen**, 0071/92, 41997/1 Brown/White
R, 23.10.91, Brschl.m.Pln.
Dl Dl Sl VBR BTR EJS <u>CACIB</u> HD0 HN FW: V
M.: Halla KS vom Pöttsiepen, 0426/88, 37426/1 Beautiful
HALLA
V.: Mondlicht KS vom Hege-Haus, 0367/89, 38733/1
Z.: Paul Kohnen, Lacher Str. 146, 42657 Solingen
2nd highest winning dog there. Wish them good luck from me
E.: Klaudia Funk, Aufderhöher Str. 189, 42699 Solingen
F.: Harald Funk, Aufderhöher Str. 189, 42699 Solingen Klaudia (wife)
Rheinland
Gruppe: _____ Formwert: _____ Bestanden: J—N

27 **Siggi vom Wasserschling**, 0984/91, 40925/1
R, 06.06.91, Brschl.
Dl Sl (oE) VBRE LN BTR IKP<u>2 SW3</u> HD0 HN FW: SG
M.: Peppy vom Wasserschling, 0762/88, 37690/1
V.: Lasso KS vom Wasserschling, 0216/86, 35565/1
Z.: Hans-Jürgen Machetanz, Gautinger Str. 34, 82131 Stockdorf
E.: wie Führer
F.: Gerrit Posthuma, Catharinadaal 7, NL-6715 KA Ede
Rheinland
Gruppe: _____ Formwert: _____ Bestanden: J—N

Both parents K.S.

28 Yard vom Hege-Haus, 0992/91, 40917/1 Brown/White
R, 23.04.91, Brschl.m.Pln.
D1 1 S1 VBR BTR IKP1 ES CACIB CAC BS ICH HD0 HN
FW: V
M.: Jelly KS vom Hege-Haus, 0522/88, 37423/1
V.: Mondlicht KS vom Hege-Haus, 0367/89, 38733/1
Z.: Karin Stramann, Waldhaus, Bergstr.47, 32361
Preussisch-Oldendorf
E.: Karin Stramann, Bergstr. 47, 32361 Preuß.-Oldendorf
F.: Paul Seegers, Oberdorf 13, 53773 Hennef
White silver grey hair, nice chap, slightly build. Sold to Greece?
Rheinland
Gruppe: _____ Formwert: _____ Bestanden: J—N

29 Arro v. d. Valleizoom, NHSB 1.639.531, 41995/1 Brown/White
R, 22.3.89, Brschl.m.Pln.
D1 S2 AZP1oIE IKP1 VBR HD0 HN FW: V
M.: Leika KS vom Wasserschling, 0224/86, 36660/1
V.: Walk KS Rothenuffeln, 1423/84, 33799/1
Z.: Geurt Oostendorp, Hogenkampseweg 178, NL-6871 JW
Renkum
E.: wie Führer
F.: Geurt B. Oostendorp, Hogenkampseweg 178, NL-6871 JW
Renkum
Rheinland from Holland
Gruppe: _____ Formwert: _____ Bestanden: J—N

30 Falco vom Löstertal, 0642/91, 41293/1
R, 22.03.91, Brschl.
D1 D1 S1 BTR IKP1 VBR HD0 HN FW: V
M.: Gundi vom Niemen, 0481/88, 37158/1
V.: Kastor KS vom Hege-Haus, 1024/88, 37772/1
Z.: Klaus Adams, Wedernerstraße 35, 66887 Wadern
E.: wie Führer
F.: Paul Maurer, In den Rübenstückern 7, 66701 Beckingen
Saar
Gruppe: _____ Formwert: _____ Bestanden: J—N

31 Igor vom Lingenauer Holz, 0975/92, 42093/1 Brown
R, 15.04.92, Br.
D1*S1 VBR HD0 HN FW: SG
M.: Barb vom Lingenauer Holz, 7056/83,
V.: Bill v. Wiesenweg, 7112/83,
Z.: Winfried Raatz, Am Heidekrug 1, 06779 Marke
E.: wie Führer
F.: Achim Klein, Straße der Einheit 15, 06369 Radegast
Sachsen-Anhalt
Gruppe: _____ Formwert: _____ Bestanden: J—N

32 Gero vom Lingenauer Holz, DDR 900906, 42092/1
R, 28.12.90, Brschl.
D1 S1 VBR HD0 HN FW: SG
M.: Birke vom Lingenauer Holz, DDR 1160/85, 23230
V.: Bill vom Wiesenweg, 7112/83
Z.: Winfried Raatz, Am Heidekrug 1, 06779 Marke
E.: wie Führer
F.: Holger Hagel, Rößbach 8, 06571 Wiehe
Sachsen-Anhalt
Gruppe: _____ Formwert: _____ Bestanden: J—N
Very young dog

33 Ivan vom Wittekind, 0740/92, 41644/1 Brown/White
R, 03.03.92, Brschl.m.br.K.u.Pln.
D1 S1 (oE) VBRE BTR SW1 HD0 HN FW: SG
M.: Dolle vom Wittekind, 1193/89, 39734/1 sister of Dolf
V.: Orka Birkenwald, 9998/90, 39990/1 I bred him, (Karli son)
Z.: Udo Zimmermann, Schipperkamp 50, 31717 Nordsehl
E.: wie Führer
F.: Christina Preußendorff, Schloßweg 15, 32429 Minden
Schaumburg-Lippe
Gruppe: _____ Formwert: _____ Bestanden: J—N

Both parents KS.

34 **Xito vom Hege-Haus**, 0899/91, 40039/1 Brown/White
R, 07.04.91, Brschl.m.Pln.
D1 D1 S1 S3 BTR IKP1 VBR HD0 HN FW: V
M.: Nike KS vom Hege-Haus, 0373/89, 39732/1
V.: Onyx KS vom Hege-Haus, 0785/89, 38329/1
Z.: Karin Stramann, Waldhaus, Bergstr.47, 32361
Preussisch-Oldendorf
E.: Karin Stramann, Bergstr. 47, 32361 Preuß.-Oldendorf
F.: Siegfried Hofstetter Altenstr. 14, 79336 Herbolzheim
Schaumburg-Lippe
Gruppe: _____ Formwert: _____ Bestanden: J—N

Both parents K.S.

35 **Iwan von der stolzen Au**, 0724/91, 41641/1 Brown/White
R, 23.03.91, Brschl.m.br.K.u.Pl.
D1 S1 (oE) VBRE IKP2 VBR HD0 HN FW: V
M.: Holle KS von der stolzen Au, 0727/87, 37080/1
V.: Kastor KS vom Hege-Haus, 1024/88, 37772/1
Z.: Heinrich Seele, Färberstr.3, 31547 Rehburg-Loccum 2
E.: wie Führer
F.: Fritz Brandt, Kampstr. 12, 31655 Stadthagen
Schaumburg-Lippe
Gruppe: _____ Formwert: _____ Bestanden: J—N
Future Halla Husband?

36 **Grix vom Wittekind**, 0685/91, 41288/1
R, 01.04.91, Brschl.m.br.K.u.Pln.
D1 S1 (oE) VBRE BTR IKP1 VBR HD0 HN FW: SG
M.: Luckilady vom Hege-Haus, 0117/89, 38163/1
V.: Donnerwetter vom Wittekind, 1190/89,
Z.: Udo Zimmermann, Schipperkamp 50, 31717 Nordsehl
E.: Fritzi Misch, Austr. 20, 90763 Fürth
F.: Werner Lampe, Lühehorst 6, 31547 Rehburg-Loccum
Schaumburg-Lippe
Gruppe: _____ Formwert: _____ Bestanden: J—N

Both parents K.S.

37 Aron vom Meynautal, 0689/90, 40297/1 Brown/White
R, 24.03.90, Brschl.m.br.K.u.Pln.
D1 S1 BTR IKP1 VBR HD0 MS FW: V
M.: Jola KS Engholms, 0198/85, 35357/1
V.: Birko KS von der Weiherwiese, 1255/85, 34027/1
Z.: Margitta/Thomas Albertsen, Hauptstrasse 22, 24969
Kleinwiehe
E.: wie Führer
F.: Jens-Diedrich Schmidt, Hoxtrup 2b, 25884 Viöl
Schleswig-Holstein
Gruppe: _____ Formwert: _____ Bestanden: J—N

38 Arco von der Schachenfluh, 9999/94, 41219/1
R, 13.05.91, Brschl.m.Pln.
D2 D1 S1 Swl HD0 HN FW: SG
M.: Espe vom Niederfeld, 1022/88,
V.: Wimm KS vom Eichelspitz, 1030/87, 37693/1
Z.: Hans Schaerli, Rest. Schachenpinte, CH-6154 Hofstatt
E.: Petra Hauser, Stalterstr.58, 79822 Titisee-Neustadt
F.: Horst Riedl, Haslachfeld 6, 79868 Feldberg
Südwest
Gruppe: _____ Formwert: _____ Bestanden: J—N

74 Brace

39 Utz Waidmanns, 0095/91, 41747/1 Brown
R, 12.10.90, Br.
D2 D1 S1 IKP1 VBR HD0 HN FW: V
M.: Polly Waidmanns, 0670/88, 37580/1
V.: Cox Fresena, 0141/88, 36700/1
Z.: ZG Waidmanns, Rodauerstr.62, 64372
Ober-Ramstadt-Rohrbach
E.: Dr. Jerkis, Ringstr.11, 66957 Ruppertsweiler
F.: A. Thomschke, Rodauerstr. 62, 64372 Ober-Ramstadt
Südwest
Gruppe: _____ Formwert: _____ Bestanden: J—N

40 Nic von der Wetterau, 0348/90, 39137/1 Brown
R, 22.01.90, Br.
D1 S1 <u>SW3</u> IKP1 HD0 MS FW: SG
M.: Laika von der Wetterau, 0454/87, 36856/1
V.: Lord KS vom Klostereck, 0865/84, 34063/1
Z.: Theo Gierich, Hohlweg 6, 61194 Niddatal 1
E.: wie Führer
F.: Walter Geipel, Ludwigstr. 34, 63619 Bad Orb
Südwest
Gruppe: _____ Formwert: _____ Bestanden: J—N

Both parents K.S.

41 Igor von der stolzen Au, 0720/91, 41828/1 Brown
R, 23.03.91, Br.m.Brfl.
D1 D1 S1 IKP1 VBR HD0 HN FW: V
M.: Holle KS von der stolzen Au, 0727/87, 37080/1
V.: Kastor KS vom Hege-Haus, 1024/88, 37772/1
Z.: Heinrich Seele, Färberstr.3, 31547 Rehburg-Loccum 2
E.: Claus Kiefer, Germersheimer Str. 148, 67354 Römerberg
F.: Bernd Härter, Karl-Marx-Str.31, 99195 Schloßvippach
Thüringen
Gruppe: _____ Formwert: _____ Bestanden: J—N
Future Halla husband?

42 Arco vom Mauritz, 0088/92, 41416/1
R, 05.11.91, Brschl.
D1 S1 (oE) VBRE BTR SW1 HD0 HN FW: SG
M.: Bona von der Tannenburg, 1273/86,
V.: Birko vom Dinkelhof, 1190/86, 36344/1
Z.: Willi Lütkebomert, Dorstener Str. 42, 48734 Reken
E.: wie Führer
F.: Alfred Lubjuhn, Wellwiese 62, 48734 Reken
Westfalen
Gruppe: _____ Formwert: _____ Bestanden: J—N

43 **Amigo von der Asseburg**, 0057/91, 40392/1 Brown
R, 12.10.90, Br.
D1 S1 VBR IKP1 HD0 HN FW: V
M.: Maja von der Asseburg, 0227/87, 36793/3
V.: Cox Fresena, 0141/88, 36700/1
Z.: Dr.M. Seeliger-Schiebener, Bäckergasse 5 A, 38300
WF-Wendessen
E.: wie Führer
F.: Werner Stefen, Borgstr. 32, 59597 Erwitte
Westfalen
Gruppe: _____ Formwert: _____ Bestanden: J—N
Future Halla husband?

Only ??? bothering about *Hündinnen* bitches

44 **Malomközi Baron**, 1157-89
R, 25.5.89, Brschl.m. Pln.
D1 S1 U-VGP1 VBR IKP1 HD0 HN FW: V
M.: Malomközi Tara, 136/87
V.: Graf v. Götzenburg, 4792
Z.: István Nagy, H-6000 Kecskemét
E.: Rinaldo Zambelli, Via Beltrami 8, I—Cremona
F.: Ottó Bánász, 94201 Surány-Kopec (Slovakoj)
Italien Italy
Gruppe: _____ Formwert: _____ Bestanden: J—N

45 **Gerti vom Kappelhof**, 0889/91, 40494/1 BLACK/WHITE
H, 25.05.91, Schwschl.
D1 HZP182 S1 VBR IKP1 HD0 HN FW: V
M.: Diva von der Poggenburg, 0041/86, 35369/3
V.: Kastor KS vom Hege-Haus, 1024/88, 37772/1
Z.: Josef Kappelhoff, Brink 10, 48607 Ochtrup 3
E.: wie Führer
F.: Christoph Lohmöller, Zum Desum 2, 49685 Emstek
Artland-Emsland
Gruppe: _____ Formwert: _____ Bestanden: J—N

46 **Dana vom Twentenfeld**, 0865/91, 40898/*
H, 19.05.91, Brschl.
D1*VJP76 S1 HZP (oE) 157 IKP2 VBR LN HD0 HN FW: V
M.: Adda vom Gut Brandlecht, 0525/87, 37610/1
V.: Grix Rothenuffeln, 0223/88, 37607/1
Z.: Johannes Geers, Twentenfeldweg 91, 48529 Nordhorn
E.: wie Führer
F.: Johannes Geers, Twentenfeldweg 91, 48529 Nordhorn
Artland-Emsland
Gruppe: _____ Formwert: _____ Bestanden: J—N

Brace + 34 both parents K.S.

47 **Alpenmilch vom Hege-Haus**, 0475/92, 41695/1 White
H, 12.01.92, Weiß m.br.Abz.
D1 D1 S1 S1 VBR BTR HD0 HN FW: V
M.: Proud KS vom Hege-Haus, 0398/90, 38975/1
V.: Mondlicht KS vom Hege-Haus, 0367/89, 38733/1
Z.: Karin Stramann, Waldhaus, Bergstr.47, 32361
Preussisch-Oldendorf
E.: Karin Stramann, Bergstr. 47, 32361 Preuß.-Oldendorf
F.: <u>Siegfried Hofstetter</u>, Altenstr. 14, 79336 Herbolzheim
Baden-Süd
Gruppe: _____ Formwert: _____ Bestanden: J—N

E. = Owner
F. = Handler

48 **Dora von der Feldl-Mühle**, 0554/89, 38810/1
H, 13.04.89, Brschl.m.br.K.u.Pln.
D2*D1 S3 IKP1 AZP1 VBR HD0 HN FW: SG
M.: Dunia von der Pfaffsmühle, 1346/85, 34934/1
V.: Birko KS von der Weiherwiese, 1255/85, 34027/1
Z.: August Feldl, Mühlenweg 4, 8066 Bergkirchen 2
E.: wie Führer
F.: Josef Heitmeier, Ascherbachweg 3, 85221 Dachau
Bayern
Gruppe: _____ Formwert: _____ Bestanden: J—N

49 **Ronda vom Wasserschling**, 0756/90, 39550/1
H, 15.04.90, Brschl.
S1J D1, 1 IKP1 SW3 HD0 MS FW:V
M.: Peppy vom Wasserschling, 0762/88, 37690/1
V.: Lasso KS vom Wasserschling, 0216/86, 35565/1
Z.: Hans-Jürgen Machetanz, Gautinger Str. 34, 82131 Stockdorf
E.: wie Führer
F.: Hans—Jürgen Machetanz, Gautinger Str. 34, 82131 Stockdorf
Bayern Son of famous Wasserschling" breeder.
Gruppe: _____ Formwert: _____ Bestanden: J—N

50 **Rackel vom Wasserschling**, 0752/90, 41832/1
H, 15.04.90, Brschl.
D1 S1 IKP1 SW2 HD0 HN FW: SG
M.: Peppy vom Wasserschling, 0762/88, 37690/1
V.: Lasso KS vom Wasserschling, 0216/86, 35565/1
Z.: Hans—Jürgen Machetanz, Gautinger Str. 34, 82131 Stockdorf
E.: wie Führer
F.: Helmut Wiesböck, Amselhof 1, 83101 Rohrdorf
Bayern
Gruppe: _____ Formwert: _____ Bestanden: J—N

No. 3 + Brace

51 **Aba Silesia**, 0379/90, 39538/1
H, 28.01.90, Brschl.m.Pl.
D1 S1 VBR SW1 HD0 HN FW: V
M.: Lona Silesia, 0830/87, 38508/1
V.: Asso Pöttmes, 0802/87, 36360/1
Z.: ZG. Hutta-Schumacher, Pfaffenrain, 97080
Würzburg-Heidingsfeld
E.: wie Führer
F.: Marica Schumacher, judges like her!!! Petite blonde, legs up
to her chinn. Engelskotten 4, 42857 Remscheid
Berlin
Gruppe: _____ Formwert: _____ Bestanden: J—N

52 Helma vom Moosbach, 0564/91, 41189/1
  H, 06.03.91, Brschl.m.br.K.u.Pln.
  D1 S1 BTR SW2 HD0 HN FW: V
  M.: Espe vom Moosbach, 1353/88, 38032/1
  V.: Graf KS vom Niemen, 0475/88, 37671/1
  Z.: Richard Matt, Oberlinder Str. 5, 95694 Mehlmeisel
  E.: wie Führer
  F.: Konrad Sendelbeck, Duerrbrunn 73, 91364 Unterleinleiter
  Franken
  Gruppe: _____ Formwert: _____ Bestanden: J—N

53 Heike vom Moosbach, 0563/91, 41187/1
  H, 06.03.91, Brschl.m.br.K.u.Pln.
  D1 S1 IKP1 BTR SW3 HD0 HN FW: V
  M.: Espe vom Moosbach, 1353/88, 38032/1
  V.: Graf KS vom Niemen, 0475/88, 37671/1
  Z.: Richard Matt, Oberlinder Str. 5, 95694 Mehlmeisel
  E.: wie Führer
  F.: Richard Matt, Oberlinder Str. 5, 95694 Mehlmeisel
  Franken
  Gruppe: _____ Formwert: _____ Bestanden: J—N

Please ask if she is for sale.

54 Aloa von der Asseburg, 0064/91, 41951/1 Brown
  H, 12.10.90, Br. Oldish!!
  D1 S1 S1 (oE) BTR IKP1 SW1 HD0 HN FW: V
  M.: Maja von der Asseburg, 0227/87, 36793/3
  V.: Cox Fresena, 0141/88, 36700/1 Ask if she has had a litter yet.
  Z.: Dr.M. Seeliger-Schiebener, Bäckergasse 5 A, 38300
  WF-Wendessen
  E.: wie Führer
  F.: Dr. Wolfgang Schmidt, Im Lochseif 19, 63517 Rodenbach
  Hannover
  Gruppe: _____ Formwert: _____ Bestanden: J—N

55 **Fina vom Ulfetal**, 0602/91, 40623/1
H, 22.03.91, Br.
D1 S1 IKP1 VBR HD0 HN FW: V
M.: Kitty von der Wetterau, 0855/84, 34441/2
V.: Birko KS von der Weiherwiese, 1255/85, 34027/1
Z.: Günter Karges, Nürnberger Str. 8, 36205 Sontra-Breitau
E.: Johann Unterreitmeier, Waldstr. 22, 85461 Bockhorn
F.: Xaver Gilnhammer, Siedlungsstr. 2, 84428 Buchbach
Niederbayern
Gruppe: _____ Formwert: _____ Bestanden: J—N

<<<MISSING PAGE 25>>>

Very both parents K.S. young bitch,

60 **Wanja von der Hansaburg**, 0395/92, 41976/1 Brown/White
H, 22.01.92, Brschl.
D1 S1 (oE) BTR SW3 VBR HD0 HN FW: V
M.: Una KS von der Hansaburg, 0195/89, 38794/1
V.: Veltin KS von der Hansaburg, 1088/90, 39944/1
Z.: Hubertus Högemann, Kirchstr.8, 26169 Friesoythe
E.: wie Führer
F.: Konrad Borgerding, Tannenkamp 30, 49456 Hausstette
Nordwest
Gruppe: _____ Formwert: _____ Bestanden: J—N

DOLF

61 **Loni vom Pöttsiepen**, 0226/92, 41209/1 Brown/White
H, 05.12.91, Brschl.m.Pl.
S1J BTR D1 IKP1 S1 VBR HD0 HN FW: V
M.: Isa vom Pöttsiepen, 0048/90, 39986/1 ½ sister to Hatz
V.: Dolf KS vom Wittekind, 1188/89, 38248/1
Z.: Paul Kohnen, Lacher Str. 146, 42657 Solingen
E.: Joachim Weeger, Rietherbach 48, 40764 Langenfeld
F.: Wilhelm Kohnen, Hauptstr. 142, 26903 Surwold
Rheinland Dolf's trainer (not Dirndel)
Gruppe: _____ Formwert: _____ Bestanden: J—N
Wish him luck and give him my love. Tell him Dolf is SUPER

62 **Cira von der Niersaue**, 0031/91, 40918/1
H, 01.10.90, Brschl.m.Pln.
D1 S1 VBR BTR IKP1 HD0 HN FW: V
M.: Elfe KS Kobow's, 0272/83, 31991/1
V.: Hannibal vom Hege-Haus, 0257/87, 37422/1
Z.: Balduin Schnitzler, Waat 47, 41363 Jüchen 1
E.: wie Führer
F.: Klaus Bommers, Burg Dürboslar, 52457 Aldenhoven
Rheinland
Gruppe: _____ Formwert: _____ Bestanden: J—N

63 Nadi Pöttmes, 0286/92, 41996/1
H, 07.01.92, Brschl.m.br.K.u.Pl.
D1 S1 VBR BTR HD0 HN FW: V
M.: Drixi Pöttmes, 0213/88, 36850/1
V.: Hasso KS vom Müggenberg, 1068/85, 33271/1
Z.: Franzi Heinen, Bahnhofstr.4, 56477 Rennerod
E.: wie Führer
F.: Leo Karduck, Rosenstr. 14, 41836 Hückelhoven
Rheinland
Gruppe: _____ Formwert: _____ Bestanden: J—N

No. 28 + Brace both parents K.S.

64 **Yelly vom Hege-Haus**, 0994/91, 40920/1 Brown
H, 23.04.91, Br.m.Brfl.
D1 D1 S1 VBR BTR IKP1CACIB HD0 HN FW: V
M.: Jelly KS vom Hege-Haus, 0522/88, 37423/1
V.: Mondlicht KS vom Hege-Haus, 0367/89, 38733/1
Z.: Karin Stramann, Waldhaus, Bergstr. 47, 32361
Preussisch-Oldendorf
E.: Karin Stramann, Bergstr. 47, 32361 Preuß.-Oldendorf
F.: Paul Seegers, Oberdorf 13, 53773 Hennef
Rheinland
Gruppe: _____ Formwert: _____ Bestanden: J—N
White silver grey haired nice chap, slightly build.
Give my regards to Frau Stramann (Head scarf tied at back of neck)
Please ask Frau Stramann if Yelly is for sale (Head Scarf)

65 Perle vom Hege-Haus, 0396/90, 40321/1

H, 17.12.89, Brschl.m.Pln.

D1*D1 AH S1/1 BTR VBR <u>WSJ</u> ES LN <u>VDHCH</u> German show CH. HD0 HN FW: V

M.: Ilex vom Hege-Haus, 0310/88, 38863/1

V.: Hannibal vom Hege-Haus, 0257/87, 37422/1

Z.: Karin Stramann, Waldhaus, Bergstr.47, 32361 Preussisch-Oldendorf

E.: wie Führer

F.: Matthias Strunk, Stollenstr. 7, 53894 Mechernich Rheinland

Gruppe: _____ Formwert: _____ Bestanden: J—N

Well Bred

66 Jestha von der stolzen Au, 0878/91, 41642/1 Brown

H, 30.04.91, Br.m.Brfl.

D1 S1 (oE) VBRE VBR IKP2 HD0 HN FW: V

M.: Grandel von der stolzen Au, 0454/85, 34045/1 Ask if she is for sale

V.: Kastor KS vom Hege-Haus, 1024/88, 37772/1

Z.: Heinrich Seele, Färberstr.3, 31547 Rehburg-Loccum 2

E.: wie Führer

F.: Dorothee Seele, Färberstr. 3, 31547 Rehburg-Loccum Schaumburg-Lippe

Gruppe: _____ Formwert: _____ Bestanden: J—N

67 Chestnut vom Hege-Haus, 1143/92, 42014/1

H, 15.04.92, Brschl.m.Pl.

D1 S1 (oE) VBR AH HD0 HN FW: V

M.: Ina von der Isarmündung, 0684/90, 40446/1

V.: Onyx KS vom Hege-Haus, 0785/89, 38329/1

Z.: Karin Stramann, Waldhaus, Bergstr.47, 32361 Preussisch-Oldendorf

E.: Heinrich Kinnius, Krümpelweg 30, 49326 Melle

F.: Wilhelm Dünnermann, Helpuper Str. 117, 32791 Lage Schaumburg-Lippe

Gruppe: _____ Formwert: _____ Bestanden: J—N

Like an American wears floppy hat with badges on. <u>Thinner</u> nigel mansel?

68 Cora vom Wittekind, 1041/88, 38681/1 Brown/White
½ Sister to Dolf
    H, 22.04.88, Brschl.m.Pln.
    D1 S3 S1 IKP1 VBR HD0 MS FW: V
    M.: Blanca KS vom Wittekind, 0657/86, 34990/1 Dolf's mother
    V.: Ferri vom Felde, 1214/86, 34617/1
    Z.: Udo Zimmermann, Schipperkamp 50, 31717 Nordsehl
    E.: wie Führer
    <u>F.: Udo Zimmermann</u>, Schipperkamp 50, 31717 Nordsehl
    Dolf's Breeder, wish him good luck from me
    Schaumburg-Lippe
    Gruppe: _____ Formwert: _____ Bestanden: J—N

69 **Jule von Bockhöft**, 0957/92, 41620/1 Brown/White very young bitch
    <u>H, 26.03.92,</u> Brschl.
    BTR AH D1 D1 S1 (oE) VBR VBRE HD0 HN FW: SG
    M.: Elva KS von Bockhöft, 1420/86, 36582/1 Both parents very good looking
    V.: Zobel KS vom Hege-Haus, 1099/85, 35628/1
    Z.: Peter Freiberg, Bockhöft, 24870 Ellingstedt-Bockhöft
    E.: wie Führer
    F.: Claus-Peter Andresen, Große Straße 98, 24855 Jübek
    Schleswig-Holstein both parents K.S.
    Gruppe: _____ Formwert: _____ Bestanden: J—N

Ruby Field can buy her!!!

70 **Yrsa Engholms**, 0683/91, 41621/1
    H, 15.03.91, Brschl.m.br.K.u.Pln.
    D1 S1 BTR VBR IKP1 HD0 HN FW: SG
    M.: Jutta Engholms, 0199/85,
    V.: Terz KS Engholms, 1140/89, 39708/1
    Z.: Carsten Petersen, Clausholmerweg 1, 25926 Westre-Engholm
    E.: wie Führer
    F.: Hans Jürgen Thaysen, Gut Fresenhagen, 25917 Leck

Schleswig-Holstein
Gruppe: _____ Formwert: _____ Bestanden: J—N

71 **Jana vom Kreuzberg**, 1005/90, 40935/1
   H, 25.05.90, Brschl.m.br.K.u.Pln.
   D1 S1 VBR IKP1 HD0 HN FW: SG
   M.: Ina vom Kreuzberg, 0112/88, 36857/1
   V.: Argus vom Schwarzen Grund, 0037/87, 35757/1
   Z.: Herbert Seemann, Schulstr. 10, 55278 Dolgesheim
   E.: wie Führer
   F.: Herbert Seemann, Schulstr. 10, 55278 Dolgesheim
   Südwest
   Gruppe: _____ Formwert: _____ Bestanden: J—N

72 **Asta vom Jägersacker**, 0967/89, 39400/1 Brown
   H, 24.05.89, Br.
   D1 S3 HZP162 BTR <u>SW1 SW/3</u> IKP1 AZP1 HD0 MS FW: SG
   M.: Porta Pöttmes, 0330/84
   V.: Arko vom Rabenberg, 9996/85, 29270/1
   Z.: Ernst Back, Nelkenstraße 1, 68535 Edingen-Neckarhausen
   E.: wie Führer
   F.: Ernst Back, Nelkenstr. 1, 68309 Mannheim
   Südwest
   Gruppe: _____ Formwert: _____ Bestanden: J—N

73 **Britta von der Fuchskaute**, 0074/91, 40320/1
   H, 06.10.90, Brschl.m.Pl.
   D1 S3 AZP1 VBR HD0 HN FW: V
   M.: Biene von der Dornburg, 1777/83, 37887/1
   V.: Birko KS von der Weiherwiese, 1255/85, 34027/1
   Z.: Gerhard Schüler, Ringstraße 4, 56479 Bretthausen
   E.: wie Führer
   F.: Gerhard Schüler, Ringstr. 4, 56479 Bretthausen
   Südwest
   Gruppe: _____ Formwert: _____ Bestanden: J—N

No. 39 + Bracie

74 **Tinka Waidmanns**, 0443/90, 41745/1
   H, 01.02.90, Brschl.
   D1 S1 IKP1 VBR HD0 MS FW: V
   M.: Irla Waidmanns, 0126/84, 33346/3
   V.: Marko KS von der Hansaburg, 1810/79, 28669/1 Birkenwald
   Nicco + Nakitas father (Import litter)
   Z.: ZG Waidmanns, Rodauerstr.62, 64372
   Ober-Ramstadt-Rohrbach
   E.: wie Führer
   F.: A. Thomschke, Rodauerstr. 62, 64372 Ober-Ramstadt
   Südwest
   Gruppe: _____ Formwert: _____ Bestanden: J—N

Both parents K.S.

75 **Pola vom Deterner Brook**, 0902/89, 40858/1 Brown/White
   H, 02.05.89, Brschl.m.br.K.u.Pln.
   D1 S1 BTR IKP1 <u>SW3</u> HD0 HN FW: SG
   M.: Danny KS von der Reiterstadt, 0089/82, 30718/1
   V.: Janusch KS Silesia, 1180/83, 32663/1
   Z.: Eduard Hansmann, Moorhauser Landstr. 2a, 28865 Lilienthal
   E.: wie Führer
   F.: Eduard Hansmann, Moorhauser Landstr. 2a, 28865 Lilienthal
   Weser Bremen
   Gruppe: _____ Formwert: _____ Bestanden: J—N

76 **Vinka vom Theelshof**, 7291/84, 41836/1
   H, 14.1.91, Brschl.
   D1 S1 SW1 IKP1 BTR HD0 HN FW: SG
   M.: Paula v. Theelshof, DDR 8793, 23416
   V.: Flott v. Bichtelwald, 245/82, 30529
   Z.: Wilhelm Theel, 14662 Wutzetz
   E.: wie Führer
   F.: Ägidius Baumgärtner, Jahnstr. 49, 74252 Massenbachhausen
   Württemberg
   Gruppe: _____ Formwert: _____ Bestanden: J—N

77 Assi von Schloß Rotenhan, 0235/88, 36855/1 Brown/White
H, 02.01.88, Brschl.m.Pl.
D1 S1 VBR HD0 HN FW: SG
M.: Bara von der Bannmühle, 0842/84, 34443/3
V.: Kosta KS vom Rheintal, 0668/83, 30943/1 His father "Varus"
is brother to my "Vassal" vom nieste tal who went to Australia
Z.: Helmut Aicher, Marktstr.19, 73765 Neuhausen
E.: wie Führer
F.: Helmut Aicher, Marktstr.19, 73765 Neuhausen
Württemberg
Gruppe: _____ Formwert: _____ Bestanden: J—N

If at all possible, copy in the results for me. They will be posted up
in the hall Sat. eve.
I want Formwert (conformation grading) and if passed or not,
(Bestanden) J = Ja (Yes) N = Nein (No)
If you have time mark in any 4H that have been awarded to which
dog and what for. ie Water (Wasser)—Suche (Hunting)—Vorstehen
(Pointing)—Nase (Nose)

Dr.-Kleemann-Zuchtausleseprüfung 1939-1992

I shall put THIS book in the post tomorrow. I have a spare book.

Year	Entered	Testet	Passed	Not Passed	Place	Club
Jahr	Gemeldet	Geprüft	Bestanden	Nicht Bestanden	Ort	Klub
39	23	23	8	15	Winningen	DK-Verband
49			5		Krefeld-Willich	Rheinland
50			4		Krefeld-Willich	Rheinland
51			4		Frankfurt	Frankfurt
52			5		Peine	Hannover
53	19	11	9	3	Frankenthal	Südwest
54	26	21	13	8	Bückeburg/Krefeld	Schaumburg-Lippe/Rheinland
55	16	14	6	8	Frankenthal	Südwest
56			4		Grevenbroich	Rheinland

57			7		Bad Lippspringe	Westfalen
58			5		Seligenstadt	Frankfurt
59	12	5	4	1	Wallerstein	Franken
61			3		Kassel	Kurthessen
62	19	18	8	10	Stadthagen	Schaumburg-Lippe
64	21	20	9	11	Speyer	Südwest
66	34	33	21	12	Bosau	Nordmark
68	30	23	10	13	Kehl	Südbaden
70	30	14	8	6	Bad Lippspringe	Westfalen
72	21	21	14	7	Stuttgart	Württemberg
74	39	39	13	26	Vluynbusch	Rheinland
76	40	29	14	15	Niebüll	Schleswig-Holstein
78	51	46	22	24	Loccum	Schaumburg-Lippe
80	31	28	18	10	Minden	Niedersachsen
82	40	32	16	16	Kehl	Südbaden
84	61	56	23	33	Kalkar-Rees	Rheinland
86	60	56	20	36	Saarlouis	Saar
88	71	66	40	26	Hannover	Hannover
90	50	47	26	21	Malente	Nordmark
92	68	64	38	26	Geldern-Walbeck	Rheinland

ALL 44 dogs get special prizes at prize giving.

Dr.-Kleemann-Zuchtausleseprüfung 1939-1992

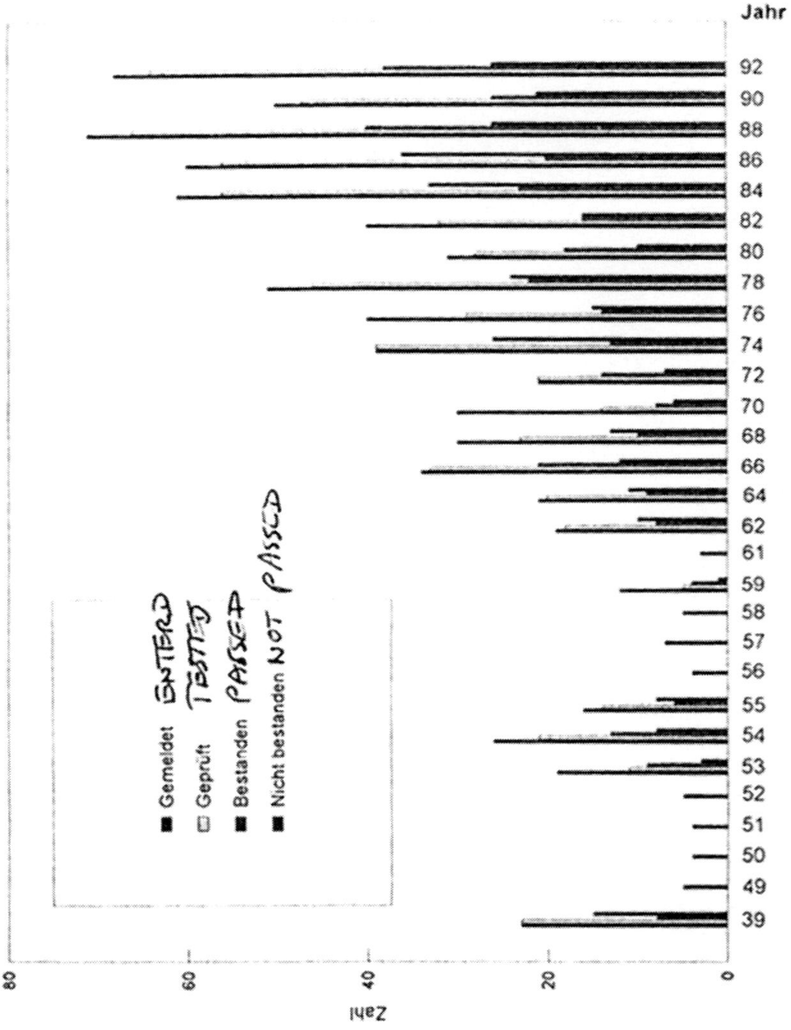

Für Ihre Notizen:

In Germany everyone knows me as <u>Hannelore</u> Gill, NOT Ann Gill.

The Stramann's sometimes still call me by my previous married name <u>Spoors</u> as I have known them longest. <u>Frau Stramann always</u> wears a head scarf, knotted at the back of the neck, (not under chinn) over very smooth auburn hair, (looks dyed) also has thin pencilled in auburn eye brows, she is medium size about 55-60. Always "<u>wears</u>" a smile! She is very chic. <u>Herr Stramann</u> is tall, very aristocratic looking, about 65-70, short cut grey hair grey goat beard, does not <u>usually</u> wear a hat, (Most other chaps do) he has very "strong" eyes. (You would'n mess <u>him</u> about!) He is not very easy to talk to. Frau Stramann is fine, BUT she will be very busy, so <u>dont pester</u> her.

All the competitors will be very up tight before the <u>trial</u>, at the <u>show</u> it is not so bad. <u>After</u> the trial they will all be leggless in the beer tent. Ruby & Jim Fields could go in the group that has the 2 Americans.

Perhaps all the others can read this book for information. (A photo copy for each ???)

Bei einer der größten englischen Zuchtschauen, der "Paignton Championchip Show", die am 11. Juli 1985 in Exeter, der Hauptstadt der Grafschaft Devon, stattfand, hatte ich mich mit dem Hauptzuchtwart des Deutschen Retriever Clubs (DRC), Frau H. Vogel, am Golden Retriever Ring verabredet. Als im Nachbarring vor einem sehr großen Interessentenkreis zahlreiche Deutsch-Kurzhaar vorgeführt worden, glaubte ich zuerst an eine Sinnestäuschung, doch die Situation war real, und als Beweis der großen Beliebtheit von DK in England—hier Short haired Pointer genannt—sende ich Ihnen dieses Foto. Der Ausstellungskatalog offenbarte dann, daß ca. 70 Deutsch-Kurzhaar gemeldet waren und von der Richterin Mrs. R. Field bewertet wurden. Die Hunde waren vorwiegend vom Braun—oder Braunschimmeltyp und hatten einen sehr ansprechenden Formwert.
???

Dr. C. Engelhardt, president of the "German Retriever Clubs" visited a large English Breed Show held in EXETER in July of last year. He send us the photo and the short notes below

On July 11th 1985 I visited one of the larger Breed Shows in England, the PAINGTON CHAMPIONSHIP SHOW, held in EXETER, in the Country of Devon.

Mrs. H. Vogel, main Breed Warden of the GERMAN RETRIEVER CLUB (DRC) met me at the golden Retriever Ring.

I couldn't believe my eyes, when in the next ring I saw several German Kurzhaar, in England they are called "Shorthaired Pointers" being shown before a large audience. But it was real, and shows how popular the Kurzhaar is in England. I enclose a photo. Over 70 Kurzhaar were entered in the catalogue. They were judged by Mrs. R. Field. The dogs were either liver or liver + white ticked + flecked, and most of them had very good conformation.

THIS WAS THE FIRST GSP REGISTEREDIN GERMANY/////

Hector I, born 1872—Prize of Honour, Berlin, 1880

germanBREAD STANDARD IN ENGLISH///

THE GERMAN BREED STANDARD IN ENGLISH////
"The Complete GSP" by
Herr H. F. Seiger
and
Dr. F. von Dewity—Colpin
1951

Chapter I

IN the following chapter we reproduce the Standard of the breed devised by E. v. Otto at the instance of the club "Shorthair", which is still now valid in all points:

(Extract from Pedigree Register "Shorthair", Volume 6, issued 1902.)

THE SHORT-HAIRED GERMAN POINTER

1. General Appearance.

"The general appearance is that of a noble symmetrical dog, whose form displays power, perseverance and speed. He shall be neither small nor strikingly big—too big dogs are long-legged in most cases and thence rarely presistent—but in medium size like the hunting horse: "though short of back, stand over much ground".

Plump and cloddy dogs are to be rejected; at first glance the dog should at once mediate the impression of being vigorous (but not nervous) and his movements appear as a whole. Systematical breeding and advancement show up not only in the anatomical equipment for moving rather than in the nobility of his whole appearance, stylish build, dry head, well carried tail and taut skin.

Well laid back shoulders and a straight stretched back, a deep chest and strong hindquarters indicate speed, while persistency is warranted by good condition in bone, an adequate width of chest and a well developed musculation all over the body.

2. Head.

Dry, not creasy, of medium size; neither too light nor too heavy.

The skull of ample breadth shows an equally rounded arch; occiput and junction of neck not strikingly developed. Back of muzzle broad, and straight or slightly arched when viewed from aside; forehead from its joint line with the muzzle gradually slanting upward: the frontal bones seen from the side, form a visible set-off.

The muzzle should be of adequate length so to enable the dog to get a firm grip on game and to carry it over long distances; too long a muzzle is as little desired as if too short. The front surface of the muzzle should nearly form a rectangle with the top line of the muzzle; pointed muzzles are therefore entirely discarded.

Flews should not overlap too much, but should form a noticeable fold at the corner of the mouth; strong jaws with well developed chops and muscles. The bite should be very powerful and all teeth sound; the molars should accurately fit into one another, the incisors touch each other for grating.

The whole of the head should never evoke the impression of tapering to a point; depth and length at the muzzle as well as in the skull itself should be in a correct proportion to each other.

3. Ears.

Moderately long, neither padded nor too fine; set on high and broad, hanging down from the head smoothly and scarcely leaving any space between; lower ends blunt and rounded.

The ears shall reach approximately as far as the corners of the mouth, if laid to the fore without tearing.

4. Eyes.

Of medium size, vivid and expressive, good-natured and yet with a definite expression; crossed exactly in the corners of the eyes, showing nothing or little of the conjunctiva tunica and not lying deeply either.

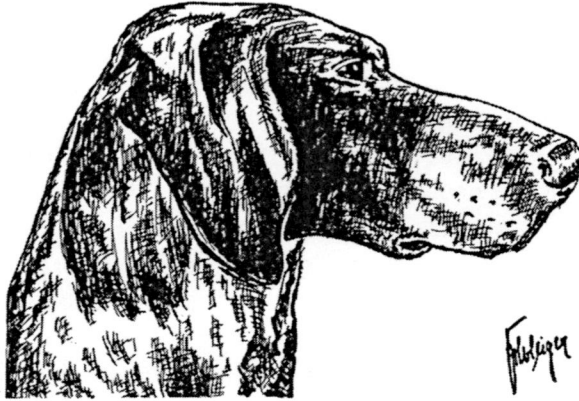

Good points: Good, well-arched skull, ideal long muzzle, with good, spacious nostrils, and close-fitting lips. Faults: Ears not wide enough set. Drawing by Fr. W. Seiger.

A GOOD HEAD

Faults: Muzzle too pointed, with too much
stop. Drawing by Fr. W. Seiger.

The best color is a beautiful brown; light yellow ("birds-of-prey") eyes are less desirable.

5. Muzzle.

Brown; the greater the better. Nostrils well opened, broad. Flesh-colored and speckled muzzles that will occur in dogs with a great deal of white, are not desirable.

6. Neck.

Of medium length, very muscular. Dry and slightly curved, gradually broadening towards the shoulders. Skin feasibly taut; free on all accounts from any noticeable dewlap.

7. Chest and Rib-cage.

The chest on a whole shall convey the impression of depth rather than breadth and withal be in correct relationship with the other parts of the body.

The rib-cage is built by well arched ribs that are not as flat as in the whippet, but are never quite round nor barrel-shaped; completely rounded ribs do not allow adequate expansion for breathing.

To the rear, the ribs extend sufficiently downward, the lower stomach line is satisfactorily tucked up to give the required space for galloping; all that without the suggestion of lankness.

The circumference of chest in the zone adjacent to the elbows towards the rear (harness depth) is and has to be less than, for example, at a hand's breadth behind the elbows in order to permit the shoulders to move freely.

8. Back.

A taut back is of ultimate importance for abrupt movements and for persistently moving as well; it must therefore not be long. The loin area should be short and but slightly curved; strong arching interferes with freedom of action and speed. Thence special stress should be put on selecting dogs from the breeding stock with a firm straight back and a short and strong loin area; dogs that are too long in back have to be eliminated.

Faults: too wide and badly set shoulder, which
overlaps the breast bone. Excells in ideal pasterns
and the best of rears. Drawing by Fr. W. Seiger.

The croup should be broad and adequately long, neither over-built nor appear cut off short, starting on equal level with the back and gradually slope down toward the tail.

9. Front Quarters.

Shoulders slanting, long, movable, exhibiting hard musculature; shoulder-blades flat lying tightly to the body. Front legs standing sufficiently under the trunk, elbows placed low, neither turned in nor out. Underarm straight and dry, adequately muscled, strong though not coarse in bone. Pasterns but little slanting, almost straight, should never stand perpendicular to the ground.

10. Hind Quarters.

Thighs well and drily muscled; correct angle between lower thigh and hock; lack in obtuseness of angle detracts from endurance. No indication of cow-hocks. The tarsus should be strongly developed and almost vertically placed under the hock joints.

11. Foot.

Strong and closed, rather rounded than tapering to the front. Tightly arched toes with strong nails. Flat toes and splay foot are repugnant. Pads must be firm and hard.

Dewclaws are not desirable, as they prejudice the perseverance of the dog in action (especially if loose, hanging down). If casually occurring, they have to be removed at an early age of the puppy.

12. Skin and Coat.

The skin shall lie tight to the body without any creases and folds. The hair should be short and dense, and feel firm and hard. It should not be noticeably longer on the lower side of the tail; its obviously appearing as a "brush" is a fault. Hair is softer, thinner and shorter on ears and head.

13. Tail.

High set and strong attachment, from where the tail then tapers to the end; of medium length, but expertly shortened (by one-third to half its length) for preventing detracting injuries. Too short a tail (stag's whisk) spoils the appearance of the dog and has to be avoided.

Neck well set on, with strong middle piece and well tucked up flank. Drawing by Fr. W. Seiger.

Ideally straight and firm back, with good, high withers, broad, level croup, good, high-set tail, and excellent, well angulated hind legs. Faults: Too small ears. Drawing by Fr. W. Seiger.

Hanging down in rest, horizontally carried when moving calmly, not placed on a level higher than the back nor strongly curved, but in vivid motion when trailing.

Too thick a tail so as to appear ignoble and clumsy is as objectionable as dewlap, bulky ears or heavily laden shoulders: faults that mostly appear in common; likewise faulty is a tail set too low, which always occurs with a croup seemingly cut off.

14. Skeleton.

It is not desired that a dog supposed to work in any kind of field and woods and demanded to be powerful, should be thin and fine in bone.

However, it is not the total of substance but the condition of the skeleton that counts; big-boned dogs are lacking in lissomeness and speed.

When breeding is perpetuated in accordance with the rules on the advancement of purebred dogs, the outer contours of the skeleton will be refined and its tissue grow more compact and firm, whereas bulky bones are porous and spongy.

15. Color.

Permissible colors are:
- (a) brown without markings
- (b) brown with few and little white or speckled markings in chest and legs
- (c) dark brown-and-mildew color with brown head, brown patches or dots

> The basic color of a dog with such markings is neither brown with white nor white with brown, but a stitch-by-stitch color, which is to say that the hair shows so sincere a mixture of brown and grey (white) as is required to lend the dog that peculiar camouflage color, which is so valuable for his practical use.
>
> The inner sides of the hind legs as well as the tail at its tip are often of a lighter color.
>
> The major or lesser number of solidly brown patches has to be considered when judging the general appearance: the fewer the patches, the better for the dog.

Good, freely moving shoulder which renders possible good trailing work. Drawing by Fr. W. Seiger.

Faults: Sloping croup, chest not deep enough, too straight pasterns in front. Drawing by Fr. W. Seiger.

Brown prevails as the color of head, though speckled (white) surface of top of muzzle and top skull as well as freckled flews are frequently met.

(d) light brown-and-mildew color with brown head, brown patches or dots.

In this coloring the brown hairs are in the minority and the white hairs are dominant. Thence the apparent lighter color of suchlike toned dogs. For the same reason also, the latter have to compete in the white-brown classes at exhibitions;

(e) white with brown head markings, brown patches or dots.

CONSTITUTION OF THE CLUB "SHORTHAIR"

It appears important to the authors that all fanciers of our German short-haired utility dog be acquainted with the entire structure of the Club "Shorthair". We should contribute thereto if only for the reason of making the readers realize in full the deep enthusiasm and how far was the goal when setting about to establish an ideal utility dog of outstanding performances in all branches of hunt in contrast to the specialized dogs.

CONSTITUTION

"Through Efficiency To Type"

Albrecht, Prince zu Solms-Braunfels

The club stands for the principle that the Type has to be conceived as the total of all physical and mental qualities and faculties such as are suitable and prove to be useful to meet the requirements of all the branches of hunt, for which the respective breed is intended to be applied in its native country. The Type is evolved from among the breeding stock by continuously using the same dogs at stud that are most efficient in hunting. Type is the result of rational breeding and therefore no longer entirely dependent on plain coincidence, if this dominant principle tending at improvement is observed. The qualities for hunt need no longer be painstakingly trained to a dog, but are vested in him by blood stronger head and neck and general muscularity appropriate in a male, is a good example of male GSP type.

3.3c. Hummel v.Lönsweg, whelped in 1980. A "V" (excellent) rated bitch, which exhibits many of the virtues of the best bitch-types in modern Germany. This bitch has substance, is free from exaggeration and is obviously feminine.

3.3d. Artemis Donald (Kl.Ausl.Prfg), whelped in 1972 (Maniz v.d. Forst Brickwedde ex Artemis Ella), a well-balanced, masculine dog of good breed-type.

It should be noted that all four dogs are free-standing, demonstrating their natural balance and proportions. I have chosen to use German dogs as illustrations in this instance, since many of the available photographs of American, British or Australian dogs picture them posed and held in position by their handlers. Nevertheless, this book contains numerous examples of GSPs of equally good type to the four illustrated here.

Head Type

Perhaps the one area in which world-wide consensus should be sought is that of head type. GSP breed books are seldom specific on this point, yet it is so often the head which distinguishes one breed from another. The structure of a good GSP head has, like its body, a lot to do with the breed's function. If a GSP is not physically capable of carrying in its mouth an animal the size of a fully grown fox, pheasant or goose for perhaps several hundred yards through reeds, water and/or heavy cover, then it is not of correct GSP type.

The long muzzle, set parallel to the skull, with its slightly aquiline profile and "stop effect" distinguishes a GSP head from that of a Pointer, with its "dished face", definite stop and shorter muzzle. The high earset and flat ear leathers distance the breed from any hound ancestry. The good temperament of the breed should be reflected in its expression. The eye shape, colour and size, help in determining this expression.

The head-studies included in this chapter demonstrate similarity in type between a father and daughter (Fig. 3.4) and a totally unrelated dog and bitch (Figs. 3.1a.and 3.1b). All four exhibit unmistakable GSP type, with appropriately masculine or feminine characteristics.

Temperament

One aspect of breed-type which I believe is of overwhelming importance is that of temperament and outlook. I believe there is a sole correct GSP type and that is described in all the breed Standards. It is a courageous, confident dog, utterly reliable with people, including small children. It is lively and enthusiastic yet tractable enough to be trained without too much difficulty. Its proud carriage gives it a look of nobility. It is neither nervous and hyperactive nor a sluggish dullard. It must be willing and able to work all day in a variety of weather and terrain. This "type", unfortunately, cannot be illustrated by a drawing or a photograph, nor can it be accurately assessed in a show ring, for to gain the

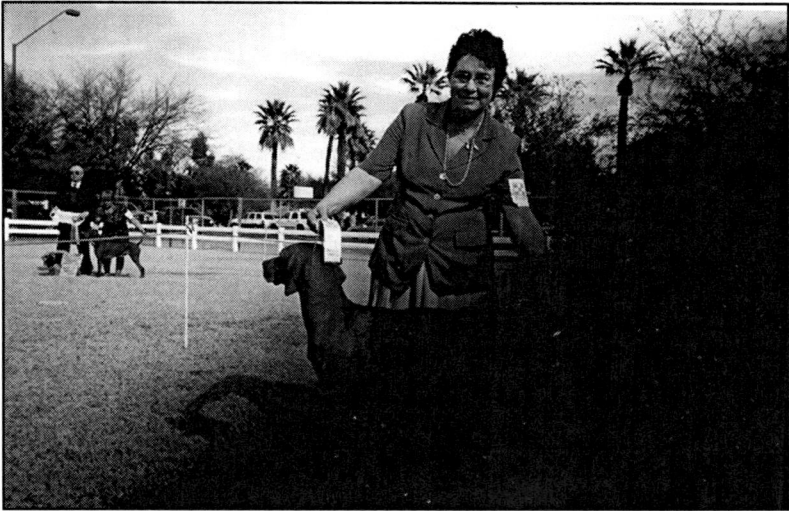

Ruby Field at Vizsla National with Mary Arsons dog
was 3rd and 3rd in open bitch with int ch misletoe

NATIONAL 2006 Tuesday, 14 May, 2013 12:14

FIRST MARY CARSON WITH RUBY LAVENDER WINNING THE OBEDIENC CLASS MARY IS NO 5 IN USA AT OBEDIENCE////

NEXTPICTUREDAY ONE OF NATIONAL HELD INSIDE IN A BALLROOM AS SO HOT//// FIRST SWEET PECAN OF DEEPTHATCH FIRST HANDLED BY MYSELF OWNED BY MARY CARSON////
NEXT CANSDIAN JUDGE BURT REYNALDSWITH VICTORIA OF DEEPTHATCH MY SELF OWNED BY MARY CARSON

NEXT PICTURE WITH CANADIAN JUDGE WITH PECAN AGAIN WON 4 PLACINGS ONE EACD UNDER 2 USA JUDGES AND 2 CANADIAN JUDGES

WON AWARD OF MERIT WITH INT CH DEEPTHATCH LASSIE ALSO HAS AMASTER HUNTERS// CERTIFICATE WITH GOOD HIPS EYE AND HEART PASSES WE BOTH WERE THE ONLY UK IN THE RING ///

MUST SAY EVERYONES HELP AND GREAT ATTITUDE TO US WAS GREAT////

obedience winner at national usa phoenix
mary carson and ruby lavender.

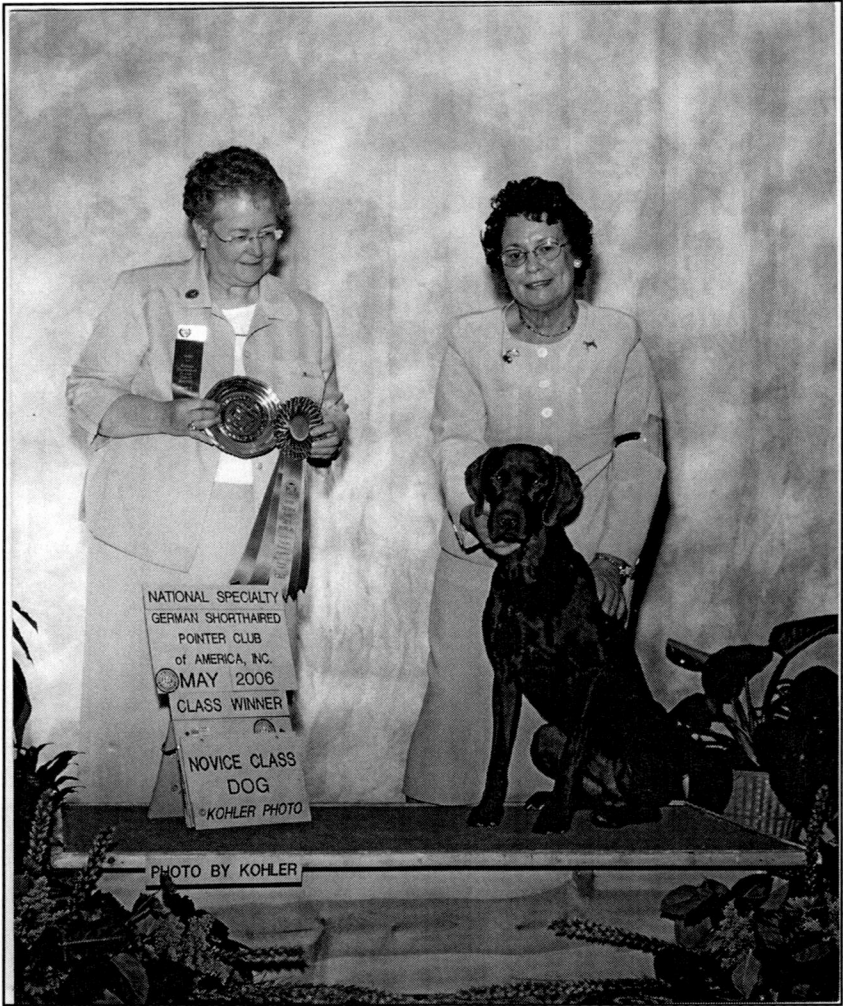

national usa phoenix judge from canada
virginia lynne my self and pecan.

At Phoenix USA National with myself and Sweet Pecan won
4 first prizes under 2 USA judges and 2 Canadian judges

NATIONAL SPECIALTY
GERMAN SHORTHAIRED
POINTER CLUB
of AMERICA, INC.
MAY 2006
PLACEMENT
NOVICE CLASS
BITCH
KOHLER PHOTO
PHOTO BY KOHLER

at national usa pecan and myself phoenix 2006.

at national usa phoenix 2006 mary carson myself
ch deepthatch lassie award of merit

THE AMERICAN KENNEL CLUB

HUNTING TEST TITLE CERTIFICATE

This certifies that

Pointer (German Shorthaired)

Deepthatch Lassie CD JH   SN39260301

bred by

Ruby Field

owned by

Mary Frances Carson & Robert D Carson

having completed the requirements on

March 16, 2002

has been officially recorded a

MASTER HUNTER

by The American Kennel Club

James P Crowley

Secretary

master hunter won by chdeepthatch lassie.

FIELD TRIAL AT TOMBSTONE Tuesday, 14 May, 2013 11:43

THESE PICTURES ARE OF TOMBSTONENEAR THE OK KORREL THEY HUNT THEN GO FOR FINDS AND RETRIEVES THEY HAVE GUNNERS NICE PRIZES////
THE PICTURES TAKEN IN MORNING ALL DOGS ON LONG CHAINS GIVEN FOOD. VERY COLD LOTS OF ODIBAR DOGS VERY WHITE SEEM TO ALL HAVE SAME HEAD AND EYES.

THE PICTURE ARE LEFT JIM FIELD NEXT JEFF CHANDLER RUGERHEIM KENNEL NEXT RUBYFIELD THEN FT HANDLERH HANGO/// NEXT LEFT HAND SIDE PHILIP CASDORPH STEVIE CASADORPH WERE PRESIDENT OF GSP OF AMERICA RUBYFIELD LEFT SIDE JIM FIELD////

tombstone fiel trial. picture jim field jaff
chandler ruby field mr hunga

tombstone usa pictures philip casdorph
stevie casdorph ruby field jim field

tombstone field trial prizes below tombstone gunners.

BOB AT SIMI VALLEY

Tuesday, 14 May, 2013 11:18

MY BOB AT SIMI VALLEY MINADO FLYN+ COULOURS
OF PALLADEN WENT BOB NEXT WEEK AT PASADENA
BECAME CHAMPION PRODUCED 5 CHAMPIONS////

ORANGE EMPIRECH SHOW// Tuesday, 14 May, 2013 11:27

AT FOOT OF SAN BERDINO MOUNTAINS BOB CHANTILLY LACE VON HAINHOLZ WITH HANDLER ERIN HOST OWNER DAISY SHEAPHER////

WINNERS DOG BOPPOSITE SEX RICHBERGMAN/////

NATIONAL USA DINNER/// HERE ARE SOME OF THE PRIZES//

Saturday, 11 May, 2013 17:53

THETABLE DURING JUDGING IN DAY AGUN///BRONZE HEAD STADY OF A GERMAN SHORTHAIR ALSO SOME LOVELY JEWLERY/// WENT TO NATIONAL DINNER SITTING AT TABLE BESIDE ME WAS ROBERT MC KOWAN WHO OWNED ADAM VON FURREHEIM NEEDED 2POINTS MORE TO BECOME ADUAL///TALKED TO ME WHAT GREAT SHOOTTING DAYS HE HAD WITH THIS DOG AND DUAL CHAMPION SCHATZIES ERIC V,.GRIEF HE IS SIRE OF HANK THE YANKDAM FC. SHATZI.V. CD NFC V. GOING BACK TO ESSERSCHICKDAUGHTER GOING BACK AGAIN TO WASSSERLING BLOODLINES HANK WAS SENT TO UK HAD 6MONTHS IN QUARANTINE MATER 2 BITCHES HERE HANK SPENT 6 MONTHS HERE IN UK THEN SENT ON TO AUSTRALIA WHERE HANK SPENT 3 MORE MONTHS IN QURANTINE BEFORE GOING TO HIS NEW OWNERS LYNN AND CAROLYN BUTLER THEN FOLLOWING YEAR WENT WITH JIM TO USA TO JUDGE HUNT TESTFOR BRITTANY CLUBIN RIGHT DOWN IN SOUTH OF CALIFORNIA VERY HOT WIND KNOW AND AGAINBLEW SAND STORMS JUDGES WERE ON HORSEBACK HANDLERS ON FOOT RUN IN PAURS THEY HAVE TO HONOUR EACH OTHER BIRDS QUAIL ARE PLANTED IN LIKE BUSHES HORSES CAME BACK AFTER EACH RUN HORSES WERE PUT IN SHADE THEY MUST HAVE MARKS AT LEAST7 OUT OF TEN IN EACH CATTERGARY ENCLOSED ARE THE CATTERGIESTHEY DO 2FOR JUNIOR HUNTERE 4 FOR SENIOR HUNTER 8 FOR MASTER HUNTER. NEXT DAY WENT ON RANGE VERY HOT AND DESSERT LIKEIN CALIFORNIA . . . ///

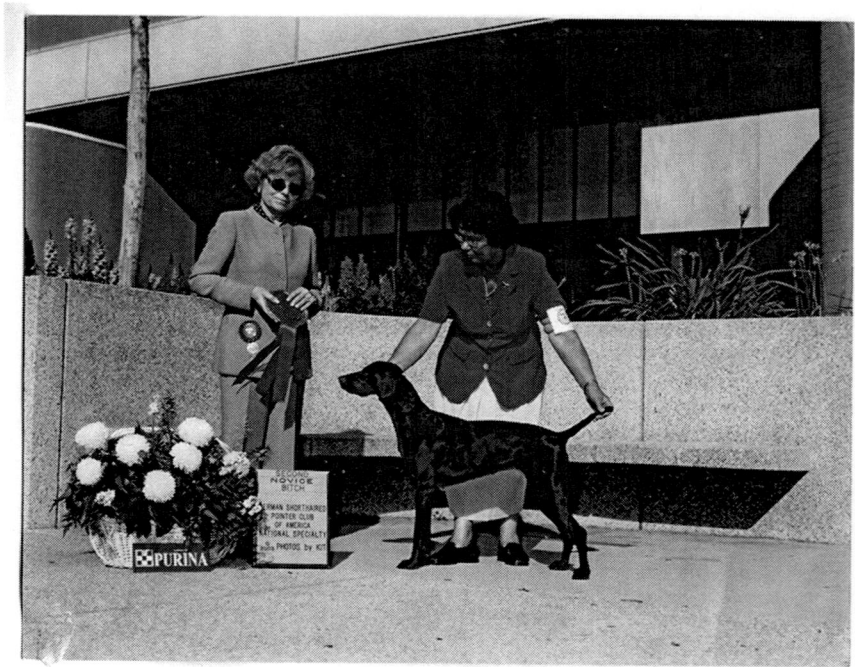

HERE IN CALIFORNIA SOUTHERN CALIFORNIA SPECIALTY MY WINNER WITH OWNER KAREN SCHOPPA 1990/////

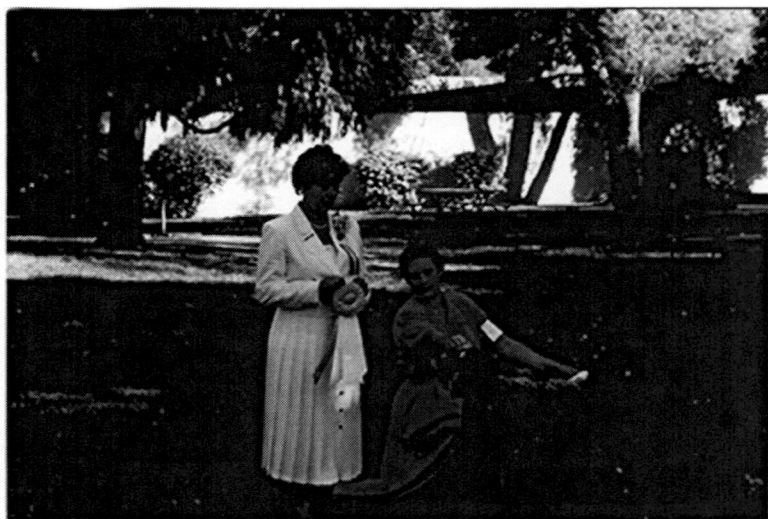

German Shorthaired Pointer Breed Standard (AKC)

The Shorthair is a versatile hunter, an all-purpose gundog capable of high performance in field and water. The judgment of Shorthair's in the show-ring should reflect this basic characteristic.

GENERAL APPEARANCE

The overall picture which is created in the observer's eye, is that of an aristocratic, well-balanced, symmetrical animal, with conformation indication power, endurance, and agility and a look of intelligence and animation. The dog is neither small nor conspicuously large. It gives the impression of medium size, but is like the proper hunter (hunter in this context refers to a horse used for hunting with pack-hounds), with a short back, but standing over plenty of ground.

Tall leggy dogs, or dogs which are ponderous or unbalanced because of excess substance should be definitely rejected. The first impression is that of keenness, which denotes full enthusiasm for work without indication of nervous or flighty character. Movements are alertly coordinated without waste of motion. Grace of outline, clean-cut head, sloping shoulders, deep chest, powerful back, strong quarters, good bone composition, adequate muscle, well-carried tail and taut coat, all combine to produce a look of nobility and an indication of anatomical structure essential to correct gait which must indicate a heritage of purposefully conducted breeding. Doggy bitches and bitchy dogs are to be faulted. A judge must excuse a dog from the ring if it displays extreme shyness or viciousness towards its handler or the judge. Aggressiveness or belligerence toward another dog is not to be considered viciousness.

SYMMETRY

Symmetry and field quality are most essential. A dog in hard and lean field condition is not to be penalized. However, overly fat or poorly muscled dogs are to be penalized. A dog well-balanced in all points is preferable to one with outstanding good qualities and defects.

HEAD

Clean-cut, neither too light nor too heavy, in proper proportion to the body. Skull is reasonably broad, arched on the side and slightly round on top. Scissura (median line between the eyes and the forehead) not too deep, occipital bone not as conspicuous as in the case of the Pointer. The foreface rises gradually from nose to forehead. The rise is more pronounced in the dog than in the bitch as befitting his sex. The chops fall away from the somewhat projecting nose. Lips are full and deep, never flewy. The chops do not fall over too much, but form a proper fold in the angle. The jaw is powerful and the muscles well developed. The line to the forehead rises gradually and never has a definite stop as that of the Pointer, but rather a stop effect when viewed from the side, due to the position of the eyebrows. The muzzle is sufficiently long to enable the dog to seize properly and to facilitate his carrying game a long time. A pointed muzzle in not desirable. The entire head never gives the impression of tapering to a point. The depth is in the right proportion to the length, both in the muzzle and in the skull proper. The length of the muzzle should equal the length of the skull. A pointed muzzle is a fault. A dish-face is a fault. Too many wrinkles in the forehead is a fault.

EYES

The eyes are of medium size, full of intelligence and expressive, good humored and yet radiating energy, neither protruding nor sunken. The eye is almond shaped, not circular. The eyelids close well. The best color is dark brown. Light yellow (Bird of Prey) eyes are not desirable, and are a fault. Closely set eyes are to be faulted. China or wall eyes are to be disqualified.

NOSE

Brown, the larger the better, nostrils well-opened and broad. Spotted nose not desirable. Flesh colored nose disqualifies.

TEETH

The teeth are strong and healthy. The molars inter-mesh properly. The bite is a true scissors bite. A perfect level bite (without overlapping) is not desirable and must be penalized. Extreme overshot or undershot bite disqualifies.

NECK

Of the proper length to permit the jaws reaching the game to be retrieved, sloping downwards on beautiful curving lines. The nape is rather muscular, becoming gradually larger towards the shoulders. Moderate hound-like throatiness permitted.

CHEST

The chest in general gives the impresison of depth rather than breadth; for all that, it should be in correct proportion to the other parts of the body with a fair depth. The chest reaches down to the elbows, the ribs forming the thorax show a rib spring and are not flat or slab-sided; they are not perfectly rounded or barrel-shaped. Ribs that are entirely round prevent the necessary expansion of the chest when taking breath. The back ribs reach well down. The circumference of the thorax immediately behind the elbows is smaller than the thorax about a hand's-breadth behind elbows, so that the upper arm has room for movement.

BACK, LOINS, AND CROUP

Back is short, strong, and straight with a slight rise from the root of tail to withers. Loin strong, of moderate length, and slightly arched. Tuck-up is apparent. Excessively long, roach or swayed back must be penalized.

FOREQUARTERS

The shoulders are sloping, movable, well-covered with muscle. The shoulder blades lie flat and are well laid back nearing a 45 degree angle. The upper arm (the bones between the shoulder and elbow joints) is as long as possible, standing away somewhat from the trunk so that the straight and closely muscled legs, when viewed from the front, appear parallel.

Elbows which stand away from the body or are too close indicate toes turning inwards or outwards, which must be regarded as faults. Pasterns are strong, short and nearly vertical with a slight spring. Loose, short-bladed or straight shoulders must be faulted. Down in the pasterns is to be faulted.

HINDQUARTERS

The hips are broad with hip sockets wide apart and fall slightly towards the tail in a graceful curve. Thighs are strong, well-muscled. Stifles well bent. Hock joints are well angulated and strong, straight bone structure from hock to pad. Angulation of both stifle and hock joint is such as to combine maximum combination of both drive and traction. Hocks turn neither in nor out. A steep croup is a fault. Cow-hocked legs are a serious fault.

FEET

Are compact, close-knot, and round to spoon-shaped. The toes sufficiently arched and heavily nailed. The pads are strong, hard and thick. Dewclaws on the hind legs must be removed. Dewclaws on the forelegs may be removed. Feet pointing in or out is a fault.

COAT AND SKIN

The skin is close and tight. The hair is short and thick and feels tough to the hand; it is somewhat longer on the underside of the tail and the back of the haunches. It is softer, thinner and shorter on the ears and the head. Any dog with long hair in the body coat is to be severely penalized.

TAIL

Is set high and firm, and must be docked leaving 40 percent of length. The tail hangs down when the dog is quiet, is held horizontally when he is walking. The tail must never be curved over the back towards the head when the dog is moving. A tail curved or bent towards the head is to be severely penalized.

BONES

Thin and fine bones are by no means desirable in a dog which must possess strength and be able to work over any and every country. The main importance accordingly is laid not so much on the size of bones, but rather on their being in proper proportion to the body. Bone structure too heavy or too light is a fault. Dogs with coarse bones are handicapped in agility of movement and speed.

WEIGHT AND HEIGHT

Dogs, 55 to 70 pounds (25 to 31.8 kgs).
Bitches, 45 to 60 pounds (20.4 to 27.2 kgs).
Dogs, 23 to 25 inches (58.4 to 63.5 cm) at the withers.
Bitches, 21 to 23 inches (53.3 to 58.4 cm) at the withers.
Deviations of 1 inch (2.5 cm) over or above the described heights are to be severely penalized.

COLOR

The coat may be solid liver or any combination of liver and white such as liver and white ticked, liver spotted and white ticked, or liver roan. A dog with any area of black, red, orange, lemon, or tan or a dog solid white will be disqualified.

GAIT

A smooth, light gait is essential. It is to be noted that as gait increases from the walk to a faster speed, the legs converge beneath the body. The tendency to single track is desirable. The forelegs reach well ahead as if to pull in the ground without giving the appearance of a hackney gait, and are followed by the back legs which give forceful propulsion. Dragging the rear feet is undesirable.

DISQUALIFICATIONS

China or wall eyes.
Flesh colored nose.
Extreme overshot or undershot.
A dog with any area of black, red, orange, lemon, or tan, or a dog solid white.

Starlite's Greif v. Kazia aka "Hank the Yank," owned by Lynn and Carolyn Butler of New South Wales and bred in the United States by Marcy Desmond, was the first American-bred GSP imported to Australia. He proved a great asset to the breed's gene pool in his new home as well as a peerless goodwill ambassador. *Lynn Butler*

Schatzi v. Heiligsepp, CD, dam of Starlite's Greif v. Kazia ("Hank the Yank"). Schatzi was owned by Marci Desmond. Hank was by Dual Ch. Schatzie's Eric v. Greif, an Adam son.

Ch. Adam v. Fuehrerheim, all-time leading sire of champions with one dual a??? two field champions and an impressive tally of 115 show champions. He ??? owned by the author Robert H. McKowen.

AKC MEET THE BREEDS®: German Shorthaired Pointer

A versatile hunter and all-purpose gun dog, the German Shorthaired Pointer possesses keen scenting power and high intelligence. The breed is proficient with many different types of game and sport, including trailing, retrieving, and pointing pheasant, quail, grouse, waterfowl, raccoons, possum, and even deer. A medium-sized breed, he has an aristocratic bearing and can be solid liver or liver and white in color.

A Look Back
The origin of the German Shorthaired Pointer is not clear, but the source of the breed seems to have been the German Bird Dog, related to the old Spanish Pointer, and various crossings with local German scent hounds and track and trail dogs. When the Germans introduced the English Pointers to lend elegance to the German Shorthaired Pointer prototype, the result was a utility dog that combined sporting virtue with clean lines, good looks and sound temperament.

Right Breed for You?
The German Shorthaired Pointer thrives as part of an active family. He is an even-tempered, intelligent and loyal family watchdog that has enthusiasm for its work. An athlete, he can adapt to his living situation, but requires consistent exercise. The GSP's short coat sheds, but grooming is minimal.

If you are considering purchasing a **German Shorthaired Pointer puppy,** learn more here.

- Sporting Group; AKC recognized in 1930.
- Average size: 55 to 70 pounds and 23 to 25 inches tall at the shoulder.
- Gun dog, family pet.

© The American Kennel Club, Inc.

German Shorthaired Pointer Breed Standard

Sporting Group

General Appearance
The German Shorthaired Pointer is a versatile hunter, an all purpose gun dog capable of high performance in field and water. The judgement of Shorthairs in the show ring reflects this basic characteristic. The overall picture which is created in the observer's eye is that of an aristocratic, well balanced, symmetrical animal with conformation indicating power, endurance and agility and a look of intelligence and animation. The dog is neither unduly small nor conspicuously large. It gives the impression of medium size, but is like the proper hunter, "with a short back, but standing over plenty of ground." Symmetry and field quality are most essential. A dog in hard and lean field condition is not to be penalized; however, overly fat or poorly muscled dogs are to be penalized. A dog well balanced in all points is preferable to one with outstanding good qualities and defects. Grace of outline, clean-cut head, sloping shoulders, deep chest, powerful back, strong quarters, good bone composition, adequate muscle, well carried tail and taut coat produce a look of nobility and indicate a adequate muscle, well carried tail and taut coat produce a look of nobility and indicate a heritage of purposefully conducted breeding. Further evidence of this heritage is movement which is balanced, alertly coordinated and without wasted motion.

Size, Proportion, Substance
Size—height of dogs, measured at the withers, 23 to 25 inches. Height of bitches, measured at the withers, 21 to 23 inches. Deviations of one inch above or below the described heights are to be severely penalized. Weight of dogs 55 to 70 pounds. Weight of bitches 45 to 60 pounds. *Proportion*—measuring from the forechest to the rearmost projection of the rump and from the withers to the ground, the Shorthair is permissibly either square or slightly longer than he is tall. *Substance*—thin and fine bones are by no means

desirable in a dog which must possess strength and be able to work over any type of terrain. The main importance is not laid so much on the size of bone, but rather on the bone being in proper proportion to the body. Bone structure too heavy or too light is a fault. Tall and leggy dogs, dogs which are ponderous because of excess substance, doggy bitches, and bitchy dogs are to be faulted.

Head

The *head* is clean-cut, is neither too light nor too heavy, and is in proper proportion to the body. The *eyes* are of medium size, full of intelligence and expression, good-humored and yet radiating energy, neither protruding nor sunken. The eye is almond shaped, not circular. The preferred color is dark brown. Light yellow eyes are not desirable and are a fault. Closely set eyes are to be faulted. China or wall eyes are to be disqualified. The *ears* are broad and set fairly high, lie flat and never hang away from the head. Their placement is just above eye level. The ears when laid in front without being pulled, should extend to the corner of the mouth. In the case of heavier dogs, the ears are correspondingly longer. Ears too long or fleshy are to be faulted. The *skull* is reasonably broad, arched on the side and slightly round on top. Unlike the Pointer, the median line between the eyes at the forehead is not too deep and the occipital bone is not very conspicuous. The foreface rises gradually from nose to forehead. The rise is more strongly pronounced in the dog than in the bitch. The jaw is powerful and the muscles well developed. The line to the forehead rises gradually and never has a definite stop as that of the Pointer, but rather a stop-effect when viewed from the side, due to the position of the eyebrows. The *muzzle* is sufficiently long to enable the dog to seize game properly and be able to carry it for a long time. A pointed muzzle is not desirable. The depth is in the right proportion to the length, both in the muzzle and in the skull proper. The length of the muzzle should equal the length of skull. A dish-shaped muzzle is a fault. A definite Pointer stop is a serious fault. Too many wrinkles in the forehead is a fault. The *nose* is brown, the larger the better, and with nostrils well opened and broad. A spotted nose is not desirable. A flesh colored nose disqualifies. The chops fall away from the somewhat projecting nose. Lips are full and deep yet are never flewy. The *teeth* are strong and healthy. The molars intermesh properly. The bite is a true scissors bite. A perfect level bite is not desirable and must be penalized. Extreme overshot or undershot disqualifies.

Neck, Topline, Body
The *neck* is of proper length to permit the jaws reaching game to be retrieved, sloping downwards on beautifully curving lines. The nape is rather muscular, becoming gradually larger toward the shoulders. Moderate throatiness is permitted. The *skin* is close and tight. The *chest* in general gives the impression of depth rather than breadth; for all that, it is in correct proportion to the other parts of the body. The chest reaches down to the elbows, the ribs forming the thorax show a rib spring and are not flat or slabsided; they are not perfectly round or barrel-shaped. The back ribs reach well down. The circumference of the thorax immediately behind the elbows is smaller than that of the thorax about a hand's breadth behind elbows, so that the upper arm has room for movement. Tuck-up is apparent. The *back* is short, strong, and straight with a slight rise from the root of the tail to the withers. The loin is strong, is of moderate length, and is slightly arched. An excessively long, roached or swayed back must be penalized. The hips are broad with hip sockets wide apart and fall slightly toward the tail in a graceful curve. A steep croup is a fault. The *tail* is set high and firm, and must be docked, leaving approximately 40% of its length. The tail hangs down when the dog is quiet and is held horizontally when he is walking. The tail must never be curved over the back toward the head when the dog is moving. A tail curved or bent toward the head is to be severely penalized.

Forequarters
The *shoulders* are sloping, movable, and well covered with muscle. The shoulder blades lie flat and are well laid back nearing a 45 degree angle. The upper arm (the bones between the shoulder and elbow joint) is as long as possible, standing away somewhat from the trunk so that the straight and closely muscled legs, when viewed from the front, appear to be parallel. Elbows which stand away from the body or are too close result in toes turning inwards or outwards and must be faulted. *Pasterns* are strong, short and nearly vertical

with a slight outwards and must be faulted. *Pasterns* are strong, short and nearly vertical with a slight spring. Loose, short-bladed or straight shoulders must be faulted. Knuckling over is to be faulted. Dewclaws on the forelegs may be removed. The *feet* are compact, close-knit and round to spoon-shaped. The toes are sufficiently arched and heavily nailed. The pads are strong, hard and thick.

Hindquarters
Thighs are strong and well muscled. Stifles are well bent. Hock joints are well angulated and strong with straight bone structure from hock to pad. Angulation of both stifle and hock joint is such as to achieve the optimal balance of drive and traction. Hocks turn neither in nor out. Cowhocked legs are a serious fault.

Coat
The hair is short and thick and feels tough to the hand; it is somewhat longer on the underside of the tail and the back edges of the haunches. The hair is softer, thinner and shorter on the ears and the head. Any dog with long hair in the body coat is to be severely penalized.

Color
The coat may be of solid liver or a combination of liver and white such as liver and white ticked, liver patched and white ticked, or liver roan. A dog with any area of black, red, orange, lemon or tan, or a dog solid white will be disqualified.

Gait
A smooth lithe gait is essential. It is to be noted that as gait increases from the walk to a faster speed, the legs converge beneath the body. The tendency to single track is desirable. The forelegs reach well ahead as if to pull in the ground without giving the appearance of a hackney gait. The hindquarters drive the back legs smoothly and with great power.

Temperament
The Shorthair is friendly, intelligent, and willing to please. The first impression is that of a keen enthusiasm for work without indication of nervous or flightly character.

Disqualifications
China or wall eyes.
Flesh colored nose.
Extreme overshot or undershot.
A dog with any area of black, red, orange, lemon, or tan, or a dog solid white.

Approved August 11, 1992
Effective September 30, 1992

German Shorthaired Pointer Links

Robert L. Holcomb
1925-1990

Dr. Jim McCue

PART II

The Holcombs arrived in Germany in the late summer of '58. Although Dean was too young for school, Mark and Grant were able to start school on time in the fall, It's not surprising that Grant's most vivid memories of Germany center on hunting with his dad and with a variety of great versatile Shorthairs—Huns, roebucks and rabbits—and, of course of his grandad Kloess.

Because of Bob's knowledge and appreciation of the breed, coupled with his outstanding training ability (a pleasant outgoing personality, a German wife and fluency in the language didn't hurt), he was taken into the **Klub Deutsch Kurzhaar** community with open arms and became a member of the Nuernberg Klub. It wasn't long before he was judging their trials. So far as I know, no other American (not of German descent) to this day, has judged more field trials in Germany or played a more active or influential role over there than Bob Holcomb—which is a strong indication of the respect the German Kurzhaar fancy had for this young **amerikanisch** soldier.

In addition to Klub activities Bob became good friends and hunting buddies with several of the legendary Shorthair breeders. An especially warm relationship developed between Bob and the wealthy and enduring old bachelor, Ernst Bleckmann (Mr. Portland Cement of Germany) of the famous **von dem Radbach's** who was then still active in the breed. Bleckmann started his Radbachs in 1921 with Atta Sand, litter-sister to the revered Artus Sand, as his "strain mother." Remember Cosak v.d. Radbach, who came to the USA back in 1935, the one Dr. Thornton called "Old Coxie"? Well, Bleckmann was still producing great ones. Bob saw that many great ones found their way to the States.

Ernst Bleckmann, von dem Radbach whose first export to the USA was to Dr. Charles Thornton in 1935. Bleckmann died in 1971.

Then there was Bleckmann's good friend and hunting buddy, Herr F. Bollhoff of the outstanding **Blitzdorf's** back of so many fine USA pedigrees. Holcomb also bought several dogs from H.F. Seiger, author of the Denlinger published "The Complete German Shorthaired Pointer," (1951) and breeder of the respected **Seiger** strain also very well-represented here. Another close friend and associate of Bob's was Gustav Machetanz (the only one still living), owner-breeder of the Shorthair's greatest all-time sire in Germany, Axel von Wasserschling. He was recently (1991) honored by the KDK for his many years of service to the Shorthair, his role as protector during the War Years and his very active role in the rebuilding process of the postwar years.

Gustav Machetanz breeder of the All-Time Top Sire in Germany Axel v Wasserschling. Still active in the breed. Recently honored.

Import Gert von dem Radbach (KS Zeus v Blitzdorf X Ruth v d Radbach). Not a great picture of this outstanding dog but the best available.

During his three year hitch in Germany, the good M/Sgt judged all of the top dogs and hunted over a good many of them as well. He gained considerable knowledge, experience and respect for the breed in the process.

While Holcomb was in Germany he exported a good many fine Shorthairs to the States—more than anyone I know. And the important point was that he was in a perfect position to know and pick the best. He was not buying "a pig in a poke"—and the record attests to his "eye for a dog." He sent 10 Shorthairs to Don Miner alone, and another 5 good ones at least to Ralph Parks of Seattle and there may have been other of which I am unaware. Don Miner also bought through Bob, Centa v Bornfeld (a KS Vito v d Radbach daughter) bred to KS Arco v Neistetal (she whelped 7 pups in the US). Space does not permit the detailing of each dog Bob sent to the States but some cannot be omitted.

Only July 1, 1959 at the Bleckmann Kennels, Beckum, W. Germany, Ruth v d Radbach whelped the "G" litter sired by Bollhoff's KS Zeus v Blitzdorf. Bob Holcomb took the pick of that litter and at three months flew it to Ralph Park, Sr., of Seattle. Gert v d Radbach arrived during the hunting season and was immediately put on wild birds in eastern Washington. All were impressed with the very young dog's intelligence, stamina, birdiness, nose and run. In the spring (1960) at 8-9 months of age he started his field trial career under Park.

In the spring of his last year in Germany (1961) Holcomb took Army leave from his duties at Nurnberg for some "dog business." First he went to Beckum to meet with Ernst Bleckmann to select a couple of pups out of a bitch he had hunted over with Bleckmann and admired, Asta vom Weidental. He knew that was going to be an outstanding litter. Bob chose two little bitch puppies out of Asta, Kara and Katja v d Radbach, sired by K S Blitz v Leisenbach. (Asta was later bred by Bleckmann and imported in whelp to the US by the author & Hubert Stipa, Boise.) Some time later Bob realized he had seen Lutz on that visit but that pup had been so young it made no impression on him.

Double Dual Radbach's Arko (Gert X Katja, both Radbach imports). Bred by Holcomb, owned by Alvin Schwager, Seattle.

Bob told me he enjoyed visiting with Mr. Bleckmann and seeing his dogs and did so as often as he could. He told me "The interesting thing about it . . . . was the opportunity to see dogs of his breeding, from 13 years to two weeks. Not just a few but many. He had a great set-up. The way he typed his dogs for size, conformation and ability was amazing to me."

After selecting the pups Holcomb attended the Derby at Westfalin and then drove with Bleckmann to Kassel to attend the Diana/Dr. Kleeman (German National). On the way they picked up Dr. Hilbrig (Vet), secretary of the Deutsche Kurahaar Klub and Shorthair student of some 60 years. That was the year Bollhoff's K S Elch v Blitzdorf, 90 H, was Kleeman-Sieger. Hilbrig passed away shortly after returning from the Nationals. Bleckmann died in 1971.

On subsequent visits to Beckum Lutz caught Bob's eye although he had not planned to buy any more pups, he could not resist just one more, Lutz. Holcomb jetted Lutz over the pole to Don Miner (VonThalberg/Saratoga, CA). The pup became deathly sick shortly after arrival (the German "crud" fortunately not seen much these days was a big large part of the problem) and Shirley Miner spend a good many sleepless nights nursing him back to health. They thought they had lost him several times over the many weeks of recovery. Don later sold Lutz, at Bob's request, to Alvin Schwager, respected Seattle lumberman, where Bob trained and handled him throughout his lifetime. Lutz is tied with Greif and DC Kay v d Wildberg (all three dogs were imported) as the Number One producer of Dual Champions in the US and Lutz is also 13th in the production of FCs. Lutz was many times among the Top Ten All Age dogs and often the Top AA dog. But it must be said that Holcomb was not, generally speaking, an All Age man.

It is no coincidence that Holcomb was associated with two of the three Top Dual Producers. Had he done no more than send these two (Lutz & Gert) to the USA his place in Shorthairdom would be assured—but he did much more. It bears repeating: in the beginning (the first 120 Dual Champions in the breed), one dual in every ten was a "Holcomb dog"; and remember Greif; and the breed's first Double Dual, Gretchen; and if you don't remember Arrak, Bimbo, Arko and all the rest, I'll remind you. There are few individuals (certainly less than 10) who had a greater or more lasting influence on the Shorthair in the USA than Bob Holcomb. It is unfortunate that newer members are unaware of his great contribution to the breed and the purpose of this piece is to overcome that ignorance. There are a few others, (very few and most dead) unknown to the present day Shorthair fancy whose contribution to the breed ranks close to Holcomb's. Some still living are Don Miner of Saratoga, CA and Richard Johns of Benton. PA have interesting stories that should be told—most in the fancy don't even recognize the names. The outstanding specimens Holcomb sent here, the quality—even the quantity—is only part of that influence, part of that contribution. Even more important was the way he maintained and concentrated that gene pool and sent it to every corner of the USA.

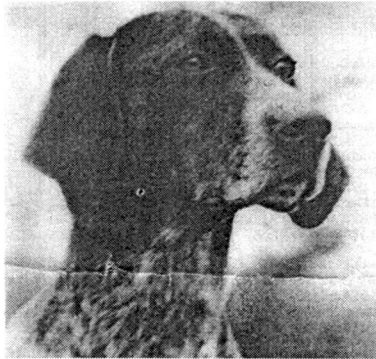

Double Dual Gert's Dena v Greif (Gert X DD Gretchen v Greif) another perfect blending of Radbach and Greif. In the same litter was another Double Dual, Gert's Duro v Greif).

This in no way lessens the contributions of others all across the country. Tradition is built on the great dogs and great individuals of the past. Their accomplishments and their contributions should be recognized and publicized. There are many here in the Northwest alone who have contributed much, many who have passed away recently (within the past 10 years) without a word in the Shorthair press. **Some** are Ralph Park, first president of the GSPCA and top producer of Duals and Double Duals, Dave McGinnis, trainer of more National Champions than any other pro, Gladys Laird, owner of the most National Champions, to mention only a few.

Holcomb returned home just in time to run Don Miner's Von Thalberg's Fritz, II (a Greif son and an all-time Top Field Trial producer) in the Nationals which were held in Ellensberg, WA in

1961. The winner that year was Don's and Fritz's next door neighbor in Saratoga (CA). Walter Seagraves' (Seagraves manufactured fire engines) Von Saalfield's Kash handled by the Michigan pro, Rusty Dixon.

One pretty fall day, soon after Holcomb's returned to the States and prior to the Nationals, the Three Musketeers (Miner, Merrell & Holcomb) were returning from a morning dove shoot (it was an annual event) when they saw a couple of men working Shorthairs in the Bakersfield alfalfa. They were impressed with what they saw and stopped to watch. The men turned out to be Buren Mayfield (Bakersfield) with his son, Mike (now a father of four, a high school teacher & coach in Pocatello. Still has good Greif Shorthairs) and the dogs were Helga and Wurtzie (FC Von Thalberg's Wurtz Greif).

Mike recalls, "Bob told me he sure liked Helga's class and movement and he'd like to train her for me. This was even before he realized that she was by Arrak v Heisterholz, one of the outstanding dogs he had sent to Ralph Park from Germany (Arrak later became an International Dual). So within about six months—well—we sent her to him. He was still working out of the Ft Ord command but was actually living off-base at Ceres, a tiny community in the big dairy area up the valley near Modesto. He was procuring milk, butter, eggs and so on for the Army—pretty nice duty. Of course he was friendly with every farmer in the valley and could hunt and train anywhere he wanted. A great deal.

Double Dual Arrak von Heisterholz sent by Holcomb from Germany to Ralph Park in Seattle as a pup—same as Gert.

A 27 months he championed her out when she won both the Gun Dog and the All Age—both major stakes—at the GSPC of Idaho trial in September 1962. Heisterholz Helga v Greif (Arrak X Gretchen) was the first field champion Bob made after returning from Germany. She was also Bob's sixth Field Trial Champion.

During this same time Bob was breaking Arrak,—and Gert v d Radbach—another great one Bob had sent to Ralph from Germany. The pair were just starting to place in broke stakes—2nd and 3rd in the Santa Clara Valley trial of April '62. He was also just starting to place Miner's Lutz v d Radbach in Puppy.

Unknown to Bob and Ralph, another pup from Ruth's "G" litter came to the US. Graf v d Radbach sent to Hubert Stipa arrived in Boise April 1960 "as sick as a dog" after a long boat trip. It took about six months to get the pup back on feed. An interesting side light is that both of Ruth's "G" pups finished their US FC on the same day—March 23, 1963. Gert at the Idaho trial in Boise handled by Bob Holcomb and the Boise dog, Graf, at Fresno, CA, handled by John Merrell.

Without going into detail on Gert's outstanding field trial and breeding record it is enough to say that his contribution to the breed can best be measured by the fact that he is the #2 producer of Dual Champions in the US.

Late in 1962 the Holcombs were transferred back "home" to Fort Lewis, WA. The same crew—Park, Brown, Gillespie, Laird, Davis, et all—was still there, plus some new ones. Jerry Peltola (who judged the National Futurity and the National Amateur Gun Dog in '90) remembers those early days well. Bob's old beat-up blue Chevey Wagon and the always over-filled tear-drop shaped dog trailer. Jerry's first contact with Bob came when Jerry was having trouble getting his first dog, an English pointer, to honor.

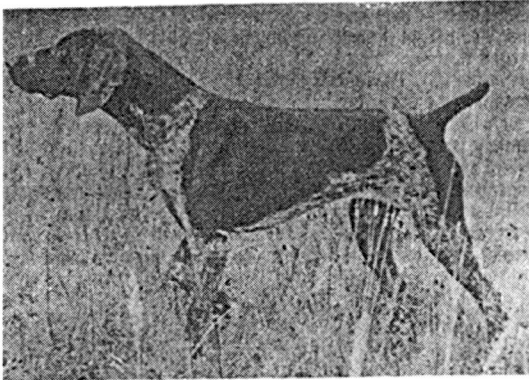

Dual Ch Janie Greif von Hesterholz (Arrak X DD Gretchen)
Elaine Stout, Denver. With a variety of consorts Double Dual
Gretchen (sandy) produced great ones. Both her father and mother
were out of old Greif. She clearly demonstrates the prepotency
of close breeding (half-sibs) when both animals are superior.

He met Bob while training in the field and asked him for help. Bob dropped everything and gave him a hand. Soon the dog was honoring without a word and with the same intensity and class she had on point. Jerry says you can't imagine how quickly Bob established rapport with a dog. It wasn't long before Bob converted Jerry to Shorthairs. He made a great many converts to Shorthairism (it is religion, you know). Jerry remembers Gert (the German papers say "Gerd" but it's pronounced the same) standing high on his hind legs to mark the fall of the bird, then returning (without a millimeter of forward movement) to his original pointing position to await the command to retrieve. He would also stand on his hind legs and bounce around to find his handler. Such activity might seem bazaar if one is unaware of the very high and heavy cover produced by some 200+ inches of rain each year—more than anywhere else in the USA. The Peltola's both have many fond memories of Bob Holcomb and those early days.

Those were the days when your dog went on point, you (and everyone else including the pros) ran to the dog as quickly as possible—and if the dog did hold and the bird was dropped, you hollered, "Fetch" a nannosecond after the shot. When Bob came along and could walk leisurely to his dog on point, it created quite a stir. When Bob kicked the bird out, he paid little apparent attention to the dog and returned to him without haste or hurry. Often he would ham it up a bit by speaking to judge or waving nonchalantly to someone in the gallery. You though he never was going to say, "fetch"—and when he did, he spoke softly. He wanted the judge—and the gallery—to know that dog was flat out broke. It was!

JKM

October, 1991

(To be continued)

1991 Breeders Stake—Canadians take home the bacon . . .

Harry & Heather Vanderzwet of Oakwood, Ontario bred the winner of the 28th National GSPCA Field Futurity **NORTHMAN'S DIXIELANDS CODY.** He is out of Gotta Go Koojo by FC (Can & US) Stormcrow in Dixieland. Cody was out of the last litter nominated in the 28th! no.239168. (28-91-68 no. indicates the 28th Futurity, run in the fall of '91, 68th litter nominated). Cody was whelped September 12, 1990, he was still a puppy, 13 months old and the youngest pup in the stake.

Cody is owned by Lou Lamaro of Richmond Hill, Ontario and the Vanderzwets and the Lamaros split the $3558 purse, Cody was handled by another Ontarian, Pro Dave King.

The runner-up was bred by Illinois Pro John Steger of Woodstock out of Directs Broadway Review by FC Monkey Shines M-Go—Blue. **Monkey Shines M-Go-Blue Bruno** was whelped January 3, 1990 and so was 22 months old at the running. Bruno was owned and handled by the well-known Mario DiMambro of Dearborn Heights, MI. John and Mario split the $2372 runner-up purse.

89 puppies out of the more than 500 pups in the 68 litters nominated for the 28th GSPCA Futurity were renominated and eligible to run in the fall event. That is about 1.3 pups per litter. 55 pups were entered and 53 ran which is about 15 per cent more than 1990.

Nomination of Dams for Futurity XXIX to run in the fall of 1992 closed the end of September with an even 100 litters enrolled.

That is up a whopping 47 per cent. That's right around 800 pups eligible for renomination. Hopefully, the second forfeit will be paid on at least 2 *pups per litter average or 200 pups total.* In that unlikely event, we would have a purse more than double that of 1991 but we are realistically estimating the 1992 purse at $8000. Renominate you XXIX pup today. All you can lose is $15.00 but you could win *three hundred times that much!* Jim McCue, Mgr.

Robert L. Holcomb
1925-1990
Dr. Jim McCue

PART III

The Holcombs were transferred back "home" to Fort Lewis in 1962. Mike Mayfield who had been training with Bob down in the Modesto area, got a summer job ('63) with a seismic crew searching for oil off the Washington and Oregon coasts. He would be at sea for two weeks and then have five days off. On his off days he'd head for Fort Lewis. If Bob wasn't at his office on the base, the Vet Colonel would pour Mike a cup of coffee and they'd shoot the bull until Bob came. It was all pretty informal. When Bob did arrive, the Colonel would tell him, "Sgt Holcomb, take this young man out and help him with his dog. It needs some work. Get going—and that's an order!" And off they'd go training. At night Mike would throw his sleeping bag down on the feed room floor and he always put on a couple of pounds eating Ottie's great German cooking. Mike learned a lot about Shorthairs and training that summer and says it was amazing how quickly Bob gained his rapport with a new dog. You could always tell that, the way the dogs came happily to the line. High tails wagging, raring to go.

Bob & Ottie at home.

The Holcomb place, home of the Radbach's, in Auburn, WA.

During this same time, there arrived in Texas another of Bleckmann's Radbacher, this one named Jessy. She had been bred in Germany to what is to this day, by the record, the greatest Shorthair sire of all time, Axel v Wasserschling. Bob Holcomb got one of the pups and called him Radbach's Bimbo. Of some two dozen Axel pups that came to the US, only two of them made great names for themselves: Radbach's Bimbo and Esser's Chick. Although Chick is fifth in all-time production of US FC, he never gained either a bench or field title here which, I suspect, was more the fault of his owner than the dog. Bimbo had enough field points to be a US FC ten times over (120 first place wins) and four times over in Canada—and he is also 10th in the all-time production of FCs. It is in a sire and dam's get that their contribution to the breed—and that of their breeder—can best be measured. Bimbo was another one of Bob's big ones. He was a joy to watch in the field. I had the pleasure of judging him on several occasions. One stands out in particular. It was an all-breed trial on a continuous course, with hour braces on wild birds. The British Columbia Centennial Trial held up in the Okanagan Country at Vernon, BC. Bimbo had more class when he lifted his hind leg than most dogs have on point.

"When Bimbo came home to live with us," Helen Peters recalls, "we had a brand new kennel and run waiting for him. However he paced so much and seemed so unhappy that he made me unhappy and nervous. He was the first dog I ever had. So shortly thereafter I went out and opened the kennel and brought him inside. He quieted down immediately, found a place that suited him and went to sleep. We were now all at peace. From that day on Mr. Bimbo never went out to the kennel again and we ultimately tore it down.

"What a lot of joy he brought to the Peters household. We were so blessed to have enjoyed him so long! He was our companion, friend and protector. We added a beautiful liver bitch, Leita, to our household and they were companions for life." It was a close-knit family affair with dad Dr. Bill, mom Helen, son Stephen, daughters Elizabeth & Susan and Shorthairs Bimbo and Leita.

Am/Can FC Radbach's Bimbo. 120 first place wins and 10th in the production of Field Champions, Hall of Famer.

Bimbo was repeatedly among the Top Ten in Both GSP News and GSPCA rankings during '68 and '72 and for that same five-year period was the Northwest Field Trial Council's Shooting Dog of the Year. A record that may never be broken. Bimbo relinquished the title to a son, Radbach's Kohoutek, the next year and the following year to a daughter, Radbach's Bridget and the year after that to Timberlane's Grit also a "Holcomb dog." The NWFTC is made up of field trial clubs of all breeds in Oregon, Washington, Idaho and British Columbia representing some 2500 field dogs and some 60 field trials a year. In 1977 Bimbo was GSPCA's Field Sire of the Year and later made the Hall of Fame. Bimbo was a great field trialer yes, Am/Can FC but he was also fabulous—and even more versatile—on a day's hunt. As much at home on the parched and barren chukar hills of Yakima Indian Reservation as in the deep blue duck waters of Puget Sound—now, that's a Shorthair!

"It was with great sadness that we put our 'Mr. Bimbo' to sleep at 16. His hind quarters were getting weak, he had been deaf for years, so when the cataracts closed in, Bill said he would not let the great animal lose any more dignity—the time had come.

"We had been preparing ourselves for this a long time, but, oh my, how the heart aches and the tears flow. We loved him so! He was a magnificent fellow who will be in our hearts always. As we look around us we see the heritage he left the breed—and his many fine sons and daughters, our own FC Radbach's Kohoutek. You can always tell a Bimbo shorthair—style, style, style, and intelligence, a joy to behold. He was aristocratic, consistent, dependable, intelligent and a gentlemen! We will never forget him."

The boys were a great help with the dogs, particularly through high school, not only in feeding, cleaning and caring but also in the training process. Here is Dean with a wheelbarrow full of "Holcomb pups."

Bob never lost his original love of horses and he had some fine field trial mounts through the years but he also owned and raced several winning thoroughbred horses and brood mares. Steve O'Donnell, Director of Racing of the Long Acres Track in Seattle, was a friend and client. Bob's middle son, Grant, now holds that same position at the Long Acres track.

You will remember Bob predicting that Asta's "K" litter in Germany would be outstanding and selected Kara and Katja v d Radbach to bring back to the U.S. Well, he was right again, KS Knirps won a huge International Trial and KS Komat became the Swiss National Champion—and when Katja was mated to Gert the result was the incomparable International Dual Champion Radbach's Arko (pictured in Part II) owned by Alvin Schwager. Schwager owned both Lutz and Arko, certainly two of the breed's finest. Alvin often trained with Bob and did the gunning well into his 80's—rarely missing a bird.

Bob loved the outdoors—hunting and fishing. In 1965 he leased a ranch and duck club near Yakima. It consisted of 80 deeded acres plus several hundred acres leased from the Yakima Indian Tribe. In addition to mallards, widgeons and pintails, there was a good to excellent population of valley quail and pheasant. When the lease expired, Bob along with a couple of dentist-clients, Drs. Marv Brown and Bob DeButts (Shorthair Club members) purchases 120 acres adjacent to the originally leased 80 deeded acres. They excavated duck ponds, grew grain in the ponds, regulated water to flood the ponds and provided perfect duck habitat and fabulous gunning.

"These were my teenage years (1963-67)," Mark told me, "They had a life-long impact on me. Dad and I hunted hard for chukar during those years—on the huge Yakima Firing Range and north in the Okanagan Country near Brewster. Much of the chukar hunting was from horseback. We hunted valley quail and pheasant as well as chukar farther north in the Coulee City area. Then back for excellent duck shooting on our leased club in the Yakima Valley. What an experience, fabulous hunting from horseback over some of the finest dogs in the world. No many teenagers—not many grown-ups either, for that matter—have experienced such living. I will never forget it as long as I live and hope to duplicate it some day."

The Northwest Field Trial Council (American Field) has honored Bob with the Annual Spring Bob Holcomb Classic. The Open Shooting Dog is the only stake in the two day classic. The huge and very beautiful Bob Holcomb Memorial Trophy is awarded the winner. The big trophy travels but each winner gets a smaller version of it to keep. Karyn Kline tells me that donations to the trophy in Bob's memory came from every corner of the country.

Holcomb's Greif/Radbach blood permeated the whole country. Although most of Bob's clients were from the West, their georgraphical distribution was wider than any pro I know— California, Oregon and Washington, north into British Columbia and Alaska and east into Idaho and Colorado. In Anchorage Milton Donner's Fritz v Trekka Radbach (a Lutz son) gained a Dual Championship and in Denver Elaine Stout's Janie Greif v Heisterholz (Arrak X Gretchen gained her Dual Championship (pictured in Part II). Elaine handled her to her show title (3/16/66). Fred Dempsey (amateur) finished her in the field. Elaine later got from Bob another big winner, Tarzan v d Radbach, a Gert X Gretchen son.

Dual Ch. Radbach's Dustcloud, owned by Harry Rich, Bellevue, WA. Note the consistency, the similiarity in color, build and class of the "Holcomb dogs" as a group. Particularly where Greif has been blended with Radbach and/ or Wasserschling (Bimbo, or Chick) to the great advantage of both. Bob knew each strain intimately—their strong points and their weaknesses. He put considerable time and effort into building and maintaining that gene pool. The beneficial results have been felt throughout the breed.

The Gert X Gretchen mating exemplified Bob's perfect blending of Greif and Radbach lines. That breeding also produced International Dual Ch Gert's Duro v Greif who in turn produced the only three-time (GSPCA/NGSPA) National Field Ch in the breed, Patricia v Frulord. Patricia was owned and often handled by another grand lady of Washington (now deceased), Gladys Laird. Patricia's kennel mate, Frulord's Tim (youngest NFC-30 months) won the National in 1976. (I remember it well, my Shilo was runner-up.) Does any other single owner hold four National (AA) Championships? The Frulord dogs were handled by Dave McGinnis (also deceased), originally of Washington and later of Idaho, a good friend and rival of Bob Holcomb and an outstanting professional.

Many Holcomb clients have told me of Bob's unique ability to break a dog and have it stay broke for years regardless who handled it, owner or passer-bye. But that's a fact I've known for 25 years— after finishing Don Miner's Holcomb-trained Von Thalberg's Radbach Queen (By Lutz out of Centa v Bornefeld, a KS Vito daughter) to her Field Championship. Bob had taken the Open Gun with Queenie and Don had planned to run her in the Amateur at the East Idaho trial but a problem arose and Miner was unable to make it to Idaho. Bob asked me to handle her at the last minute. Bob introduced me to the classic little solid liver bitch just moments before we went to to the line, "Queenie this is Doc, Doc this is Queenie, go get 'em!" I was hesitant, but I need not have been. She tore up the backcourse with two finds and an honor, then flawlessly vacuumed four birds out of the birdfield before her wide-eyed, unbelieving bracemate and handler knew what was going on. She was fast and wide and always out front but she responded so well my great granddaughter could have handled her. I don't suppose I spoke ten words to her during the whole event.

Bob had a falling out (dropped his membership after 25 years) with the GSPCA Board when they ruled that no professional could judge the National. He had no desire to do so but felt that the ruling discriminated against him and many of those best qualified to judge. After all he had been asked to judge (and did) the Brittany National twice. He also won the Brittany National twice. To be perfectly accurate, Way Kan Jeff handled by his owner, Art Stavik (retired Standard Oil distributor of Tacoma), won the Brittany National twice. Bob trained Jeff and always handled him except in the National. The wins were certainly a tribute to Bob's training ability. Not many professionals today would "trust" a client to run their own dog in the Nationals. Art's dogs were the only non-shorthairs Bob ever trained and handled as far as I know.

FC/AFC Timberlane's Grit, another great Holcomb dog.
Owned by Bob & Karyn Kline, Kingston, WA. Grit was
nationally ranked among the Top Ten in All Age, Gun Dog
and Amateur Gun Dog—all at the same time—in 1978.

Bob's influence is still being felt. Peggy Davis' FC/AFC
Timberlane's Grit's Gus, #2 Gun Dog 1990, GSPCA. Winner
1991 Region 12 Amateur Gun Dog Championship, he had
won the Regional Gun Dog Championship in 1989.

"The day came when I decided it would be fun for me to handle
Ace in the field competition, and although my pro thought I would
never be able to do it, my darling husband (who pushes, praises,
curses, and loves me) . . . encouraged me . . . . Sure, the criticism
hurt, 'Silly, little, gray-haired, lady running that dog' . . . 'Oh, my
God, there she goes' . . . 'See, he broke again.'"

Although Bob had never handled a dog for her or seen Ace in
the field, when she asked for his help, he responded immediately. He

watched her in the field, pointed out her training faults and helped her overcome them. He encouraged her, showed her how, gave her some tips—but he let her do it all herself. "If Ace and I can just hold together, we will finish this job," she said, "Ace is eight and I lead him by 50 years." And the 'silly, little, gray-haired lady' and her dog did hold together. They held together so well that Timberland's Ace became the breed's second Double Dual Champion in 1963. Bob trained and handled all Peggy Davis' dogs after Ace—and there were many good ones—most with Holcomb blood. A few were: Timberlane's Maggie, Timberlane's Fritz, Timberlane's Ruff and Tuff, Timberlane's Grit and even to this day, Timberlane's Grit's Gus.

The litter by Ruff & Tuff (who was sired by Bimbo) out of Timberlane's Krautina (whose sire & dam were both by Lutz, another half-sib mating with superior stock) was called the "Eddie Bauer litter" because all the pups, save one, went to Eddie Bauer and his executives around the country—the "Goose-down King" was a friend and client of Holcombs. The "save one" went to Bob & Karyn Kline, then of Lacey, WA, in December '75. Karyn Kline told me, "Grit was our first Shorthair and thanks to Bob Holcomb, he gave us the thrill of our lives. We've never been able to duplicate him. Thanks to Holcomb, he talked us into field trialing this dog after we refused his $2500 offer for Grit at one year of age. Bob also taught my husband (Bob) to handle Grit and Grit and my Bob brought home the bacon many times too. Now we're excited to see his son, Gus, doing so well." (FC/AFC Timberlane's Grits Gus—#2 gun Dog 1990—GSPCA).

The solid liver Grit was the only one of that Eddie Bauer litter that was field trialed and he made his FC at just over 24 months without ever running Puppy or Derby. He was among the Top Ten Gun Dogs in the Nation three years running. In '78 he was in the top All Age, Gun Dog and Amtr Gun Dog rankings—all at the same time. Has any other Shorthair done that? That same year ('78) he was NWFTC's Top Shooting Dog. Grit's best son, Timberlane's Grit's Gus, was one of the last dogs trained by Bob before he moved permanently from Seattle (Auburn) to his ranch in the Yakima Valley.

The winners Region 12 Amateur Gun Dog Championship,
January 1991, Tombstone, Arizona. Right to left: "the silly,
little, gray-haired lady" Winifred "Peggy" Davis, Shorthair's
Grand Dame, owner of Timberlane's Grit's Gus, winner of
the championship. Gus being held by Judge Dr. Jim Moreau
of Connecticut. Standing, Judge Mike Hansing of Utah.
Gailen Carothers, Pullman, WA, holds the Runner-Up,
his Snake River Lottie. Carothers also handled Gus.

In January 1991 Karyn Kline and the "Silly, little, gray-haired
lady", now in her 85th year, headed for wild and lawless Tombstone
(AZ) and the two-fisted, gun-slingin' likes of Parl Larson and
Dewey Hicks—to witness the running of the NGSPA Region 12
Championship. With a boost into the saddle, the "silly, little, gray-
haired lady" mounted her horse and followed her Gus (with Amtr.
Gailen Carothers, Pullman, WA handling) off the line. She had
difficulty seeing beyond the horses ears, but, by the grace of God
a very kind, helpful and knowledgeble field trial lady, came to her
rescue. Fran Kommenhoek, whose husband, Terry, was handling
Gus' bracemate, accompanied her and provided a running account
of the action as it took place. What a kindness, what a blessing.
Just being in the saddle, being a part of the action again brought a
flood of happy memories which were sweetened by Gus' winning
the NGSPA Regional Amateur Championship that day. (Gus had
won the Open Shooting Dog Championship in 1989, the same year

he made Top Ten Gun Dogs under the whistle of former Spokane pro, now of AZ, Bob Deitering.) As she was helped down from the saddle, Winifred "Peggy" Davis, Shorthair's Grand Dame, looked up toward heaven and smiled—she knew Bob Holcomb was watching and that he was enjoying it just as much as she was.

Good friends and happy hunting. Dr. Bill
Peters, Bob and Woody Gillespie.

Eventually Bob sold his interest in the 120 acres and later purchased the original 80 acres he had leased and fallen in love with 20 years before. The setting was perfect with year-round snow-capped Mount Adams of the Cascade Range in the background. There were pheasant and quail, and ducks galore. There was a nice home, a large barn and outbuildings and a kennel. It was a working ranch too, where Bob and youngest son, Dean, ran cattle, he had several Shorthairs including his old hunting buddy and his last Field champion, "Leroy" (FC Radbach's Kniff II), 12 who had the run of the house and slept on his bed. The ranch was his true love. A place to relax, to unwind, to enjoy life, to enjoy friends—equine, canine and human—to be close to the good, rich earth of his childhood.

Bob was totally unaware of the seriousness of his condition until the very end. He complained that his past hip operation was not improving, he had some pain with it. He knew he should see to it but he kept putting it off. It wasn't that serious, he thought—and actually it wasn't. He had a lot more than a bum hip to worry about. Dean finally convinced his father that he must go to the hospital for tests. Dean took him in early May. The results came as a terrible shock to both of them. They were completely unprepared for the swiftness of the final verdict.

It was May 30th, 1990. Because of his Service, Memorial Day had always been special with Bob. The ranch flag had fluttered in a light breeze and bright sunshine all day long. Bob sat on the ranch steps. Leroy sat beside him, his head resting on Bob's knee. Together they watched the western sky turn pink and slowly darken. As recently as a couple of weeks ago their evening ritual was a walk down past the barn, over to the pond and back by the corrals but now Bob had difficulty just getting out of bed.

The two sat quietly together. Bob's mind wondered back through the pages of his life and recalled with sadness some of the favorite hunting spots that he would never visit again, the faces of friends he would never see again and great dogs he would never shoot over again. "Leroy, it's not fair," At the sound of his name, the dog's tail started thumping lightly against the step.

They got up slowly. Bob took down the flag, folded it by the book and put it carefully away. The two of them headed for bed. They didn't lay awake long. Bob reached over and rubbed the soft brown ears, "Good night, pardner, see you in the morning." The tail started to thump again on the covers. Soon both were dreaming.

FC Radbach's Kniff II, "Leroy"—Bob's last hunting buddy is still hunting, just a little slower than in the old "horseback days." Leroy & Dean in chukar country.

The field stretched as far as the eye could see, there were no briars or cactus, the cover was ideal and there were birds galore. The day was bright. The breeze was light. A smile came over Bob's face. He was hunting again over Greif and Yunga, Sandy and Gert, Lutz and Bimbo and Arko and all the rest. Each dog took its turn while the others honored. The birdwork was perfect, the gunning flawless, the retrieves quick and tender—and it went on and on until every dog had his chance.

Bob did not awaken on the morning of May 31st, 1990.

JGM

—Finis—

ranchrosamond california Sunday, 12 May, 2013 20:45

well here we are LOOKED AT KENNELS FULL OF GSPS KARL
OUR SON AND JIM TOGETHER ONLY SAW ONE I REALLY
LIKED A BITCH ABOUT 4 MONTHS OLD AFEW YEARS
LATER I JUDGED AT ORANGE EMPIRE GSPS THIS LITTLE
BITCH WAS IN OPEN BEING SHOWN WITH PROFESSIONAL
HANDLER DIDNT KNOW IT WAS THE ONE I DAW ON
THE RANCH GAVE HER WINNERS BITCH AND BOB SAW
HOW THEY TRAINED THERE GSPS SHOWING THEM
GAME TO POINT AND FIND BEFORE THE CONTROL AND
OBEDIENCE WHICH WE DO./ THEN I SAW THERE DUAL
CHAMPION DOG YBOLD AND GERMAN DUAL HAD MY
PICTURE WITH HIM THE ONLY ONE USA AND GERMAN
DUAL GETTING OLD AND BIG TO UK STANDARDS
SAW THE PEWTER PLATE HE HAD WON IN GERMANY
WON WINNERS DOG AT SANTA BARBARA UNDER BILL
PARKINSON. THEY HAVE GOLF BUGGIES TO EXERCISE
THE DOGS ONE AT FRONT LEFT AND RIGHT WATCHING
OUT FOR SNAKES QUITE FRIGHTENING

THEN THAT EVENING WE ALL WENT TO DINNER ON
THE WAY PICK UP SHERIFF WIFE HAD TREE LEOPARDS
AND BIG CATS IN BIG CAGES/?///SHERRIFF HAD A BAR
A STUFFED LADY SITTING IN A CHAIR WITH A HOLE IN
HER BLACK DIAMOND SHAPE TIGHTS. THEN NEXT STOP
WHERE THEY MADE HORSE SADDLES AND GUN COVERS
THEN GOT TO SKI RESTUARANT ALL LITTLE LIGHTS JOB
TO READ MENU THE SHIRRIFF SAT NEXT TO ME LITE
UP HIS LIGHTER TO SEE MENU ALL GENTELMEN KEPT
THERE COWBOY HATS ON. WELL WE ALL HAD NICE
MEAL AND MADE OUR JOURNEY BACK TO RANCH WHAT
SOME MEMORIES///

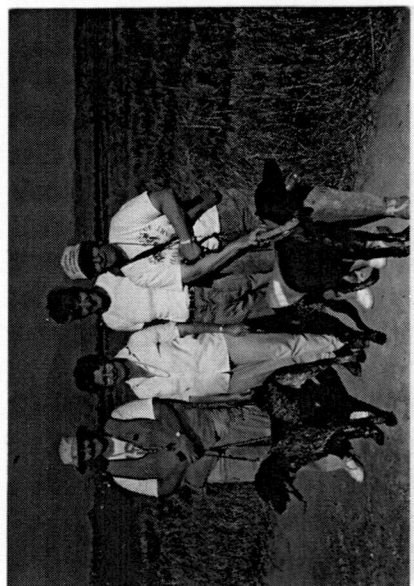

OFFICIAL AKC SCORECARD
HUNTING TESTS FOR
POINTING BREEDS

INDICATE WHETHER JUNIOR, SENIOR, MASTER

DOG'S NAME _____

BRACE# _____

HANDLER _____

SCORE ALL CATEGORIES OF ABILITY ON THE BASIS OF 0-10. DO NOT SCORE RETRIEVING AND HONORING IN JUNIOR.

1.	HUNTING	
2.	BIRD FINDING ABILITY	
3.	POINTING	
4.	TRAINABILITY	
5.	RETRIEVING NOT APPLICABLE IN JUNIOR	
6.	HONORING NOT APPLICABLE IN JUNIOR	
	TOTAL	
	AVERAGE*	

* DIVIDE TOTAL BY 4 IN JUNIOR, AND DIVIDE BY 6 IN SENIOR AND MASTER FOR OVERALL AVERAGE.

IN ORDER TO RECEIVE A QUALIFYING SCORE A DOG MUST ACQUIRE A MINIMUM OF NOT LESS THAN 5 ON EACH OF THE CATEGORIES OF ABILITY (4 CATEGORIES IN JUNIOR, 6 IN SENIOR AND MASTER) WITH AN OVERALL AVERAGE OF NOT LESS THAN 7. JUDGES MUST AGREE ON WHICH DOGS WILL QUALIFY AND WHICH DOGS WILL NOT QUALIFY BEFORE SCORES ARE TURNED IN.

YBOLD

"Deepthatch" Dual Purpose German Shorthaired Pointers

International Championship Show Judge

MRS R. FIELD

Tel. 01869 347538

7 Farriers Road
Middle Barton
Chipping Norton
Oxon OX7 7EU

National German Shorthaired Pointer Association, Inc.

THE NGSPA: ITS EARLY YEARS

By: Don Kidd

While the general field trial fraternity would not be expected to know the history of the National German Shorthaired Pointer Association, Inc., (NGSPA), the sad truth is that many Shorthair field trial enthusiasts have little or no knowledge of the origins of this association. When German Shorthairs were first imported into the United States in 1925, they were originally promoted as an "every use" dog, a super-dog with some type of canine superiority. This type of exploitation may have induced some individuals to purchase dogs at inflated prices, but it did little to improve the breed. Fortunately, such elaborate promotion did not keep sincere breed enthusiasts from logically and sensibly endeavoring to bring out the true qualifications of the German Shorthaired Pointer.

Although limited in number, Shorthair field trial enthusiasts started to occasionally enter their breed in field trial competition. As early as 1931 a German Shorthair was braced with Mary Blue in an All-Age event soon after this Teagle Pointer had won the National Championship at Grand Junction, Tennessee. The majority of Shorthair field trialers, however, were content to run in shooting dog competition in stakes either for their own breed or in events judged along gun dog lines.

Ultimately, several factors converged to create the NGSPA and its affiliation with the American Field. Unlike today, there was an abundance of wild birds immediately following World War II. Young men who had fought in either the European or Pacific theaters returned home and started to again hunt upland game birds. Some of these men acquired German Shorthairs, field trials became an extension of their hunting experience, and the breed saw the development of its first professional handlers. Although field trial competition for the breed was increasing, several of these individuals were not satisfied with the Shorthair competition that was most readily available.

The typical field trial format was a walking trial run on a single course with a bird field. The emphasis was on a dog working in a windshield wiper pattern with extreme subservience to the gun. Since scouting was not allowed, there was little or no emphasis on the ability of a dog to independently select and run to logical objectives. Judges at the time frequently penalized a handler who attempted to sing to a dog that was reaching out on the course.

It was against this backdrop that knowledgeable amateur and professional handlers discussed the future of this breed in the late 1940's. These men frequently met after a trial and in huddled conversations discussed the need for field trial competition that offered the opportunity to test this breed under more natural conditions. These individuals were determined that the natural qualities of the breed—pointing, backing, and retrieving—should be retained while encouraging wider and faster moving dogs able to more effectively hunt upland game birds. These men also recognized that if American Field competition were available to their breed, it would expand their field trial opportunities.

While some men may dream and talk about what might be, there are other men that can lead. Every individual who has blown a whistle over a German Shorthaired Pointer in any type of field trial competition owes a debt of gratitude to a man most of them never knew existed. It was this individual who was almost solely responsible for the formation of the NGSPA, the first breed National Championship and, most important, the constant and continued development of the German Shorthaired Pointer as a bird dog.

Virgil Valdosta VanDivort was born on May 20, 1909, at Mansfield, Ohio, raised in Pennsylvania, spent his early life in Texas, and then returned to Toledo, Ohio, where he started work as an independent distributor for the Toledo Times, a newspaper which was then owned by the Toledo Blade. In 1947 VanDivort became an employee of the Times and over the years would hold positions as district manager in the circulation department, city circulation manager, and home delivery manager. VanDivort, on his employment application with the Times, described his hobbies as field trialing, bird dogs, riding horses, photography, fly fishing and almost any kind of bird shooting.

VanDivort was an excellent horseman and was quite knowledgeable of pointer-setter trials, having ridden the major circuit trials on several occasions. In keeping with his interests, he would operate a commercial kennel, judge all types of pointing dog competition, and frequently acknowledge that his first love was bird dogs. Lou Campbell, a sports writer for the Toledo Times, became a close friend and on occasion VanDivort would write an article for Campbell's Waters and Woods newspaper section.

VanDivort's passion for hunting, bird dogs, and field trials, along with his association with the newspaper business, led him into contact with William F. Brown who was then editor of The American Field. It was through this association that the idea of the National German Shorthaired Pointer Association, Inc., was born. VanDivort was a member of the old Toledo German Shorthaired Pointer Club. In this era there were a great number of pheasants in the Toledo area, and the Toledo club had a large and active membership. After hunting season was over, the members would run dogs on the weekend and would then gather together at their clubhouse located on Rancamp Road for cookouts, parties, and other social activities. Paul Sharp, a bulk distributor for City Services Gasoline, who would serve as the first president of the NGSPA of Toledo and VanDivort, the first club secretary, would utilize the existing Toledo club membership as a basis for an American Field club. The original constitution and by-laws for the National German Shorthaired Pointer Club of Toledo were modeled after those of the Amateur Field Trial Clubs of America and were written in Paul Sharp's office in 1951 at the club's first meeting. This NGSPA club would be soon followed by the Defiance NGSPA and the Tri-City

NGSPA, consisting of individuals from Saignaw, Bay City, and Midland, Michigan.

In 1952 these three clubs conducted the American Field sanctioned Mid-Western Open Challenge Stake. The Challenge Stake was the first American Field German Shorthaired Pointer all-age stake ever run in the United States that had a $500.00 guaranteed purse. The trial attracted 14 entries, was run on the club grounds of the old Toledo club in November 1952, and was judged by Dr. Richard Jackson of Toledo, Ohio, and R.L. "Cap" Mulder of Worthington, Ohio. Fritz Condon, owned and handled by Fred Condon of Toledo, Ohio, took first place in the trial. Russell "Lefty" Dixon, who was then operating out of St. Clair Shores, Michigan, garnered second with Dixon's Skiddoo, and Al Summers of Detroit, Michigan, captured third with Dixon's Starlite II. This stake fulfilled The American Field requirements that the sponsoring clubs had proven their knowledge and ability to stage a classic type trial and attract dogs worthy of running in such an event. This trial set the stage for the first NGSPA Championship.

A significant factor in the success of any field trial is adequate grounds to show a bird dog. In 1952 the Ohio Department of Natural Resources began the purchase of a natural basin of prairie in Wyandot and Marion Counties. This land acquisition would eventually grow to 8,627 acres and be known as the Killdeer Plains Wildlife Area. The October 24, 1953, issue of The American Field proclaimed that the National German Shorthaired Pointer Association was running its First National Championship Stake for German Shorthaired Pointers on November 14 and 15, 1953, over 6,000 acres of wonderful cover with an abundance of game birds. This inaugural NGSPA National Championship would be the third field trial run on these now famous grounds, the first continuous course trial ever held at Kildeer Plains, and the first bird dog field trial championship at this venue.

A total of 14 dogs went to the line in this first NGSPA Championship, which was judged by Dr. Richard W. Jackson of Toledo, Ohio, and G. Fred Hill of Crooksville, Ohio. Kildeer Plains, this November 1953, was extremely dry, and Ohio had unreasonably warm weather. Del Schmeltz, a local area professional trainer, and V.V. VanDivort had laid out five one-hour courses. C.L. "Kip" Kiple brought horses from Toledo mainly for the judges and a few guests. A number of handlers walked and this practice would be followed for almost ten years. Since there were no facilities on the grounds, a portable power generator had been brought in to help Ann VanDivort prepare lunches. On Saturday, November 14, 1953, the NGSPA hosted the first of many subsequent dinners at the Evergreens near Upper Sandusky, Ohio.

Dixon's Shelia had the class race of the stake—forward, and finishing strong but birdless. Dixon Star Lite II put down a good forward pattern with one find, a stop to flush, and a nonproductive. Hauptman v Dusseldorf's race was excellent for 45 minutes, but he had to be pushed to finish the hour. Hauptman had a stop at command on a bracemate's bump, a stop to flush, and one well-established stylish find. Dixon's Skiddoo scored early with one well-handled find, three stops to flush, and one nonproductive. Skiddoo ran a level race but lacked the punch and drive that was expected. There were dogs that lacked range, dogs with erratic races, and dogs that pushed wild birds into the air. On occasion, the flush of several pheasants at one time caused dogs to forget their manners.

At the conclusion of the trial, Dixon's Shelia was called back for another effort. She lacked the drive that carried her the day before and when the opportunity came on birds she did not take advantage of it. Four dogs were then called back to test their retrieving ability. Dixon's Star Lite II completed the land retrieve but failed to retrieve from water. Hauptman v Dusseldorf refused the land retrieve. Dixon's Skiddoo, while a bit slow in picking up the birds, made an acceptable delivery of the bird in both land and water tests. Max v Schulenberg marked his bird down well, retrieved smartly from land and water, but dropped his bird just short of the handler's hand.

In the first NGSPA Championship the title was withheld. Dixon's Skiddoo, dog, 485084, by Meadow v Reichenberg—Dixon's Star Lite, owned and handled by Lefty Dixon of St. Clair Shores,

Michigan, was named the stake winner. Max v Schulenberg, 505602, dog, by Count vd Schulenberg—Kathryn v Sievers, owned and handled by Henry F. Weiss of Toledo, Ohio, was named runner-up. Virgil V. VanDivort vowed that the Championship would return next year and no one should doubt that the NGSPA would demand a Championship performance before one would be named.

On April 28, 1954, the NGSPA incorporated as not-for-profit corporation in the State of Ohio. While authorized to do business in other states, Toledo, Ohio, still remains the principal place of business of the NGSPA. Paul L. Sharp, was the first president, and Virgil V. VanDivort was the initial secretary of the NGSPA. Henry L. Weiss, who owned and operated a baking company in the Toledo area, served as vice-president, and Leonard Hansen, the fire chief at an army ordinance depot near Toledo, Ohio, served as treasurer. The initial board of directors consisted of the foregoing individuals along with Paul Radde, James Baker, Gilbert Cross, Mahlon Tibbitts, Oscar VandenBosch, Martin Walter, H.G. Hogle, Dan Thornton, Charles Rogers, George Reimlinger, and William Wooten. A total of 114 individuals signed on as initial charter members including several that would make significant contributions to this organization.

On November 6, 1954, a total of ten dogs went to the line to compete for the second NGSPA Championship. VanDivort was concerned about the small entry and the way that the Shorthair fancier viewed this trial. In his article in the American Field VanDivort wrote words that have served as a guidepost for the NGSPA: "It was a distinct departure from the usual one-course trial and in the minds of these officers the only true test of a bird dog. We can watch all the work in the world on planted or just-released pen-raised birds and we'll never determine what the average dog owner wants to know about the breed; that is, the dog's ability to perform as a hunting dog."

After running an excellent race through any and all likely objectives, Fritz v Strauss emerged as the first NGSPA National Champion. Fritz's bracemate at 11 minutes worked a bird to the end of a feed strip where it flushed wild. Frtiz stopped. At 16 minutes Fritz backed his bracemate on a wild covey find. At 20 minutes both dogs were on point in the same area, but birds were not produced. At 22 minutes Fritz had a find with manners all in order at the shot. Fritz was sent on, took one step, and stopped. Two more birds rose in front of him with manners still in order. At 40 minutes Fritz found and handled a covey of quail with excellent deportment. At 48 minutes both dogs encountered several wild flushing pheasants in a feeder strip. Both dogs stood during several flushes and shots with Murdock alone flushing seven birds with no more than two rising at one time. In the second series, consisting of only a land retrieve, Fritz handled his retrieve in a credible manner. Dixon's Shelia had run a strong first hour with a good pattern which resulted in four solid finds and one stop to flush. Shelia performed well in the second series proving her ability during the shot, kill, and retrieve.

Fritz v Strauss, 512073, dog, by Otto v. Strauss-Ritz's Coco, owned by Carl Kemritz and handled by Joe Murdock, a retired engineer turned dog trainer of Downers Grove, Illinois, was declared the first NGSPA National Champion on November 6, 1954. The owner, Carl Kemritz, an Eastern airline pilot, was originally from Toledo, Ohio, but was then residing in Evergreen Park, Illinois. Kemritz, who liked to hunt upland birds, had been introduced to the breed by VanDivort. Dixon's Shelia, bitch, 509521, by Max v Schulenberg-Dixon's Star Lite, owned and handled by Lefty Dixon was named runner-up. On December 8, 1956, Vitality Dry Dog Food would run an advertisement featuring Fritz v. Strauss on the cover page of The American Field, the first of his breed to appear there.

The third NGSPA Championship was held on November 12, 1955, at Kildeer Plains Wildlife Area, again with an entry of only 10 dogs. VanDivort wrote in The American Field, dated December 31, 1955, at page 755 that the entry of ten dogs drawn to start was disappointing but the stake lacked nothing in quality. More dogs could have been obtained from a couple of sources, but they would have added nothing except numbers to the trial. But, this apparent lack of interest by breeders and trainers gave the officers of the organization cause to stop and ponder whether or not their efforts were worth it.

The trial was blessed with wonderful weather, and the courses for the most part were excellent. While the cover was too high in certain areas, the Ohio Division of Wildlife had established an excellent program of pheasant propagation that was ensuring an adequate supply of game birds for hunters as well as those who were utilizing the grounds for field trial activity.

Dixon's Sheila, owned and handled by professional Lefty Dixon of New Haven, Michigan, was awarded the Championship with "a sparking ground heat during which she really poured on the coal in her search for game." The course she had drawn was not the best, but she had opportunities on birds and her manners and style were exemplary at all times. Cast off at 2:05 she hit pay dirt in 11 minutes with a solid find. At 35 minutes she was out of ken for eight minutes. At 46 minutes she was observed working on a running pheasant, which got too near one of the horses and flushed. The dog stopped and remained until the command was given. Two minutes later Sheila backed her bracemate who was on point in a fencerow. Before the handlers could get in, the birds flushed with both dogs displaying good manners. Sheila was braced with Tell v Pinecrest, owned and handled by James Baker of Toledo, Ohio. Tell had a find at nine, the location of the covey of quail, and a find in a fencerow at 55.

Dixon's Sheila, Tell v Pinecrest, Kay Starr, and Dixon's Skiddoo were called back for a second series. Sheila and Kay Star were braced together and Sheila honored Starr on an unproductive. Sheila then scored on two birds, which she retrieved smartly when sent. On her second point, Starr refused to honor, went by Sheila, and stole point. Tell and Skiddoo both pointed, backed, and retrieved in the second series, but Tell's first series ground heat gave him the nod. Judges G. Fred Hill of Crooksville, Ohio, and James C. Tallmadge of Jeromesville, Ohio, named Sheila the Champion and Tell v Pinecrest, dog, 513037 by Max v Schulenberg—Vesta v Maribeth, runner-up.

After the running a meeting of the NGSPA was held at the Evergreens in Upper Sandusky, Ohio. Martin Walter of Defiance, Ohio, was named president, Earl Cutler of Reese, Michigan, was elected vice-president, Virgil V. VanDivort was again named secretary, and Mahlon Tibbitts of Toledo was elected treasurer. While the future of the NGSPA and its Championship seemed uncertain, these officers vowed to continue with a trial that would prove the worth of this breed as a bird dog.

The fourth annual NGSPA Championship was held on November 10-11, 1956. Much of the Killdeer Plains Wildlife Area, again dry with wide cracks that had opened in the black earth, had become unusable because of high heavy weed growth that had taken over the fields. Ohio had a dry autumn with a 40-day drought, causing the cat-tails and bull thistle to rattle as a dog moved through the cover. However, Len Hansen, Whit LeMay, and Virgil VanDivort were still able to lay out three one-hour courses. A total of 18 dogs were entered in the championship which was judged by Richard S. Johns of Benton, Pennsylvania, and Lee G. Vollrath of Findlay, Ohio. Edward Van Tassel, Jim Baker, Virgil VanDivort, and Ed Haughn, and the NGSPA trustees, were enthusiastic about an increased interest in the trial.

In the first one-hour series Dixon's Sheila had run an enthusiastic race and was found on point by Judge Johns. She remained high and steady for Dixon's flush and shot. Lotte v. Heidelberg, running in the first brace, had a stop to flush at 11. From then on Lotte was a little hard to control but scored another find before the end of the hour with manners in order. A total of eight dogs were called back for the second series in a bird field. Dixon's Sheila cleaned the birdfield with three finds and two retrieves with one bird being missed. Lotte v. Heidelberg had two finds. On the first she moved just a bit and was whoaed, causing her to be slow to retrieve. On the second bird she did not move a hair and made a snappy return of the bird. These were the only two dogs that came through the second series without serious error.

As Sheila lacked the opportunity to honor, a dog was placed on point on a planted bird. Dixon cut Sheila away about 75 yards away from the dog on point. Sheila immediately backed upon observing the pointing dog. It was a worthy performance for the defending champion. Dixon's Sheila, owned and handled by Lefty Dixon of New Haven, Michigan, was again named the winner of the NGSPA Championship. Lotte v Heidelberg, handled by Joe Murdock, was named runner-up. Lotte, owned by Frank Vetter of Milwaukee, Wisconsin, was no stranger to field trial circles since Frank's father had previously entered her into field trial competition. After the senior Vetter died, his son, who had never seen her run, continued to campaign her—thus fulfilling the dog's promise.

Lefty Dixon, who also retired the first NGSPA rotating trophy with this his third win of the stake, was no stranger on the field trial circuit. Lefty was born and raised in the Dexter, Missouri, area and grew up quail hunting. Although of relatively small stature, Lefty was recruited to attend college at Louisiana State University to play football. His college gridiron career was cut short when it was learned that he had already played the sport professionally. Lefty then played baseball out of Popular Bluff, Missouri, pitching left handed for the old Southern League. In 1930 Lefty moved to Detroit, ostensibly to obtain employment with the United States Rubber Company but principally to play baseball for this corporation when such organizations placed a premium on company teams. World War II would find Dixon in the United States Army as a K-9 handler in the Pacific Theater.

After the war, Dixon would return to Detroit, Michigan, to work for his former employer. Dixon, as well as his father, were devoted quail hunters and his father bought Lefty a pointer and then a shorthair. The shorthair was registered as Dixon's Bell and would prove to be an outstanding hunting dog that would also have a great impact as a brood bitch. Her blood ran through many of the entries in the early years of the NGSPA Championship. Dixon turned professional in 1948 first operating his kennel out of St. Clair Shores and then, with the financial support of Henry F. Weiss, relocating to better facilities at New Haven, Michigan. Lefty, a tough competitor, was a strong supporter of the NGSPA.

In the first brace of the fifth renewal of the NGSPA Championship Kay Star, bitch, 547113 by Captain v Falkenhorst—Dixon's Star Lite II, owned and handled by Levi F. Summers of Detroit, Michigan, went away at 8:32 on October 9, 1957. Kay faced rugged conditions. Heavy rains on the previous day left some of the fields covered with water that had frozen into icy puddles through which dogs broke at every jump. Unless woods screened the course, the wind was a steady 30 to 40 miles per hour without letup.

Kay showed her mettle all the way. At 8:43 she swung off along a side road and found a pheasant where no bird really should have been on such a day. She pointed it with intensity and style to spare but took a couple of steps when the shot was fired. VanDivort reported that it would have been wrong to say she broke on this one as those two steps, perhaps made to better mark the flight, surely could not be construed as a break except by those who are just too narrow in their thinking. At 9:08 Kay had a mannerly stop on a bird which had been worked to a stop to flush by her bracemate. At 9:30 she again nailed a bird in a clump of weeds, and Summers went in to flush. The bird moved toward her and flushed near her head, but Kay remained steady. Kay's heady forward hour race set a standard for this stake.

Caudle's Leader, 550379, dog, by Dixon's Skiddoo—Ladie II, owned and handled by Edward B. Caudle, went to the post at 4:25 in the last brace on Saturday. Leader had a hard-driving race except for a couple of slow moments when he was trying to unravel some mystery of wind-scattered scent. At six minutes he had a stop to flush on a large bevy of quail. With the wind pouring across the backs of this brace, they topped a rise to see the birds leave. Leader was mannerly. At 4:38 he again stopped on the rise of one of the scattered coveys, and again the wind precluded any possibility of the dog handling the birds. At 4:57 all hands were searching heavy cover for Leader. He was discovered standing high and intent after Judge Johns had ridden up a bird. When Caudle approached, another bird rose in front of the dog and Leader was all manners at the shot. Leader also had an opportunity to stylishly back his bracemate on course.

A total of six dogs were called back for the second series. The first brace consisted of Kay Star and Caudle's Leader, who had made the trip to Kildeer Plains in the same dog box. After a short back course to warm up, the dogs were brought into a large alfalfa field where birds had been planted. Kay went to a bird almost immediately and pointed positively and with lots of character. She needed no word during the flush and kill and made a good retrieve when sent, dropping the bird momentarily to get a better hold, before bringing it to hand. Leader nailed a bird at the edge of tall weeds and his retrieve was snappily executed and to hand. Marko Radbach v Lindenwald, Dixie v Heidebrink, Fritz of Sleepy Hollow, and Duke v Strauss all came through the second series with good manners.

A total of 20 dogs had been entered in this fifth renewal which was judged by Paul J. Teadway of Berkley, Michigan and Richard Johns. Kay Star was named the winner of this Championship, and Caudle's Leader was named runner-up. In winning this one, Kay recorded the first leg on the Ann VanDivort memorial trophy. Ann VanDivort had been a vital part of the early Championship trials at Kildeer Plains, preparing food and making coffee for the trial participants. She passed away on October 3, 1956, after an illness of two years. Virgil VanDivort had taken a poll to determine what type trophy would be most suitable and had commissioned Alfred Carl of Sylvania, Ohio, to execute one. When presented the trophy, tears appeared when Summers tried to say a few words of acceptance. Levi Summers, the first and one of the few amateurs to win this championship, was as gracious in victory as he had previously been in defeat.

Leonard Hansen again marshalled this stake. Jim Zander, George Roberts, Martin Walters, Bill Wooten, Jim Baker, Paul Radde, Eddie Haughn, and Virgil VanDivort lent hands wherever needed. These individuals were elated not only because of the success of this Championship, regarded as having many outstanding pieces of bird work by several dogs, but also because The American Field had given the NGSPA permission to run the first field futurity for German Shorthaired Pointers in 1958. Leonard Hansen was the first Futurity Manager but Paul Kile of the Defiance, Ohio, would shortly take over the futurity and run it for several years. The NGSPA's elected new officers were President, Eddie Haughn of Ridgeville Corners, Ohio; Vice-President, Frank Summers of Detroit, Michigan; Secretary, Virgil V. VanDivort, and Treasurer, Dr. Henry Fredericks of Cleveland, Ohio.

The Sixth NGSPA Championship was run on November 8-9, 1958, at Kildeer Plains Wildlife Area. Four one-hour courses were laid out which offered a variety of cover. The Ohio Division of Wildlife had been emphasizing a program of cover control and game management that was benefiting not only hunters but also field trialers. The weather was once more a significant factor in this trial for it was raw and windy during the running with spots of sleet and a great deal of rain. A high wind kept the birds more than unusually skittish, and the trial featured more than its share of unproductive points where handlers could not produce birds, which caused lengthy relocations and bumped birds.

A total of twenty dogs went to the line in this Championship judged by Richard Johns and Charles Hendricks. Dixon's Susie Q, 559152, bitch, by Dixon's Skiddoo—Audy Girl, owned by Howard F. Confer of Detroit, Michigan, and handled by Lefty Dixon was named Champion. Susie Q, who had taken top honors at the German Pointing Dog National Championship at Ohio, Illinois, the previous month, was described as the "new" type of German Shorthair in stature and build. She was streamlined, on the fine side, having good depth of chest, and standing up on her legs the way a dog should in order to move attractively and easily. She ran with a high head and moved into her birds without going to the ground. Susie showed the judges the type of race they wanted to see. She had a back on her bracemate's unproductive, a legitimate stop to flush with the wind across her back, and a solid pheasant find with manners all in order.

In the second series, consisting of a twenty minute back course ending in a bird field. Susie Q hunted her away around and climaxed her work with a solid find and good retrieve. Fritz v Strauss, the 1954 Champion, was named runner-up. In the first series Fritz had three well-handled pheasant finds and one creditable stop to flush, but his race had not measured up to what was expected in the stake. In the second series Fritz had a slow back course but hit his bird with style and made his retrieve properly.

A total of six dogs had been called back for the second series. VanDivort explained that in these call-backs the judges had to recall enough dogs to protect themselves in case the leading contenders failed to come through. However, if Susie Q and Fritz had not come through, he felt certain that no title would have been awarded.

Notwithstanding the elements, Eddie Haughn, Bill Wooten, Mart Walter, Jim Zander, George Roberts, Jim Baker, Dan Mast, Levi Summers and Ed Caudle did all sorts of jobs to ensure that this trial was a good one. The NGSPA officers elected for 1959 consisted of Eddie Haugh, president; Stanley Chiras, vice-president, Dr. H.H. Fredrick, treasurer; and Virgil V. VanDivort, secretary.

The 1959 NGSPA Championship would end the early years of this organization. Clubs from Cleveland, Toledo, and western Ohio along with the Golden Gate, Northern New York, Southern California, Michigan, and the Middle-Atlantic Regional Shorthair Club were now affiliated with the NGSPA. The one-hour stake run on wild birds was not only attracting more interest from field trial enthusiasts but was also influencing the manner in which professional handlers were having to develop their dogs. While the previous winners were the best of the breed, they were, in reality, only Shorthair shooting dogs. The Seventh NGSPA Championship would change that.

Kay V D Wilburg, dog, 571273, by Pol v Blitzdorf—Cora v Wesertor, was imported from Germany by Bodo S. Winterhelt of Port Colborne, Ontario, Canada, with money fronted by Walter Kogut of Brantford, Ontario, Canada. Winterhelt and Kogut were interested in a field trial dog, and this pup was not suitable for conditions in Germany because of his range. Winterhelt started working the dog, but Kogut obtained full title to Kay and placed him with Bill Bowers, a pointer-setter handler of Cross Junction, Virginia. Bowers not only placed this dog but also won with him in some pretty fast pointer-setter open derby competition. In the 1958 Championship, Kay, handled by Bowers, had started strong, had the class race of the stake, suffered an unproductive, and then took a bird—giving extended chase. Nevertheless, Kay was called back for the second series, had two unproductives on the backcourse, and did not find a bird. After this championship, Kogut would subsequently place the dog with Dick Johns who handled the dog to a pointer-setter open shooting dog placement as well as wins and placements in shorthair competition.

The Seventh NGSPA Championship was originally scheduled for two days, but a total of 33 dogs were entered in this stake with entries from Canada, Cuba, California, Washington, Virginia, Ohio, Michigan, Illinois, Kentucky, New York, Vermont, and Connecticut. The stake was again run at Killdeer Plains starting on October 30 and running through November 1. The grounds were in good condition, and the pheasant and quail populations were excellent on the four one-hour courses which had been laid out. Weather was excellent with sunshine and temperatures in the 50's and 60's. The trial was judged by G. Fred Hill of Crooksville, Ohio, and James C. Tallmadge of Jeromesville, Ohio.

Ed Haughn served as stake manager and received assistance from Henry and Edna Frederick, Martin Walter, Dan Mast, Len Hansen, Bill Wooten, and Fred Hunt. Curt Elarton had brought in a number of horses and VanDivort, who could not attend the trial for personal reasons, sent down his horses. At the annual NGSPA meeting, held at the Evergreens Restaurant, Edward Haughn was elected president, Dan Mast, first vice-president, Stanley Chiras was elected secretary, and Dr. H.H. Fredrick was elected treasurer. In addition, Don Briggs and Dick Johns were elected to the newly created positions of second vice-president and third vice-president, respectively.

Kay V D Wilburg was braced with Dixon's Sheila on the second day of the trial. Kay broke away at tremendous speed and started a cast down a woods line, reaching out to all likely objectives. Kay made eyes pop when he leaped a fence without breaking stride and shortly thereafter slammed into a stylish point. Johns produced three pheasants with Kay's manners exemplary. Johns led Kay a short distance away, and a minute later Kay pointed again with the handler having difficulty flushing the bird. Kay was sent on to relocate and as Kay pointed, Sheila, whose race had lacked the intensity of Kay's, bumped the pheasant. Kay then had an unproductive on a running pheasant. Kay went away running at exceptional range with long reaching strides cracking his tail up and down with each jump. Kay pointed again after time was called. A true shorthair all-age race had been witnessed, and those in attendance were well aware of the fact. Kay V D Wilburg had won this championship, and Stanley Chiras would write that Kay could wear this crown proudly.

Shenna v Feldstrom, the runner-up, bitch, 571273, by Ulk v d Radbach—Ginnie v Feldstrom, owned by Ed Caudle and Dr. Clark Lemley of Detroit, Michigan, and handled by Caudle, was braced with Skiddoo's Bee after lunch on the third day. This brace featured a large riding gallery taking advantage of sunshine and comfortable 55 degree weather. Bee jumped merrily at good range, pointed at three but then corrected. Sheena ran stylishly at good range, and applied herself well. Sheena pointed at 18 and had a beatiful relocation and displayed exemplary manners on a cock pheasant. Four minutes later Sheena was in motion as a pheasant took to the air beyond a corn feeder strip. Sheena stopped and a pair of pheasants then lifted. At 33 Bee had a stop to flush and Sheena backed. Sheena was found on point at 40 minutes and remained steady to wing and shot on the rooster. Sheena pointed again at 43 and was sent for a relocation. She made a big swing with head held high; as Sheena looped her turn back into the wind, a rooster flushed and she stopped. Sheena pointed again at 45 and was mannerly as the pheasant was produced. Sheena later had another legitimate stop to flush before the end of the hour.

A total of six dogs—Sergent v Dusseldorf, Sandra v Hohen Tann, Kay V D Wildburg, Riga v Hohen Tann, Sheena v Feldstrom, and Bobo Gradenbruch Beckum—were called back for the second series. While this series was originally deemed necessary to fulfill the requirements of the Championship, the NGSPA and its member clubs had decided the second series was somewhat artificial and were giving serious thought to the matter. Nevertheless, Kay went into the second series with tremendous drive, had a nice find in the birdfield, and remained mannerly. Kay was sent on the retrieve and he returned the bird merrily. Likewise, Sheena pinned a bird, exhibited perfect manners, and retrieved on command. The performance of both dogs had made them worthy of the title of NGSPA Champion and runner-up.

The two individuals who handled Kay and Sheena have been significant in the history of the NGSPA. Dick Johns, born and raised in Pennsylvania, was soon hunting grouse at an early age with bird dogs. As a young adult, Johns would be training bird dogs and horses for a living. World War II would find Johns with the United States Army in Europe. At the conclusion of the war, Johns was assigned to a horse cavalry unit with the task of locating dogs for pheasant hunting for senior officers. This role would acquaint him with the German Shorthaired Pointer, and he would import specimens of this breed to the United States upon his return. Johns would resume the training of hunting and field trial bird dogs near Benton, Pennsylvania, and would become an active professional handler competing with different breeds in both open pointer-setter and shorthair competition. Dick Johns actively promoted the NGSPA Championship by judging, competing and winning in this competition, and serving as an officer in this organization.

Edward Caudle, who handled Sheena, was born in Atkins, Arkansas, but his family subsequently relocated to Reeves, Missouri, and then to Caruth, Missouri, where they farmed to survive the depression. His early hunting experience was born of an economic necessity to help fill the family larder. World War II would find Caudle in the United States Marine Corps in the Pacific theater. Upon his discharge Caudle would return to Missouri, but he would soon relocate to Detroit, Michigan, to seek employment. He became a friend of Levi Summers and their hunting association led to Caudle's purchase of a German Shorthaired Pointer in 1949. This dog led him into a life as a professional handler when in 1952 he began operating a kennel and boarding operation out of Canton, Michigan. While not the first, Caudle was one of the early shorthair trainers who started taking this breed to the prairies for development. As a promoter of the breed, Caudle was a charter member of the NGSPA, worked at the early championship trials, served as a trustee for many years, and on two occasions presided as president of this association. His ideas about judges, judging, bird dogs, and the proper conduct of a class trial influenced many of the modern shorthair trainers more than they care to admit.

The NGSPA would now start a new era and many different individuals would come forward to participate in the Championship and work for this organization that has grown in strength and prestige. Like all field trial clubs, this association would experience the good times as well as the turbulent ones. Although the names of the dogs and the faces have changed, a debt of gratitude is owed to these early pioneers who wanted field trial competition that would realistically test this breed as a bird dog.

Joe Murdock, the handler of the first NGSPA Champion, would retire in Sarasota, Florida, but would remain active with shorthairs judging several Florida trials prior to his death. Lefty Dixon would retire to his winter headquarters, Ocala, Florida, in 1963 where he would enjoy quail hunting for several years. He died on December 31, 1995, in Rock Hill, South Carolina, the home of his stepson, Kenneth Johnston. This article could not have been written without the assistance of Ed Caudle of Canton, Michigan, Dick Johns of Benton, Pennsylvania, and Bill Wooten of Toledo, Ohio, also a charter member and former trustee of the NGSPA, all of whom still maintain an active interest in this organization. In addition, Barbara Teare and Gary Lockee of the Bird Dog Foundation in Grand Junction, Tennessee, were most gracious in helping my wife and myself locate and copy materials. The Foundation's growing collection of bird dog literature and memorabilia is invaluable to anyone attempting to research the history of field trials and its participants.

Virgil V. VanDivort, the individual most responsible for the National German Shorthaired Pointer Association and its championships, would be diagnosed with cancer. VanDivort had taken care of his first wife, Ann, for almost two years prior to her death from this same dreaded disease. In the last days prior to his death he would place telephone calls to or visit many of his field trial friends and express to them his appreciation for their friendship over the years. On January 10, 1968, VanDivort placed a telephone call to the Sheriff's Office in Toledo, Ohio. When a deputy sheriff responded, VanDivort's body was found. Dr. Harry Mignerey, a local coroner, ruled the death a suicide from a self-inflicted gunshot wound.

At the time of his death, VanDivort was active in many civic projects and fraternal orders, a member of the Outdoor Writers Association of America, and was still active in the affairs of the NGSPA. He had also served as vice president of the Ohio Field Trial Association and worked with some of his bird dog friends, who loved pheasant hunting, field trials, and Killdeer Plains, to create a stake that would develop into what came to be known as the International Pheasant Championship.

VanDivort has been quoted and misquoted about the NGSPA and his desire for this breed. He wrote in The American Field in 1954 at page 634 that "the thinking that went into the building of this stake was the result of a few persons with coinciding ideas about the Shorthair. We believed them to the capable of much more in the way of becoming bird dogs than we had seen demonstrated in many trials. We knew of and had the utmost faith in the nose of these dock-tailed imports. We knew, too, that they could be bred to have some of the drive, the bounce, the intensity in action through the fields and in their bird contacts that makes handling any bird dog a really thrilling experience even without a gun in one's hand.

This we have attempted to do. We have not tried to do anything further."

that come within their sight. They ask for a dog that looks right because it is built right to move right. Mere flashiness may catch the judges who don't know—"mug-catchers," we call dogs of such a flashy description where I hail from—but it never catches the ones who do know. The ones who know look for elegance in all-over appearance, the sloping shoulders that shape the short back, the long upper arms that facilitate movement, the rib cage that makes place for heart and lungs, the clean legs that provide the movement, and the sound, thick, arch-toed feet that carry the load. They look for the kind, wise eyes of a temperamentally sound dog, and the tail that emphasizes what the eyes have said. These indicators, fore and aft, are the proof of "intelligence and animation."

Dr. Kleeman has pointed out that the rules of structural engineering are also the rules of nature. To work right, a dog must be built right. To be built right, it has first to be born right. Mighty simple, if one comes to think of it . . . .

HEAD: (A.K.C. Standard)

Clean-cut, neither too light nor too heavy, in proper proportion to the body. Skull is reasonably broad, arched on side and slightly round on top. Scissura (median line between the eyes at the forehead) not too deep, occipital bone not as conspicuous as in the case of the Pointer. The foreface rises gradually from nose to forehead. The rise is more strongly pronounced in the dog than in the bitch as befitting his sex. The chops fall away from the somewhat projecting nose. Lips are full and deep, never flewy. The chops do not fall over too much, but form a proper fold in the angle. The jaw is powerful and the muscles well developed. The line to the forehead rises gradually and never has a definite stop as that of the Pointer, but rather a stop-effect when viewed from the side, due to the position of the eyebrows. The muzzle is sufficiently long to enable the dog to seize properly and to facilitate his carrying game a long time. A pointed muzzle is not desirable. The entire head never gives the impression of tapering to a point. The depth is in the right proportion to the length, both in the muzzle and in the skull proper. The length of the muzzle should equal the length of skull. A pointed muzzle is a fault. A dish-faced muzzle is a fault. A definite Pointer stop is a serious fault. Too many wrinkles in forehead is a fault.

GOOD HEADS
"A" AND "B"

POOR HEADS
"C" AND "D"

"C" HAS A COARSE EAR, TOO MUCH CHOP AND A FLEWY LIP.

"D" HAS EARS THAT ARE TOO LONG AND POINTED, A POINTED SNIPY MUZZLE, IS TOO ROUNDED IN SKULL AND HAS A POOR EYE SET.

BOTH LACK BALANCE, ARE SHORT IN MUZZLE, HAVE TOO MUCH STOP.

AUTHOR'S COMMENT: In the practical sense, as is to be observed, the variation of head type within the German Shorthaired Pointer breed is extremely wide, not only in American-bred dogs, but also in the dogs imported from overseas. There appears here to be a variation from the widest of "Pointer" skulls to the finest of "Setter"—to quote the extreme opposites. Between, one finds every possible variation on those themes, adding up to the reasonable belief that head type in the breed is not as yet exactly fixed, and that each line-bred strain tends to favor a head type of its own. Actually, most heads seem to sit suitably on the front ends of the dogs that own them, so that the vagueness of the opening sentence of the Standard, as it applies to this part of the dog, reasonably caters to them all. "Neither too light nor too heavy, in proper proportion to the body" . . ."skull should be reasonably broad," leaves much to the discretion of a judge. How little is "too light"? How much is "too heavy"? What is "reasonable breadth"? In the listing of the faults, further along, heads are held less desirable if they are "too large, with too many wrinkles in forehead, dish-faced, snipy muzzle." But how *many* wrinkles are too many? How large *is* too large? Certainly, such wordage presents some good arguments for the compilation of dog breed Standards in a pictorial medium rather than in words.

With the head the seat of character and intelligence, inevitably it can make or mar a dog. It is the first thing looked at, by the buyer in the yard, the trainer at the kennels, the judge in the show ring. If the head displeases in that first going-over, the rest of the dog may even be dismissed without any great amount of further consideration—it happens. The bitterest wrangling of the pioneer German breeders was in respect to the head the developing utility breed should have. The first direction to prevail was for a head described as "Grecian" in profile, as near as could be a straight line, nose to occiput. In the view of many strong supporters of this type of head, it was considered to favor trailing-keeping (which meant hound) abilities, as distinct from the dished profile of the high-scenting Pointer. Many of the best of the early-day dogs, pillars of the breed such as Wodan Hektor II v. Lemgo, and Tell aus der Wolfsschlucht, had definitely Roman-nosed heads. The tendency to a "bump" on the bridge has come down the generations with a persistency that not even the disapproval of the original Standard here has been able wholly to thwart. One still sees many a German Shorthaired Pointer with the same bumpy profile as, say, K.S. Michel v.d. Goldenen Mark had in his prepotent day. Such inheritances are not lightly scotched.

Over the years intervening since such dogs as Tell and K.S. Michel, there came to be emphasis on the signs of working qualities, such as a skull really broad enough to contain brains and the ole-factory (scenting) nerves; a lower jaw long, deep and strong enough to bite to kill when necessary, as well as to bear heavy weights over long-distance carries. It is just such a head that the present-day Standard seems to define, the good honest head of a useful working dog. However, the wording could possibly be made clearer for the novices. One useful way would be to delete references of comparison with the Pointer. The modern American field trial Pointer is not the familiar sight in Shorthair competition that he was when the first breed Standard was compiled in 1946. Many novice Shorthair owners may never actually have seen a true Pointer-type head, though modern resurgence in show competition has brought many classic examples to the fore. But the average Pointer seen at Field Trials may have a head in which any resemblance to classic breed type is purely coincidental. For these reasons, the comparison as worded provides little help in making the definition clear to German Shorthaired Pointer novices.

EARS: (A.K.C. Standard)
Ears are broad and set fairly high, lie flat and never hang away from the head. Placement is just above the eye level. The ears, when laid in front without being pulled, meet the lip angle. In the case of heavier dogs, the ears are correspondingly longer. Ears too long or fleshy are to be faulted.

K.S. Kara v. Hohenfeld at Kleeman Auslese Prufung, 1968. This superbly beautiful Axel v. Wasserschling daughter was refused top rating in conformation for low ear placement, a fault German judges never overlook. Many U.S. judges would not give it a thought! All standards ask for Shorthair ears to be "broad and set fairly high, never hang away from the head."—*C. Bede Maxwell*

AUTHOR'S COMMENT: Now, *there's* some dog Standard writing at its very best. Every word means exactly what it says, and no confusing comparisons dragged in—nor any comparisons needed. The Germans, perhaps still influenced by the preoccupation of the pioneer breeders with ear shape, spell the requirements right out— ears shall be neither too thick nor too fine, and lower ends shall be blunted and round. Well, the A.K.C. Standard takes care of that description as well, bracketing it in the fault column, spelling out exactly what German Shorthaired Pointer ears shall *not* be.

Closer to home, a writer in the A.K.C. *Gazette* has truthfully described the ear as "the one part of the dog that cannot tell a lie." In many animals, as a matter of fact, the ears are the barometers of emotion. Who doubts the message conveyed by the flattened ears of the horse, or those of the family tomcat? Similarly, the dog can convey his feelings by the movement even of such pendant lugs as grace the heads of the sporting dogs as a group.

Ears in this breed, as in all smooth-coated, pendant-eared breeds, are cruelly vulnerable. Flaps suffer in cover, get chewed in fights, are prey to flies. Absence of feather helps the entrance of grass seeds, foreign bodies. Blows can produce painful, bulging hematomas, and allergic reactions do the strangest things. I am reminded of a fine young bitch greeting me one morning with her ears swollen literally inches thick through, and heavy as lead—a condition (oedema) that vanished as rapidly and as mysteriously as it came, within a few hours.

Looking over the ears of the German Shorthaired Pointer breed, one may discover them to be as varied in type as heads—ears long, ears short, sometimes even folded. However, the Standard directions are excellently plain, so no confusion should be experienced by breeder or by judge as to how those ears *should* be.

EYES: (A.K.C. Standard)
The eyes are of medium size, full of intelligence and expressive, good humored and yet radiating energy, neither protruding nor sunken. The eye is almond shaped, not circular. The eyelids close well. The best color is dark brown. Light yellow (Bird of Prey) eyes are not desirable and are a fault. Closely set eyes are to be faulted. China or wall eyes are to be disqualified.

THE NGSPA: ITS EARLY YEARS

By: Don Kidd

While the general field trial fraternity would not be expected to know the history of the National German Shorthaired Pointer Association, Inc., (NGSPA), the sad truth is that many Shorthair field trial enthusiasts have little or no knowledge of the origins of this association. When German Shorthairs were first imported into the United States in 1925, they were originally promoted as an "every use" dog, a super-dog with some type of canine superiority. This type of exploitation may have induced some individuals to purchase dogs at inflated prices, but it did little to improve the breed. Fortunately, such elaborate promotion did not keep sincere breed enthusiasts from logically and sensibly endeavoring to bring out the true qualifications of the German Shorthaired Pointer.

Although limited in number, Shorthair field trial enthusiasts started to occasionally enter their breed in field trial competition. As early as 1931 a German Shorthair was braced with Mary Blue in an All-Age event soon after this Teagle Pointer had won the National Championship at Grand Junction, Tennessee. The majority of Shorthair field trialers, however, were content to run in shooting dog competition in stakes either for their own breed or in events judged along gun dog lines.

Ultimately, several factors converged to create the NGSPA and its affiliation with the American Field. Unlike today, there was an abundance of wild birds immediately following World War II. Young men who had fought in either the European or Pacific theaters returned home and started to again hunt upland game birds. Some of these men acquired German Shorthairs, field trials became an extension of their hunting experience, and the breed saw the development of its first professional handlers. Although field trial competition for the breed was increasing, several of these individuals were not satisfied with the Shorthair competition that was most readily available.

The typical field trial format was a walking trial run on a single course with a bird field. The emphasis was on a dog working in a windshield wiper pattern with extreme subservience to the gun. Since scouting was not allowed, there was little or no emphasis on the ability of a dog to independently select and run to logical objectives. Judges at the time frequently penalized a handler who attempted to sing to a dog that was reaching out on the course.

It was against this backdrop that knowledgeable amateur and professional handlers discussed the future of this breed in the late 1940's. These men frequently met after a trial and in huddled conversations discussed the need for field trial competition that offered the opportunity to test this breed under more natural conditions. These individuals were determined that the natural qualities of the breed—pointing, backing, and retrieving—should be retained while encouraging wider and faster moving dogs able to more effectively hunt upland game birds. These men also recognized that if American Field competition were available to their breed, it would expand their field trial opportunities.

While some men may dream and talk about what might be, there are other men that can lead. Every individual who has blown a whistle over a German Shorthaired Pointer in any type of field trial competition owes a debt of gratitude to a man most of them never knew existed. It was this individual who was almost solely responsible for the formation of the NGSPA, the first breed National Championship and, most important, the constant and continued development of the German Shorthaired Pointer as a bird dog.

Virgil Valdosta VanDivort was born on May 20, 1909, at Mansfield, Ohio, raised in Pennsylvania, spent his early life in Texas, and then returned to Toledo, Ohio, where he started work as an independent distributor for the Toledo Times, a newspaper which was then owned by the Toledo Blade. In 1947 VanDivort became an employee of the Times and over the years would hold positions as district manager in the circulation department, city circulation manager, and home delivery manager. VanDivort, on his employment application with the Times, described his hobbies as field trialing, bird dogs, riding horses, photography, fly fishing and almost any kind of bird shooting.

VanDivort was an excellent horseman and was quite knowledgeable of pointer-setter trials, having ridden the major circuit trials on several occasions. In keeping with his interests, he would operate a commercial kennel, judge all types of pointing dog competition, and frequently acknowledge that his first love was bird dogs. Lou Campbell, a sports writer for the Toledo Times, became a close friend and on occasion VanDivort would write an article for Campbell's Waters and Woods newspaper section.

VanDivort's passion for hunting, bird dogs, and field trials, along with his association with the newspaper business, led him into contact with William F. Brown who was then editor of The American Field. It was through this association that the idea of the National German Shorthaired Pointer Association, Inc., was born. VanDivort was a member of the old Toledo German Shorthaired Pointer Club. In this era there were a great number of pheasants in the Toledo area, and the Toledo club had a large and active membership. After hunting season was over, the members would run dogs on the weekend and would then gather together at their clubhouse located on Rancamp Road for cookouts, parties, and other social activities. Paul Sharp, a bulk distributor for City Services Gasoline, who would serve as the first president of the NGSPA of Toledo and VanDivort, the first club secretary, would utilize the existing Toledo club membership as a basis for an American Field club. The original constitution and by-laws for the National German Shorthaired Pointer Club of Toledo were modeled after those of the Amateur Field Trial Clubs of America and were written in Paul Sharp's office in 1951 at the club's first meeting. This NGSPA club would be soon followed by the Defiance NGSPA and the Tri-City NGSPA, consisting of individuals from Saignaw, Bay City, and Midland, Michigan.

In 1952 these three clubs conducted the American Field sanctioned Mid-Western Open Challenge Stake. The Challenge Stake was the first American Field German Shorthaired Pointer all-age stake ever run in the United States that had a $500.00 guaranteed purse. The trial attracted 14 entries, was run on the club grounds of the old Toledo club in November 1952, and was judged by Dr. Richard Jackson of Toledo, Ohio, and R.L. "Cap" Mulder of Worthington, Ohio. Fritz Condon, owned and handled by Fred Condon of Toledo, Ohio, took first place in the trial. Russell "Lefty" Dixon, who was then operating out of St. Clair Shores, Michigan, garnered second with Dixon's Skiddoo, and Al Summers of Detroit, Michigan, captured third with Dixon's Starlite II. This stake fulfilled The American Field requirements that the sponsoring clubs had proven their knowledge and ability to stage a classic type trial and attract dogs worthy of running in such an event. This trial set the stage for the first NGSPA Championship.

A significant factor in the success of any field trial is adequate grounds to show a bird dog. In 1952 the Ohio Department of Natural Resources began the purchase of a natural basin of prairie in Wyandot and Marion Counties. This land acquisition would eventually grow to 8,627 acres and be known as the Killdeer Plains Wildlife Area. The October 24, 1953, issue of The American Field proclaimed that the National German Shorthaired Pointer Association was running its First National Championship Stake for German Shorthaired Pointers on November 14 and 15, 1953, over 6,000 acres of wonderful cover with an abundance of game birds. This inaugural NGSPA National Championship would be the third field trial run on these now famous grounds, the first continuous course trial ever held at Kildeer Plains, and the first bird dog field trial championship at this venue.

A total of 14 dogs went to the line in this first NGSPA Championship, which was judged by Dr. Richard W. Jackson of Toledo, Ohio, and G. Fred Hill of Crooksville, Ohio. Kildeer Plains, this November 1953, was extremely dry, and Ohio had unreasonably warm weather. Del Schmeltz, a local area professional trainer, and V.V. VanDivort had laid out five one-hour courses. C.L. "Kip"

Kiple brought horses from Toledo mainly for the judges and a few guests. A number of handlers walked and this practice would be followed for almost ten years. Since there were no facilities on the grounds, a portable power generator had been brought in to help Ann VanDivort prepare lunches. On Saturday, November 14, 1953, the NGSPA hosted the first of many subsequent dinners at the Evergreens near Upper Sandusky, Ohio.

Dixon's Shelia had the class race of the stake—forward, and finishing strong but birdless. Dixon Star Lite II put down a good forward pattern with one find, a stop to flush, and a nonproductive. Hauptman v Dusseldorf's race was excellent for 45 minutes, but he had to be pushed to finish the hour. Hauptman had a stop at command on a bracemate's bump, a stop to flush, and one well-established stylish find. Dixon's Skiddoo scored early with one well-handled find, three stops to flush, and one nonproductive. Skiddoo ran a level race but lacked the punch and drive that was expected. There were dogs that lacked range, dogs with erratic races, and dogs that pushed wild birds into the air. On occasion, the flush of several pheasants at one time caused dogs to forget their manners.

At the conclusion of the trial, Dixon's Shelia was called back for another effort. She lacked the drive that carried her the day before and when the opportunity came on birds she did not take advantage of it. Four dogs were then called back to test their retrieving ability. Dixon's Star Lite II completed the land retrieve but failed to retrieve from water. Hauptman v Dusseldorf refused the land retrieve. Dixon's Skiddoo, while a bit slow in picking up the birds, made an acceptable delivery of the bird in both land and water tests. Max v Schulenberg marked his bird down well, retrieved smartly from land and water, but dropped his bird just short of the handler's hand.

In the first NGSPA Championship the title was withheld. Dixon's Skiddoo, dog, 485084, by Meadow v Reichenberg—Dixon's Star Lite, owned and handled by Lefty Dixon of St. Clair Shores, Michigan, was named the stake winner. Max v Schulenberg, 505602, dog, by Count vd Schulenberg—Kathryn v Sievers, owned and handled by Henry F. Weiss of Toledo, Ohio, was named runner-up. Virgil V. VanDivort vowed that the Championship would return next year and no one should doubt that the NGSPA would demand a Championship performance before one would be named.

On April 28, 1954, the NGSPA incorporated as not-for-profit corporation in the State of Ohio. While authorized to do business in other states, Toledo, Ohio, still remains the principal place of business of the NGSPA. Paul. L. Sharp, was the first president, and Virgil V. VanDivort was the initial secretary of the NGSPA. Henry L. Weiss, who owned and operated a baking company in the Toledo area, served as vice-president, and Leonard Hansen, the fire chief at an army ordinance depot near Toledo, Ohio, served as treasurer. The initial board of directors consisted of the foregoing individuals along with Paul Radde, James Baker, Gilbert Cross, Mahlon Tibbitts, Oscar VandenBosch, Martin Walter, H.G. Hogle, Dan Thornton, Charles Rogers, George Reimlinger, and William Wooten. A total of 114 individuals signed on as initial charter members including several that would make significant contributions to this organization.

On November 6, 1954, a total of ten dogs went to the line to compete for the second NGSPA Championship. VanDivort was concerned about the small entry and the way that the Shorthair fancier viewed this trial. In his article in the American Field VanDivort wrote words that have served as a guidepost for the NGSPA: "It was a distinct departure from the usual one-course trial and in the minds of these officers the only true test of a bird dog. We can watch all the work in the world on planted or just-released pen-raised birds and we'll never determine what the average dog owner wants to know about the breed; that is, the dog's ability to perform as a hunting dog."

After running an excellent race through any and all likely objectives, Fritz v Strauss emerged as the first NGSPA National Champion. Fritz's bracemate at 11 minutes worked a bird to the end of a feed strip where it flushed wild. Frtiz stopped. At 16 minutes Fritz backed his bracemate on a wild covey find. At 20 minutes both dogs were on point in the same area, but birds were not produced. At 22 minutes Fritz had a find with manners all in order at the shot.

Fritz was sent on, took one step, and stopped. Two more birds rose in front of him with manners still in order. At 40 minutes Fritz found and handled a covey of quail with excellent deportment. At 48 minutes both dogs encountered several wild flushing pheasants in a feeder strip. Both dogs stood during several flushes and shots with Murdock alone flushing seven birds with no more than two rising at one time. In the second series, consisting of only a land retrieve, Fritz handled his retrieve in a credible manner. Dixon's Shelia had run a strong first hour with a good pattern which resulted in four solid finds and one stop to flush. Shelia performed well in the second series proving her ability during the shot, kill, and retrieve.

Fritz v Strauss, 512073, dog, by Otto v. Strauss-Ritz's Coco, owned by Carl Kemritz and handled by Joe Murdock, a retired engineer turned dog trainer of Downers Grove, Illinois, was declared the first NGSPA National Champion on November 6, 1954. The owner, Carl Kemritz, an Eastern airline pilot, was originally from Toledo, Ohio, but was then residing in Evergreen Park, Illinois. Kemritz, who liked to hunt upland birds, had been introduced to the breed by VanDivort. Dixon's Shelia, bitch, 509521, by Max v Schulenberg-Dixon's Star Lite, owned and handled by Lefty Dixon was named runner-up. On December 8, 1956, Vitality Dry Dog Food would run an advertisement featuring Fritz v. Strauss on the cover page of The American Field, the first of his breed to appear there.

The third NGSPA Championship was held on November 12, 1955, at Kildeer Plains Wildlife Area, again with an entry of only 10 dogs. VanDivort wrote in The American Field, dated December 31, 1955, at page 755 that the entry of ten dogs drawn to start was disappointing but the stake lacked nothing in quality. More dogs could have been obtained from a couple of sources, but they would have added nothing except numbers to the trial. But, this apparent lack of interest by breeders and trainers gave the officers of the organization cause to stop and ponder whether or not their efforts were worth it.

The trial was blessed with wonderful weather, and the courses for the most part were excellent. While the cover was too high in certain areas, the Ohio Division of Wildlife had established an excellent program of pheasant propagation that was ensuring an adequate supply of game birds for hunters as well as those who were utilizing the grounds for field trial activity.

Dixon's Sheila, owned and handled by professional Lefty Dixon of New Haven, Michigan, was awarded the Championship with "a sparking ground heat during which she really poured on the coal in her search for game." The course she had drawn was not the best, but she had opportunities on birds and her manners and style were exemplary at all times. Cast off at 2:05 she hit pay dirt in 11 minutes with a solid find. At 35 minutes she was out of ken for eight minutes. At 46 minutes she was observed working on a running pheasant, which got too near one of the horses and flushed. The dog stopped and remained until the command was given. Two minutes later Sheila backed her bracemate who was on point in a fencerow. Before the handlers could get in, the birds flushed with both dogs displaying good manners. Sheila was braced with Tell v Pinecrest, owned and handled by James Baker of Toledo, Ohio. Tell had a find at nine, the location of the covey of quail, and a find in a fencerow at 55.

Dixon's Sheila, Tell v Pinecrest, Kay Starr, and Dixon's Skiddoo were called back for a second series. Sheila and Kay Star were braced together and Sheila honored Starr on an unproductive. Sheila then scored on two birds, which she retrieved smartly when sent. On her second point, Starr refused to honor, went by Sheila, and stole point. Tell and Skiddoo both pointed, backed, and retrieved in the second series, but Tell's first series ground heat gave him the nod. Judges G. Fred Hill of Crooksville, Ohio, and James C. Tallmadge of Jeromesville, Ohio, named Sheila the Champion and Tell v Pinecrest, dog, 513037 by Max v Schulenberg—Vesta v Maribeth, runner-up.

After the running a meeting of the NGSPA was held at the Evergreens in Upper Sandusky, Ohio. Martin Walter of Defiance, Ohio, was named president, Earl Cutler of Reese, Michigan, was elected vice-president, Virgil V. VanDivort was again named secretary, and Mahlon Tibbitts of Toledo was elected treasurer. While the future of the NGSPA and its Championship seemed uncertain, these officers vowed to continue with a trial that would prove the worth of this breed as a bird dog.

The fourth annual NGSPA Championship was held on November 10-11, 1956. Much of the Killdeer Plains Wildlife Area, again dry with wide cracks that had opened in the black earth, had become unusable because of high heavy weed growth that had taken over the fields. Ohio had a dry autumn with a 40-day drought, causing the cat-tails and bull thistle to rattle as a dog moved through the cover. However, Len Hansen, Whit LeMay, and Virgil VanDivort were still able to lay out three one-hour courses. A total of 18 dogs were entered in the championship which was judged by Richard S. Johns of Benton, Pennsylvania, and Lee G. Vollrath of Findlay, Ohio. Edward Van Tassel, Jim Baker, Virgil VanDivort, and Ed Haughn, and the NGSPA trustees, were enthusiastic about an increased interest in the trial.

In the first one-hour series Dixon's Sheila had run an enthusiastic race and was found on point by Judge Johns. She remained high and steady for Dixon's flush and shot. Lotte v. Heidelberg, running in the first brace, had a stop to flush at 11. From then on Lotte was a little hard to control but scored another find before the end of the hour with manners in order. A total of eight dogs were called back for the second series in a bird field. Dixon's Sheila cleaned the birdfield with three finds and two retrieves with one bird being missed. Lotte v. Heidelberg had two finds. On the first she moved just a bit and was whoaed, causing her to be slow to retrieve. On the second bird she did not move a hair and made a snappy return of the bird. These were the only two dogs that came through the second series without serious error.

As Sheila lacked the opportunity to honor, a dog was placed on point on a planted bird. Dixon cut Sheila away about 75 yards away from the dog on point. Sheila immediately backed upon observing the pointing dog. It was a worthy performance for the defending champion. Dixon's Sheila, owned and handled by Lefty Dixon of New Haven, Michigan, was again named the winner of the NGSPA Championship. Lotte v Heidelberg, handled by Joe Murdock, was named runner-up. Lotte, owned by Frank Vetter of Milwaukee, Wisconsin, was no stranger to field trial circles since Frank's father had previously entered her into field trial competition. After the senior Vetter died, his son, who had never seen her run, continued to campaign her—thus fulfilling the dog's promise.

Lefty Dixon, who also retired the first NGSPA rotating trophy with this his third win of the stake, was no stranger on the field trial circuit. Lefty was born and raised in the Dexter, Missouri, area and grew up quail hunting. Although of relatively small stature, Lefty was recruited to attend college at Louisiana State University to play football. His college gridiron career was cut short when it was learned that he had already played the sport professionally. Lefty then played baseball out of Popular Bluff, Missouri, pitching left handed for the old Southern League. In 1930 Lefty moved to Detroit, ostensibly to obtain employment with the United States Rubber Company but principally to play baseball for this corporation when such organizations placed a premium on company teams. World War II would find Dixon in the United States Army as a K-9 handler in the Pacific Theater.

After the war, Dixon would return to Detroit, Michigan, to work for his former employer. Dixon, as well as his father, were devoted quail hunters and his father bought Lefty a pointer and then a shorthair. The shorthair was registered as Dixon's Bell and would prove to be an outstanding hunting dog that would also have a great impact as a brood bitch. Her blood ran through many of the entries in the early years of the NGSPA Championship. Dixon turned professional in 1948 first operating his kennel out of St. Clair Shores and then, with the financial support of Henry F. Weiss, relocating to better facilities at New Haven, Michigan. Lefty, a tough competitor, was a strong supporter of the NGSPA.

In the first brace of the fifth renewal of the NGSPA Championship Kay Star, bitch, 547113 by Captain v Falkenhorst—Dixon's Star Lite II, owned and handled by Levi F. Summers of Detroit, Michigan, went away at 8:32 on October 9, 1957. Kay faced rugged conditions. Heavy rains on the previous day left some of the fields covered with water that had frozen into icy puddles through which dogs broke at every jump. Unless woods screened the course, the wind was a steady 30 to 40 miles per hour without letup.

Kay showed her mettle all the way. At 8:43 she swung off along a side road and found a pheasant where no bird really should have been on such a day. She pointed it with intensity and style to spare but took a couple of steps when the shot was fired. VanDivort reported that it would have been wrong to say she broke on this one as those two steps, perhaps made to better mark the flight, surely could not be construed as a break except by those who are just too narrow in their thinking. At 9:08 Kay had a mannerly stop on a bird which had been worked to a stop to flush by her bracemate. At 9:30 she again nailed a bird in a clump of weeds, and Summers went in to flush. The bird moved toward her and flushed near her head, but Kay remained steady. Kay's heady forward hour race set a standard for this stake.

Caudle's Leader, 550379, dog, by Dixon's Skiddoo—Ladie II, owned and handled by Edward B. Caudle, went to the post at 4:25 in the last brace on Saturday. Leader had a hard-driving race except for a couple of slow moments when he was trying to unravel some mystery of wind-scattered scent. At six minutes he had a stop to flush on a large bevy of quail. With the wind pouring across the backs of this brace, they topped a rise to see the birds leave. Leader was mannerly. At 4:38 he again stopped on the rise of one of the scattered coveys, and again the wind precluded any possibility of the dog handling the birds. At 4:57 all hands were searching heavy cover for Leader. He was discovered standing high and intent after Judge Johns had ridden up a bird. When Caudle approached, another bird rose in front of the dog and Leader was all manners at the shot. Leader also had an opportunity to stylishly back his bracemate on course.

A total of six dogs were called back for the second series. The first brace consisted of Kay Star and Caudle's Leader, who had made the trip to Kildeer Plains in the same dog box. After a short back course to warm up, the dogs were brought into a large alfalfa field where birds had been planted. Kay went to a bird almost immediately and pointed positively and with lots of character. She needed no word during the flush and kill and made a good retrieve when sent, dropping the bird momentarily to get a better hold, before bringing it to hand. Leader nailed a bird at the edge of tall weeds and his retrieve was snappily executed and to hand. Marko Radbach v Lindenwald, Dixie v Heidebrink, Fritz of Sleepy Hollow, and Duke v Strauss all came through the second series with good manners.

A total of 20 dogs had been entered in this fifth renewal which was judged by Paul J. Teadway of Berkley, Michigan and Richard Johns. Kay Star was named the winner of this Championship, and Caudle's Leader was named runner-up. In winning this one, Kay recorded the first leg on the Ann VanDivort memorial trophy. Ann VanDivort had been a vital part of the early Championship trials at Kildeer Plains, preparing food and making coffee for the trial participants. She passed away on October 3, 1956, after an illness of two years. Virgil VanDivort had taken a poll to determine what type trophy would be most suitable and had commissioned Alfred Carl of Sylvania, Ohio, to execute one. When presented the trophy, tears appeared when Summers tried to say a few words of acceptance. Levi Summers, the first and one of the few amateurs to win this championship, was as gracious in victory as he had previously been in defeat.

Leonard Hansen again marshalled this stake. Jim Zander, George Roberts, Martin Walters, Bill Wooten, Jim Baker, Paul Radde, Eddie Haughn, and Virgil VanDivort lent hands wherever needed. These individuals were elated not only because of the success of this Championship, regarded as having many outstanding pieces of bird work by several dogs, but also because The American Field had given the NGSPA permission to run the first field futurity for German Shorthaired Pointers in 1958. Leonard Hansen was the first Futurity Manager but Paul Kile of the Defiance, Ohio, would shortly take over the futurity and run it for several years. The NGSPA's elected new officers were President, Eddie Haughn of Ridgeville Corners, Ohio; Vice-President, Frank Summers of Detroit, Michigan; Secretary, Virgil V. VanDivort, and Treasurer, Dr. Henry Fredericks of Cleveland, Ohio.

The Sixth NGSPA Championship was run on November 8-9, 1958, at Kildeer Plains Wildlife Area. Four one-hour courses were laid out which offered a variety of cover. The Ohio Division of Wildlife had been emphasizing a program of cover control and game management that was benefiting not only hunters but also field trialers. The weather was once more a significant factor in this trial for it was raw and windy during the running with spots of sleet and a great deal of rain. A high wind kept the birds more than unusually skittish, and the trial featured more than its share of unproductive points where handlers could not produce birds, which caused lengthy relocations and bumped birds.

A total of twenty dogs went to the line in this Championship judged by Richard Johns and Charles Hendricks. Dixon's Susie Q, 559152, bitch, by Dixon's Skiddoo—Audy Girl, owned by Howard F. Confer of Detroit, Michigan, and handled by Lefty Dixon was named Champion. Susie Q, who had taken top honors at the German Pointing Dog National Championship at Ohio, Illinois, the previous month, was described as the "new" type of German Shorthair in stature and build. She was streamlined, on the fine side, having good depth of chest, and standing up on her legs the way a dog should in order to move attractively and easily. She ran with a high head and moved into her birds without going to the ground. Susie showed the judges the type of race they wanted to see. She had a back on her bracemate's unproductive, a legitimate stop to flush with the wind across her back, and a solid pheasant find with manners all in order.

In the second series, consisting of a twenty minute back course ending in a bird field. Susie Q hunted her away around and climaxed her work with a solid find and good retrieve. Fritz v Strauss, the 1954 Champion, was named runner-up. In the first series Fritz had three well-handled pheasant finds and one creditable stop to flush, but his race had not measured up to what was expected in the stake. In the second series Fritz had a slow back course but hit his bird with style and made his retrieve properly.

A total of six dogs had been called back for the second series. VanDivort explained that in these call-backs the judges had to recall enough dogs to protect themselves in case the leading contenders failed to come through. However, if Susie Q and Fritz had not come through, he felt certain that no title would have been awarded.

Notwithstanding the elements, Eddie Haughn, Bill Wooten, Mart Walter, Jim Zander, George Roberts, Jim Baker, Dan Mast, Levi Summers and Ed Caudle did all sorts of jobs to ensure that this trial was a good one. The NGSPA officers elected for 1959 consisted of Eddie Haugh, president; Stanley Chiras, vice-president, Dr. H.H. Fredrick, treasurer; and Virgil V. VanDivort, secretary.

The 1959 NGSPA Championship would end the early years of this organization. Clubs from Cleveland, Toledo, and western Ohio along with the Golden Gate, Northern New York, Southern California, Michigan, and the Middle-Atlantic Regional Shorthair Club were now affiliated with the NGSPA. The one-hour stake run on wild birds was not only attracting more interest from field trial enthusiasts but was also influencing the manner in which professional handlers were having to develop their dogs. While the previous winners were the best of the breed, they were, in reality, only Shorthair shooting dogs. The Seventh NGSPA Championship would change that.

Kay V D Wilburg, dog, 571273, by Pol v Blitzdorf—Cora v Wesertor, was imported from Germany by Bodo S. Winterhelt of Port Colborne, Ontario, Canada, with money fronted by Walter Kogut of Brantford, Ontario, Canada. Winterhelt and Kogut were interested in a field trial dog, and this pup was not suitable for conditions in Germany because of his range. Winterhelt started working the dog, but Kogut obtained full title to Kay and placed him with Bill Bowers, a pointer-setter handler of Cross Junction, Virginia. Bowers not only placed this dog but also won with him in some pretty fast pointer-setter open derby competition. In the 1958 Championship, Kay, handled by Bowers, had started strong, had the class race of the stake, suffered an unproductive, and then took a bird—giving extended chase. Nevertheless, Kay was called back for the second series, had two unproductives on the backcourse, and did not find a bird. After this championship, Kogut would subsequently place the dog with Dick Johns who handled the dog to a pointer-setter open shooting dog placement as well as wins and placements in shorthair competition.

The Seventh NGSPA Championship was originally scheduled for two days, but a total of 33 dogs were entered in this stake with entries from Canada, Cuba, California, Washington, Virginia, Ohio, Michigan, Illinois, Kentucky, New York, Vermont, and Connecticut. The stake was again run at Killdeer Plains starting on October 30 and running through November 1. The grounds were in good condition, and the pheasant and quail populations were excellent on the four one-hour courses which had been laid out. Weather was excellent with sunshine and temperatures in the 50's and 60's. The trial was judged by G. Fred Hill of Crooksville, Ohio, and James C. Tallmadge of Jeromesville, Ohio.

Ed Haughn served as stake manager and received assistance from Henry and Edna Frederick, Martin Walter, Dan Mast, Len Hansen, Bill Wooten, and Fred Hunt. Curt Elarton had brought in a number of horses and VanDivort, who could not attend the trial for personal reasons, sent down his horses. At the annual NGSPA meeting, held at the Evergreens Restaurant, Edward Haughn was elected president, Dan Mast, first vice-president, Stanley Chiras was elected secretary, and Dr. H.H. Fredrick was elected treasurer. In addition, Don Briggs and Dick Johns were elected to the newly created positions of second vice-president and third vice-president, respectively.

Kay V D Wilburg was braced with Dixon's Sheila on the second day of the trial. Kay broke away at tremendous speed and started a cast down a woods line, reaching out to all likely objectives. Kay made eyes pop when he leaped a fence without breaking stride and shortly thereafter slammed into a stylish point. Johns produced three pheasants with Kay's manners exemplary. Johns led Kay a short distance away, and a minute later Kay pointed again with the handler having difficulty flushing the bird. Kay was sent on to relocate and as Kay pointed, Sheila, whose race had lacked the intensity of Kay's, bumped the pheasant. Kay then had an unproductive on a running pheasant. Kay went away running at exceptional range with long reaching strides cracking his tail up and down with each jump. Kay pointed again after time was called. A true shorthair all-age race had been witnessed, and those in attendance were well aware of the fact. Kay V D Wilburg had won this championship, and Stanley Chiras would write that Kay could wear this crown proudly.

Shenna v Feldstrom, the runner-up, bitch, 571273, by Ulk v d Radbach—Ginnie v Feldstrom, owned by Ed Caudle and Dr. Clark Lemley of Detroit, Michigan, and handled by Caudle, was braced with Skiddoo's Bee after lunch on the third day. This brace featured a large riding gallery taking advantage of sunshine and comfortable 55 degree weather. Bee jumped merrily at good range, pointed at three but then corrected. Sheena ran stylishly at good range, and applied herself well. Sheena pointed at 18 and had a beatiful relocation and displayed exemplary manners on a cock pheasant. Four minutes later Sheena was in motion as a pheasant took to the air beyond a corn feeder strip. Sheena stopped and a pair of pheasants then lifted. At 33 Bee had a stop to flush and Sheena backed. Sheena was found on point at 40 minutes and remained steady to wing and shot on the rooster. Sheena pointed again at 43 and was sent for a relocation. She made a big swing with head held high; as Sheena looped her turn back into the wind, a rooster flushed and she stopped. Sheena pointed again at 45 and was mannerly as the pheasant was produced. Sheena later had another legitimate stop to flush before the end of the hour.

A total of six dogs—Sergent v Dusseldorf, Sandra v Hohen Tann, Kay V D Wildburg, Riga v Hohen Tann, Sheena v Feldstrom, and Bobo Gradenbruch Beckum—were called back for the second series. While this series was originally deemed necessary to fulfill the requirements of the Championship, the NGSPA and its member clubs had decided the second series was somewhat artificial and were giving serious thought to the matter. Nevertheless, Kay went into the second series with tremendous drive, had a nice find in the birdfield, and remained mannerly. Kay was sent on the retrieve and he returned the bird merrily. Likewise, Sheena pinned a bird, exhibited perfect manners, and retrieved on command. The performance of both dogs had made them worthy of the title of NGSPA Champion and runner-up.

The two individuals who handled Kay and Sheena have been significant in the history of the NGSPA. Dick Johns, born and raised in Pennsylvania, was soon hunting grouse at an early age with bird dogs. As a young adult, Johns would be training bird dogs and horses for a living. World War II would find Johns with the United States Army in Europe. At the conclusion of the war, Johns was assigned to a horse cavalry unit with the task of locating dogs for pheasant hunting for senior officers. This role would acquaint him with the German Shorthaired Pointer, and he would import specimens of this breed to the United States upon his return. Johns would resume the training of hunting and field trial bird dogs near Benton, Pennsylvania, and would become an active professional handler competing with different breeds in both open pointer-setter and shorthair competition. Dick Johns actively promoted the NGSPA Championship by judging, competing and winning in this competition, and serving as an officer in this organization.

Edward Caudle, who handled Sheena, was born in Atkins, Arkansas, but his family subsequently relocated to Reeves, Missouri, and then to Caruth, Missouri, where they farmed to survive the depression. His early hunting experience was born of an economic necessity to help fill the family larder. World War II would find Caudle in the United States Marine Corps in the Pacific theater. Upon his discharge Caudle would return to Missouri, but he would soon relocate to Detroit, Michigan, to seek employment. He became a friend of Levi Summers and their hunting association led to Caudle's purchase of a German Shorthaired Pointer in 1949. This dog led him into a life as a professional handler when in 1952 he began operating a kennel and boarding operation out of Canton, Michigan. While not the first, Caudle was one of the early shorthair trainers who started taking this breed to the prairies for development. As a promoter of the breed, Caudle was a charter member of the NGSPA, worked at the early championship trials, served as a trustee for many years, and on two occasions presided as president of this association. His ideas about judges, judging, bird dogs, and the proper conduct of a class trial influenced many of the modern shorthair trainers more than they care to admit.

The NGSPA would now start a new era and many different individuals would come forward to participate in the Championship and work for this organization that has grown in strength and prestige. Like all field trial clubs, this association would experience the good times as well as the turbulent ones. Although the names of the dogs and the faces have changed, a debt of gratitude is owed to these early pioneers who wanted field trial competition that would realistically test this breed as a bird dog.

Joe Murdock, the handler of the first NGSPA Champion, would retire in Sarasota, Florida, but would remain active with shorthairs judging several Florida trials prior to his death. Lefty Dixon would retire to his winter headquarters, Ocala, Florida, in 1963 where he would enjoy quail hunting for several years. He died on December 31, 1995, in Rock Hill, South Carolina, the home of his stepson, Kenneth Johnston. This article could not have been written without the assistance of Ed Caudle of Canton, Michigan, Dick Johns of Benton, Pennsylvania, and Bill Wooten of Toledo, Ohio, also a charter member and former trustee of the NGSPA, all of whom still maintain an active interest in this organization. In addition, Barbara Teare and Gary Lockee of the Bird Dog Foundation in Grand Junction, Tennesee, were most gracious in helping my wife and myself locate and copy materials. The Foundation's growing collection of bird dog literature and memorabilia is invaluable to anyone attempting to research the history of field trials and its participants.

Virgil V. VanDivort, the individual most responsible for the National German Shorthaired Pointer Association and its championships, would be diagnosed with cancer. VanDivort had taken care of his first wife, Ann, for almost two years prior to her death from this same dreaded disease. In the last days prior to his death he would place telephone calls to or visit many of his field trial friends and express to them his appreciation for their friendship over the years.

On January 10, 1968, VanDivort placed a telephone call to the Sheriff's Office in Toledo, Ohio. When a deputy sheriff responded, VanDivort's body was found. Dr. Harry Mignerey, a local coroner, ruled the death a suicide from a self-inflicted gunshot wound.

At the time of his death, VanDivort was active in many civic projects and fraternal orders, a member of the Outdoor Writers Association of America, and was still active in the affairs of the NGSPA. He had also served as vice president of the Ohio Field Trial Association and worked with some of his bird dog friends, who loved pheasant hunting, field trials, and Killdeer Plains, to create a stake that would develop into what came to be known as the International Pheasant Championship.

VanDivort has been quoted and misquoted about the NGSPA and his desire for this breed. He wrote in The American Field in 1954 at page 634 that "the thinking that went into the building of this stake was the result of a few persons with coinciding ideas about the Shorthair. We believed them to the capable of much more in the way of becoming bird dogs than we had seen demonstrated in many trials. We knew of and had the utmost faith in the nose of these dock-tailed imports. We knew, too, that they could be bred to have some of the drive, the bounce, the intensity in action through the fields and in their bird contacts that makes handling any bird dog a really thrilling experience even without a gun in one's hand. This we have attempted to do. We have not tried to do anything further."

NATIONAL USA DINNER/// HERE ARE SOME OF THE PRIZES//

THETABLE DURING JUDGING IN DAY AGUN///BRONZE HEAD STADY OF A GERMAN SHORTHAIR ALSO SOME LOVELY JEWLERY/// WENT TO NATIONAL DINNER SITTING AT TABLE BESIDE ME WAS ROBERT MC KOWAN WHO OWNED ADAM VON FURREHEIM NEEDED 2POINTS MORE TO BECOME ADUAL///TALKED TO ME WHAT GREAT SHOOTTING DAYS HE HAD WITH THIS DOG AND DUAL CHAMPION SCHATZIES ERIC V., GRIEF HE IS SIRE OF HANK THE YANKDAM FC. SHATZI.V. CD NFC V.GOING BACK TO ESSERSCHICKDAUGHTER GOING BACK AGAIN TO WASSSERLING BLOODLINES HANK WAS SENT TO UK HAD 6MONTHS IN QUARANTINE MATER 2 BITCHES HERE HANK SPENT 6 MONTHS HERE IN UK THEN SENT ON TO AUSTRALIA WHERE HANK SPENT 3 MORE MONTHS IN QURANTINE BEFORE GOING TO HIS NEW OWNERS LYNN AND CAROLYN BUTLER THEN FOLLOWING YEAR WENT WITH JIM TO USA TO JUDGE HUNT TESTFOR BRITTANY CLUBIN RIGHT DOWN IN SOUTH OF CALIFORNIA VERY HOT WIND KNOW AND AGAINBLEW SAND STORMS JUDGES WERE ON HORSEBACK HANDLERS ON FOOT RUN IN PAURS THEY HAVE TO HONOUR EACH OTHER BIRDS QUAIL ARE PLANTED IN LIKE BUSHES HORSES CAME BACK AFTER EACH RUN HORSES WERE PUT IN SHADE THEY MUST HAVE MARKS AT LEAST7 OUT OF TEN IN EACH CATTERGARY ENCLOSED ARE THE CATTERGIESTHEY DO 2FOR JUNIOR HUNTERE 4 FOR SENIOR HUNTER 8 FOR MASTER HUNTER. NEXT DAY WENT ON RANGE VERY HOT AND DESSERT LIKEIN CALIFORNIA . . . ///

Tuesday, 14 May, 2013 13:27

USA SCENE OF BLOODLINES

BETTY ECHEN LIVED IN CALIFORNIA NR OREGEN
WORKED HER DOGS MORE THAN SHOW THEM GAVE
ME ALL THE PEDIGREES OF EARLY IMPORTS OF DOGS
ENCLOSING SOME OF THEM INTERESTING SHE HAD
DOGS THEN FROM RADBACK BRICKWEDDA AND
WASSERCHLING THEN AS HER PROGRAMME OF GOOD
BLOODLINES GOD BLESS HER///

Betty Eschen:

QUIETLY MAKING AN IMPACT ON THE SHORTHAIR WORLD

By Patte Titus

The Shorthair world and Parent Club lost a longtime friend when Merit Member Betty Eschen died in April. Well respected by her peers, she will be greatly missed as a quiet but lasting influence in the Shorthair world.

During WWII as a Civil Servant, she worked at Fort Richardson, Alaska and the McKinley National R&R Center. Then as a member of the Red Cross she worked in Army hospitals on the West Coast and in Japan after which she returned to Carmel, CA where she resided for the past 45 years.

In Carmel, she worked with the Community Hospital of the Monterrey Pennisula until her retirement in 1983 afterward she continued to work with the local blood bank.

Betty was highly regarded for her integrity, breed knowledge and expertise with an acknowledged good eye for a dog or bitch.

She trained and handled her own dogs whether it was for the show ring or the local field trials held at Ft. Ord, CA. which at the time, other than obedience, were the only events in which one could compete with their dog.

She was a member of the GSPCA during its formative and reorganization process to become the AKC licensed member Parent Club and was also active in the GSP Club of Central California and All Breed Del Monte KC.

One only has to look through C. Bede Maxwell's books to find pictures of Betty's dogs or their get. Her foundation bitch Ch. Liza von Greif (FC Greif von Hundsheimerkogel x Ch. Yunga War Bride) was the 1959 Westminster KC Best Opposite Sex at 22 months of age having finished at 14 months with 5 straight wins.

Another noteworthy bitch was Ch. Gina Braun von Greif (Dominic Radbach von Greif x Ch. Kanichen von Braun) that was BOS at the 1969 GSPCA NSS. Gina was a littermate to the very well known Dual Champion sisters pictured in Maxwell's book that were owned by Gene & Erica Harden.

Betty never establish a kennel name and the registered names of the dogs she owned and bred indicated their lineage. She was also very fond of older dogs and would often take them when the circumstances warrented.

In 1977 Betty judged the GSPCA 6th annual National Sweepstakes hosted by the Eastern GSPC in Bridgewater, NJ and selected Berta von Graufles bred by Marilyn K. Gates for Best in Sweeps.

In 1982 she judged the GSPCA 5th annual National Futurity hosted by the GSPC of California in San Mateo and picked Jim & June Burns Kingswood's Miss Chiff for her Best in Futurity winner.

In 1987 she was asked to judge the GSPCA 10th annual National Futurity in Wisconsin when Helen Shelley was unable to judge due to the untimely death of her husband. Her Best in Futurity winner was Fieldfines Snomel Alpha bred by Stephanie Snyder.

Lasting friendships formed in these early years of the GSPCA and during the National Events. These friend would look forward to each National Field Trial and Specialty Show when they would get together, have dinner and enjoy one another's company, the competition and their dogs. If a new face showed up they took them under their wing and made sure they were taken care of and more friendships were formed. The Shorthair world will miss Betty as will her friends.

Above: Betty Eschen with CH Gina Braun von Greif going Best of Opposite Sex at the 1969 GSPCA National Specialty Show under Judge C. Bede Maxwell; below, Betty with all of her dogs (Becky, Nicky, Gina, Tullah and Jody) at the Fort Ord, CA field trial grounds.

Kay v.d. Schrummer Heide 723y 7975	K.S. Bill II Raven 187q 6826	Hasso v. Wilseder Berg 2268n	K.S. Frei Südwest 63f 4003	Argus von der Weihermühle 452b 2767 11
				Drossel Südwest 341d 2
			K.S. Asta Raven 481i 5684	K.S. Unkas vom Wilseder Berg 301e 3
				Heidejägers Stolze Wanda 335d 4
		Ella Raven 1619o	Armin v. Sülfmeister 767h	K.S. Bill vom Hirschfeld 16c 2855 5
				Gerlinde von der Heidelust 813g 6
			Heidejägers Stolze Wanda 235d	Tasso vom Winterhauch 345Y 2038 7
				Freya Luhetal 238c 8
	Doris v.d. Wurth 869x	Arno vom Winkelbauer 357s	K.S. Bodo v. Grimmstal 502p 6956	Arco vom Grimmstal 2094m 9
				Kalla von der Wolfskuhle 1501 1 10
			Jnga v. Gröningen 1260p	Hanno von Gröningen 1475n 11
				Flora von Oßmannstedt 15570 12
		Asta Georgis 16u	K.S. Bodo v. Grimmstal 502p 6956	Arco vom Grimmstal 2094m 13
				Kalla von der Wolfskuhle 1501 1 14
			Bella vom Sandfall 518n	K.S. Bodo von dem Radbach 190h 4173 15
				Zilla vom Fuchspass 757k 16
Ruth von dem Radbach 1771x	K.S. Adel von dem Assegrund 268v 7585	Junos vom Heidebrink 335r	Greif vom Heidebrink 235p	K.S. Arthur vom Scheperhof 1006k 5607 17
				Cilli vom Heidebrink 737 1 18
			Bärbel v. Reußenstein 2195m	K.S. Bodo vom Veronikaberg 536k 1811 19
				K.S. Kalla von der Lußhardt 979i Vbr. 20
		Pierette Roggenstein gen. Toska 183v	Seigers Prinz 3ö8t	Markus Freising 1668n 6588 21
				Seigers Jna 311n 22
			Nixe Roggenstein 40t	Mirko Freising 1672n 6280 23
				Freya Patria=Zürich 507i 24
	Ondra v.d. Radbach 842q	Claus vom Veronikaberg 322 1 5543	K.S. Junker Goldbeck 63e 3606	Artus Sand 1830V 1638 25
				Bessie vom Hamelsberg 364c 26
			Lotte Fuchssiepen 630h	Dux Ringsheim 180b 27
				Erle Mauderode=Westerholt 703c 28
		Klio v.d. Radbach 2000n	K.S. Seigers Zett 491m Vbr.	Seigers Widu 441 1 5278 29
				Seigers Werra 442 1 30
			Bella Rothenburg 1763 1	K. S. Frei Südwest 63f 4003 31
				Jolla Sankt Ewaldi 642g 32

Table 1

Arco vom Grimshal 2094m	K. S Bill v. Hirschfeld 16e DII y I 2855	Wehrwolf v.d goldenen Mark 465Z 2011	Held Farve 217 X 1591	Widu v.d. goldenen Mark 1270 T 1370
				Thyra v. Farmsen 125iU
			Eller v.d. goldenen Mark 1277T.	Edelmann v.d. goldenen Mark 424 S.
				Madel v. Lindau 153 o.
		Frigg II Sand 581 y 2050	Artus Sand 1830 v 1638	Yelmos Gotz v. Kauffungen 21T 1244
				Ella Sand 543N
			Frigga Sand 104P.	K.S. Michel v.d. goldenen Mark 422M
				K.S. Erra Cannstatt—Sand 489H
	Lore v. Fuchspass 200 h ??? SI 4170	K.S. Rino vom Schornbusch 153L 3204	Heido Holstenperle 1141 Y 2174	Held v Farve 257-X 59
				Lutjenburgerin 451 X
			Brune Ringsheim 1076Z	Argo von Lamborn 20W 1478
				Adda Ringsheim 1126X
		Fee vom Fuchspass 449Z 3637	Sur Ringsheim 180b.	Heido Holstenperle 1141 Y 2174
				Adda Ringsheim 1126X
			Cara Sudwest 1c	Heide vom Winterhauch 447Z 2254
				Freidel Sudwest 226T 1295

Table 2

Erle Mauderode Westerholt 703 c	Rino Forst 1685U 1502	Mars Altenau 69 d m 20	Nestor Altenau 226 o	Rino Altenau 31H 200
				Hertha III Pfaffendorf 645K
			Fasme 68p.	Hassan Altenau 712K
				Ina v.d. Wessnitz 712k
		Forster's Senta 269	Hessa's ??? Rosenburg 232p.	Waldo Raven 654 M.
				Bella vom Syratal 505k.
			Försters Hertha II 109 o.	Tell v.d. Wolfsschlucht 358 H.
				Forsters Hertha 308k.
	Aster Manderode 69 Z. 2120	Artus Sand 1830 v. 1638	Yelmos Gotz von Kauffungen 21T. 1244	Lump Mauderode 154o
				Lusi v. Kauffungen 16Q
			Ella Sand 543 v 1472	Rino Weisseritztal v.d. Wessnitz 131 s. 1127
				Frigga Sand 104P.
		Hella Travemunde 752 v.	Pleck Hirschfeld 33Q 1139	K.S ???? v.d. Wessnitz 9M 990
				Hertha v.d. goldenen Mark 595H
			Lissy v.d. Wessnitz 83Q	K.S. ??? v.d. Wessnitz 9 M. 990
				??? v.d. Wessnitz 101k

Page 235 in a separate file (520014_p235_table.docx)
'ESSER'S CHICK (German Import) 8th and 9th Generations
(SIRE'S SIDE)
(Numbers in left margin keyed to 7th generation numbers)

	8	9
1	KS Wehrwolf vd goldenen Mark Frigga II Sand	Held v Farve & Eller vd goldenen Mark Artus Sand & Frigga Sand
	Patz v Bardenhof Rina v Schwentinetal	Trio Holstenperle & Bonnscheins Corela Artus v Gottorp & Diana Holstenperle
2	KS Wehrwolf vd goldenen Mark Frigga II Sand	Held v Farve & Eller vd goldenen Mark Artus Sand & Frigga Sand
	Artus v Gottorp Diana Holstenperle	Artus Sand & Karin v Furstenmoor Held v Farye & Lutienburgerin-genannt Zilla
3	KS Junker v Bomlitztal Eule v Runenstein	Prinz v Schlosshof & Arna Sand Artus Sand & Biene v Runenstein
	KS Rino Forst (Buir) Aster Mauderode	Mars Altenzu & Forster's Senta Artus Sand & Hella v Travemunde
4	KS Wehrwolf vd goldenen Mark Frigga II Sand	Held v Farve & Eller vd goldenen Mark Artus Sand & Frigga Sand
	Arno v Schneppengrund Aster Mauderode	Hestas Arminius & Lona v Buchwald Artus Sand & Hella v Travemunde
5	KS Wehrwolf vd goldenen Mark Frigga II Sand	Held v Farve & Eller vd goldenen Mark Artus Sand & Frigga Sand
	KS Rino v Schornbusch KS Fee v Fuchspass	Heido Holstenperle & Brune Ringsheim KS Dux Ringsheim & Cara Sudwest
6	Cay v Wieler See Dina v Brocklandsau	Satan vd goldenen Mark & Bessie v Wieler See Treffer v Hamdorf & Sentagreta vd Brocklandsau
	KS Kobold Mauderode-Westerholt Coralle v Fuchspass	KS Magnet v Ockerbach & Edda Mauderode-Westerholt KS Junker v Bomlitztal & Cara Sudwest
7	KS Magnet v Ockerbach Edda Mauderode-Westerholt	KS Junker v Bomlitztal & Eule v Runenstein KS Rino Forst (Buir) & Aster Mauderode
	Artus Sand Werra v Syratal	Yelmos Gotz v Kauffungen & Ella Sand Atila v Choren & Norita v Syratal
8	KS Dux Ringsheim Kalla Ringsheim	Heido Holstenperle & Adda Ringsheim KS Klaus v Fuchspass & KS Dura Ringsheim
	KS Benno v Schlossgarten Cori Sudwest	Bob v Winterhauch & Fatuma Kamerun Mars v Winterhauch & Zilly Sudwest
9	Junos Heidebrink Pierette Roggenstein	Greif v Heidebrink & Barbel v Ruessenstein Seigers Prinz & Nixe Roggenstein
	Monarch Beckum Sagitta Beckum	Horst Beckum & Rita vd Radbach Panther v Wittekind & Nanny Beckum
10	Greif v Heidebrink Barbel v Ruessenstein	KS Arthur v Scheperhof & Cilli v Heidebrink KS Bodo v Veronikaberg & KS Kalla vd Lusshardt
	Seigers Prinz Nixe Roggenstein	KS Markus Freising & Seigers Ina Mirko Freising & Freya Patria Zurich
11	KS Bill v Hirschfeld Lori v Fuchspass	KS Wehrwolf vd goldenen Mark & Frigga II Sand KS Rino v Schornbusch & KS Fee vd Fuchspass

	Ajax v Krupunder See		Cay v Wieler See & Dina vd Brocklandsau
	Grille v Travemunde		KS Kobold Mauderode-Westerholt & Coralle v Fuchspass
12	KS Kobold Mauderode-Westerholt		KS Magnet v Ockertachnd Edda
	Diana v Syratal		Mauderode-Westerholt
			Artus Sand & Werra v Syratal
	Otto v Fuchspass		KS Dux Ringsheim & Kalla Ringsheim
	KS Friedel Sudwest		KS Benno v Schlossgarten & Cori Sudwest
13	RS Drall v Dreieck-Mulheim		Roland Campf & Biene v Dreieck-Mulheim
	KS Leberechts Donau		Mars v Fuchspass & Leberechts Bussa
	Seydels Hill		Jagers Nasso & Seydels Betty
	KS Hussa v alten Postweg		Ajax v Laupendahl & Betti v Kocksbusch
14	WS & RS Heidi vd Beeke		Treff v Waldhausen & Diana v Landsherrn
	Junogoldbach		KS Hasso vd Schwarzen Kuhle & Dianaahlen
	Seydels Arno		KS Don vd Schwarzen Kuhle & WS Hella v
	Alli vd Paulusburg		Bohmer Wald-
			Ajax v Seefeld & Kara vd goldenen Mark
			Gothersitz
15	Kanto v Gottorp		Artus Sand & Rita v Schwentinetal
	Jagers Irade		Argo v Laachersee & Jagers Elite
	WS & RS Heidi vd Beeke		Treff v Waldhausen & Diana v Landsherrn
	Karin vd Corley		KS Don vd Schwarzen Kuhle & Gemse vd
			Gorley
16	KS Bill v Hirschfeld		KS Wehrwolf vd goldenen Mark & Frigga II
	Senta v Holm		Sand
			Patz v Bardenhof & Rina v Schwentinetal
	KS Murr Sudwest		KS Frei Sudwest & Kuni Sudwest
	Cora v Feldhof		WS & RS Heidi vd Beeke & Rauke vd Forst
			Brickwedde
17	KS Frei Sudwest		Argus vd Weihermuhle & Drossel Sudwest
	Cally v Veronikaberg		KS Junker Goldbech & Lotte Fuchssiepen
	KS Don vd Schwarzen Kuhle		Wodan Peppenhoven & Hertana Papinghausen
	Lore Beckum		Horst Beckum & Wanderhevdt
18	WS & RS Heidi vd Beeke		Treff v Waldhausen & Diana v Landsherrn
	Junogoldbach		KS Hasso vd Schwarzen Kuhle & Dianaahlen
	KS Dax v Veronikaberg		KS Frei Sudwest & Cally v Veronikaberg
	Adria v Blitzdorf		KS Don vd Schwarzen Kuhle & Lore Beckum
19	Treff v Waldhausen		Manfred v Waldhausen & Edda v Waldhausen
	Diana v Landsherrn		Etzel vd Beeke & Ilka v Landsherrn
	KS Hasso vd Schwarzen Kuhle		Held v Farve & Hertana Papinghausen
	Dianaahlen		Treff v Wittekind & Amsel v Spahenfelde
20	Wodan Peppenhoven		Axel v Schnepfengrund & Pille Sand
	Hertana Papinghausen		Heidi Esterhof & Jutta Papinghausen
	Horst Beckum		Zeus vd Bode & Freva Beckum
	Wanderheydt		Tiro Immerrath & Xilly Altenbach
21	KS Arthur v Scheperhof		KS Don vd Schwarzen Kuhle & Seigers Thea
	Cilli v Heidebrink		Harro v Weserstrand & Lea v Seckachtal
	KS Bodo v Veronikaberg		KS Junker Goldbeck & Lotte Fuchsstepen
	KS Kalla vd Lusshardt		KS Frei Sudwest & Hexe vd Lusshardt
22	KS Marcus Freising		KS Marko v Schaumberg & Juno Freising
	Seigers Ina		KS Klaus v Veronikaberg & KS Seigers Werra
	Mirko Freising		KS Marko v Schaumberg & Juno Freising
	Freya Patria Zurich		KS Kobold Mauderode-Westerholt & Carin v
			Fuchspass

23	Artus Sand		Yelmos Gotz v Kauffungen & Ella Sand
	Bessie v Hammelsberg		Borneblitz vd Bode & Hexe v Lenz
	KS Dux Ringsheim		Heido Holstenperle & Adda Ringsheim
	Erle Mauderode-Westerholt		KS Rino Forst (Buir) & Aster Mauderode
24	KS Seigers Widu		Treff v Waldhausen & Dolly Heisenstein
	KS Seigers Werra		Treff v Waldhausen & Dolly Heisenstein
	KS Fred Sudwest		Argus vd Weihermuhle & Diossel Sudwest
	???		???
25	Adel v Stukenberge		KS Murr Sudwest & Arga v Finkenbusch
	Turne v Holle		Basco v Feldhof & Astra v Fensterberg
	Falk v Wasserschling		Seydels Hill & Marga vd Radbach
	Puschka v Hellerau		KS Komet v Spehteshart & Geescha v Dreieck
26	Falk v Wasserschling		Seydels Hill & Marga vd Radbach
	Puschka v Hellerau		KS Komet v Spehteshart & Geescha v Dreieck
	Till vd Beeke		KS Alf v Manhagen & Lissi vd Beeke
	Adda v Pfingsttal		KS Carlo vd Rheinau & Anny v Theimsburg Forst
27	Jagers Naso		KS Frei Sudwest & Jagers Jo
	Saydels Adda		KS Don vd Schwarzen Kuhle & WS Hella v Bohmerwald-G.
	Basco v Feldhof		WS & RS Heidi vd Beeke & Rauke vd Forst Brickwedde
	Seydels Karin		Arno v Gunztal & KS Seydels Hella
28	KS Alf v Manhagen		KS Bill Hirschfeld & Senta Holm
	Lissi vd Beeke		Bill Woldenhorn & Cita vd Sule
	Benno v Bruhler Tor		KS Carlo vd Rheinau & Asta v Bruhler Tor
	Edda v Briesensee		Axel v Briesensee & Cora v Briesensee
29	KS Frei Sudwest		Argus vd Weihermuhle & Drossel Sudwest
	Okka Ringsheim		KS Bill v Hirschfeld & Junora Ringsheim
	Cito Furstenmoor		
	Olga (Aischal)		
30	KS Frei Sudwest		Argus vd Weihermuhle & Drossel Sudwest
	Okka Ringsheim		KS Bill v Hirschfeld & Junora Ringsheim
	KS Kraft v Syratal		KS Kobold Mauderode-Westerholt & Dianna v Syratal
	Berka v Muhlenfeld		WS Tell v Wilsederberg & Greta ad Kaspel
31	Jagers Nasso		KS Frei Sudwest & Jagers Jo
	Seydels Betty		KS Bill v Hirschfeld & Seydels Asta
	Ajax v Laupendahl		KS Rauck Mauderode-Westerholt & KS Jagers Norma
	Betty Kocksbusch		KS Don vd Schwarzen Kuhle & Berns Freya
32	Seydels Hill		Jagers Nasso & Seydels Betty
	Marga vd Radbach		WS & RS Heidi vd Beeke & KS Dea vd Radbach
	KS Romet v Spehteshart		KS Kobold Mauderode-W. & Elda vd Romerstadt
	Geescha v Dreieck		KS & RS Bodo vd Radbach & KS Freja vd Dreieck

ESSER'S CHICK (German Import) 8th and 9th Generations (DAM'S SIDE)
(Numbers in left margin keyed to 7th generation numbers)

33	Roland Campf		Troll Kaltenscheid & Anni Campf
	Biene v Dreieck-Mulheim		Gero Sand & Bianka v Hirschfeld

	Mars v Fuchspass Leberechts Bussa	Roland vd Lindenhole & Vita v Weinbiet Leberechts Ambose & Bonna v Grafenstein
34	Jagers Nasso Seydels Betty	KS Frei Sudwest & Jagers Jo KS Bill v Hirschfeld & Seydels Asta
	Ajax v Laupendahl Betty v Kocksbusch	KS Rauck Mauderode-Westerholt & KS Jagers Norma KS Don vd Schwarzen Kuhle & Berns Freya
35	Treff v Waldhausen Diana v Landsherrn	Manfred Waldhausen & Edda v Waldhausen Etzel vd Beeke & Ilka v Landsherrn
	KS Hasso vd Schwarzen Kuhle Dianaahlen	Held v Farve & Hertana Papinghausen Treff v Wittekind & Amsel v Spahenfelde
36	KS Don v Schwarzen Kuhle WS Hella v Bohmerwald-Gothersitz	Wodan Peppenhoven & Hertana Papinghausen Aspodlesi (as vom unter-w.) & Flora (v Lind.-schl.)
	Ajax v Seefeld Kara v goldenen Mark	KS & RS Bodo vd Radbach & Afra v Schlachtental Strolch v Gottorp & Hummel vd goldenen Mark
37	Held v Farve Eller vd goldenen Mark	Widu vd goldenen Mark & Thyra v Farmsen Edelmann vd goldenen Mark & Madel v Lindau
	Artus Sand Frigga Sand	Yelmos Colz v Kauffungen & Ella Sand KS Michel vd goldenen Mark & Erra Cannstatt-Sand
38	Trio Holstenperle Bernscheins Corela	Held v Farve & Lutjenburger-genannt Zilla Prinz v Schlosshof & Lona Siegerblut
	Artus Gottorp Diana Holstenperle	Artus Sand & Karin v Furstenmoor Held v Farve & Lutjenburger-genannt Zilla
39	KS Wehrwolf vd goldenen Mark Frigga II Sand	Held v Farve & Eller vd goldenen Mark Artus Sand & Frigga Sand
	KS Dux Ringsheim Cara Sudwest	Heido Holstenperle & Adda Ringsheim Heidi v Winterhauch & Trudel Sudwest
40	Artus Sand Bella vd Beeke	Yelmas Cotz v Kauffungen & Ella Sand Heidi Esterhof & Diana vd Jaglitz
	Heidi Esterhof Amsel vd Beeke	Mars Altenau & Cora v Merkenich Esterhof Lump Mauderode & Diana vd Jaglitz
41	Axel v Schnepfengrund Pille Sand	Hestas Arminius & Erchen v Interlaken KS Rino Weisseritztal vd Wessnitz & Frigga Sand
	Heidi Esterhof Sutta Papinghausen	Mars Altenau & Cora v Merkenich Esterhof Frey III v Freithof & Juno Cramer
42	Asmiradiste Mora Skagerrak	Frei Kwasner & Freya Skagerrak Harras Pichtberg & Drossel v Kauffungen
	Arno v Doschen Wixe (Hohne)	Blitz vd Lowengrude & Lissi v Leonorenhof Blitz II Rabinstein & Lola Rabenstein
43	Treff v Waldhausen Diana Landsherrn	Manfred v Waldhausen & Edda v Waldhausen Etzel vd Beeke & Ilka v Landsherrn
	KS Klaus v Hellerau Sirena v Hummling	KS & RS Bodo vd Radbach & Freya v Fuchspass KS Furst v Fuchspass & Opal v Hummling
44	Heido Holstenperle Brune Ringsheim	Held v Farve & Lutjenburger-genannt Zilla Argo v Samborn & Adda Ringsheim
	KS Benno v Schlossgarten Gilly Zieverich	Bob v Winterhauch & Fatuma Kamerun Heido Holstenperle & Minka v Parlshof
45	Manfred v Waldhausen Hilda v Waldhausen	Besso v Wilkenburg & Hella v Echenhorst Waldhausen Nordstern vd Stolzen & Suse v Hohnsen

	Lizel vd Beeke Mike v Landsherrn		Artus Sand & Bella vd Beeke ??? v Ritterhaus & Bella v Brochstreek
46	??? RS Bodo vd Radbach ??? v Fuchspass		ES Kobold Mauderode ??? KS Hussa vd Radbach KS Dux Ringsheim Cara Sudwest
	??? Furst v Fuchspass Opal v Hummling		KS Dux Ringsheim & Cara Sudwest Wodan Peppenhoven RS Gisela v Hummling
47	KS Junker Coldbeck Lotte Fuchsseipen		Artus Sand & Bessie v Hamelsberg KS Dux Ringsheim & Eren Mauderode-Westerholt
	KS Fred Sudwest ??? vd ???		Argus vd Weihermule & Drossel Sudwest KS Benno v Schlossgarten & Bicke v Schroterhof
48	Argus vd Weihermuhle Drossel Sudwest		Artus Sand & Bessie vd Weihermuhle KS Tasso v Winterhauch & Zilly Sudwest
	KS Kobold Mauderode-Westerholt KS Friedel Sudwest		KS Magnet v Ockerbach & Edda Mauderode-Westerholt KS Benno v Schlossgarten & Cori Sudwest
49	KS Don vd Schwarzen Kuhle Seigers Thea		Wodan Peppenhoven & Hertana Papinghausen Treff v Waldhausen & Herta Winzler
	Harro v Weserstrand Lea v Seckachtal		Rubin III Stdzen Au & Kleinchen Sentein v Hastedt Eurst v Frankenwald & Flora v Seckachtal
50	KS Junker Goldbeck Lotte Fuchsseipen		Artus Sand & Bessie v Hammelsberg KS Dux Ringsheim & Free Mauderode-Westerholt
	KS Frei Sudwest Hexe vd Lusshardt		Argus vd Weihermuhle & Drossel Sudwest KS Benno v Schlossgarten & Birke v Schroterhof
51	KS Marko v. Schaumberg Juno Freising		KS Kobold Mauderode-Westerholt & KS Kascha v Schlossgarten Harrasgern & Freya v Veitshof
	KS Claus v Veronikaberg KS Seigers Werra		KS Junker Goldbeck & Lotte Fuchsseipen Treff v Waldhausen & Dolly Heisenstein
52	KS Marko v Schaumberg Juno Freising		KS Kobold Mauderode-Westerholt & KS Kascha v Schlossgarten Harrasgern & Freya v Veitshof
	KS Kobold Mauderode-Westerholt Carin v Fuchspass		KS Magnet v Ockerbach & Edda Mauderode-Westerholt KS Junker v Bomlitzal & Cara Sudwest
53	KS Don vd Schwarzen Kuhle Jagers Hansa KS Furst v Fuchspass Frigga v Runenstein		Wodan Peppenhoven & Hertana Papinghausen Ajax Frankfurt-Main & Senta v Thalham
	KS Furst v Fuchspass Frigga v Runenstein		KS Dux Ringsheim & Cara Sudwest Prinz v Schlosshof & Biene v Ruenstein
54	Marko v Waldmoos Birke v Stockbach		KS Furst v Fuchspass & Frigga v Ruenstein KS Kobold Mauderode-Westerholt & Bessie v Groningen
	KS Furst v Fuchspass Frigga v Runenstein		KS Dux Ringsheim & Cara Sudwest Prinz v Schlosshof & Biene v Ruenstein
55	Artus Sand Bessie y Hamelsberg		Yelmos Gotz v Kauffungen & Ella Sand Borneblitz vd Bode & Hexe v Lenz

	Borneblitz vd Bode	Punsch vd Bode & Pitti vd Bode
	Tanna vd Bode	Artus Sand &
56	KS Junker Goldbeck	Artus Sand & Bessie v Hamelsberg
	Lotte Fuchssiepen	KS Dux Ringsheim & Erle Mauderode-Westerholt
	Arno v Juraalp	Greif v Schlossgarten & Trine (Haus Kallhardt)
	Bella v Sch Au Ins Land	KS Frei Sudwest & Ossi v Interlaken
57	KS Dux Ringsheim	Heido Holstenperle & Adda Ringsheim
	Cara Sudwest	Heide v Winterhauch & Trudel Sudwest
	Artus Sand	Yelmos Gotz v Kauffungen & Ella Sand
	Anni vd Forst Brickwedde	Treff Kalthof & Korya
58	KS & RS Bodo vd Radbach	KS Kobold Mauderode-Westerholt & KS Hussa vd Radbach
	Freya v Fuchspass	KS Dux Ringsheim & Cara Sudwest
	KS Furst v Fuchspass	KS Dux Ringsheim & Cara Sudwest
	Opal v Hummling	Wodan Peppenhoven & RS Gisela v Hummling
59	KS Magnet v Ockerbach	KS Junker v Bomlitztal & Eule v Runenstein
	Edda Mauderode-Westerholt	KS Rino Forst (Buir) & Aster-Mauderode
	Artus Sand	Yelmos Gotz v Kauffungen & Ella Sand
	Werra v Syratal	Atilla v Choren & Norita Syratal
60	KS Furst v Fuchspass	KS Dux Ringsheim & Cara Sudwest
	Cora vd Forst Brickwedde	Artus Sand & Anni vd Forst Brickwedde
	KS Furst v Fuchspass	KS Dux Ringsheim & Cara Sudwest
	Opal v Hummling	Wodan Peppenhoven & RS Gisela v Hummling
61	KS Rino v Schornbusch	Heido Holstenperle & Brune Ringsheim
	Asta Zieverich	Held v Farve & Minka v Parlshof
	KS Don vd Schwarzen Kuhle	Wodan Peppenhoven & Hertanna Papinghausen
	Berns Freya	Jagers Isgo & Amsel v Schornbusch
62	Treff v Waldhausen	Manfred v Waldhausen & Edda v Waldhausen
	Diana v Landsherrn	Etzel vd Beeke & Ilka v Landsherrn
	KS & RS Bodo vd Radbach	KS Kobold Mauderode-Westerholt & KS Hussa vd Radbach
	Bessie v Hamelsberg	Borneblitz vd Bode & Hexe v Lenzen
63	KS Kobold Mauderode-Westerholt	KS Magnet v Ockerbach & Edda Mauderode-Westerholt
	KS Hussa vd Radbach	Hasso v Nibelungenhort & Richa vd Radbach
	KS Dux Ringsheim	Heido Holstenperle & Adda Ringsheim
	Cara Sudwest	Heide v Winterhauch & Trudel Sudwest
64	KS Rino Forst (Buir)	Mars v Altenau & Forster's Senta
	Bella v Suppling	
	Taps v Usingen	
	Juno Odinshain	

Recall that:

Artus Sand was pointer endowed.

Mars Altenan's maternal great grandsire was a pointer.

K.S. Edelman Giftig's sire was said to have been a pointer.

(Addendum) Notes to ESSER'S CHICK'S Nine Generation Pedigree

The extended pedigree of an active stud is a useful reference for breeders, to denote the bloodlines of the performing/producing dogs used by the Germans for breeding purposes.

Chapters 2 through 8 of the book <u>The</u> <u>Complete</u> <u>German</u> <u>Shorthaired</u> <u>Pointer</u> by Herr H.F. Seiger and Dr. F. von Dewitz Colpin and chapters 1 through 4 of C. Bede Maxwell's book, <u>The</u> <u>New</u> <u>German</u> <u>Shorthaired</u> <u>Pointer</u> are most useful and meaningful when studying extended pedigrees of the better German bred dogs.

Artus Sand, Mars Altenau and their great grandson, KS Kobold Mauderode-Westerholt, are conceded to be the most famous of 20th century breed pillars. These and their famous progeny, along with KS Edelman Giftig and KS Michel v.d. goldenen Mark and their distinguished get, would be found many more times in a longer pedigree of ESSER'S CHICK.

Prinz Schlosshof-Artus Sand & Mars Altenau-Artus Sand are the paternal and maternal great grandsires respectively of <u>KS</u> <u>Kobold</u> <u>Mauderode</u>-<u>Westerholt</u>. <u>Prinz</u> <u>Schlosshof</u> is a Mars Altenau grandson.

Held v. Farve & Artus Sand are the paternal and maternal grandsires of <u>KS</u> <u>Dux</u> <u>Ringsheim</u>.

Hestas Arminius-KS Rino Weissertztal v.d. Wessnitz & Mars Altenau-Frey III v. Freithof are paternal and maternal great grandsires respectively of <u>KS</u> <u>Don</u> <u>v.d.</u> <u>Schwarzen</u> <u>Kuhle</u>.

Held v. Farve-Artus Sand & Trio Holstenperle-Artus v. Gottorp are the paternal and maternal great grandsires respectively of <u>KS</u> <u>Alf</u> <u>v.</u> <u>Manhagen</u>.

Treff v. Waldhausen is the sire and Artus Sand is the maternal grandsire of <u>WS</u> <u>&</u> <u>RS</u> <u>Heidi</u> <u>v.d.</u> <u>Beeke</u>.

KS Edelman Giftig (sire of Edelman v.d. goldenen Mark) and KS Michel v.d. goldenen Mark are great grandsires of Held v. Farve; and are the paternal and maternal grandsires of Eller v.d. goldenen Mark.

Mars Altenau and KS Edelman Giftig are paternal and maternal grandsires of Bornscheims Corela, whose sire is Prinz Schlosshof.

Mars Altenau is a double great grandsire and triple great great grandsire of WS Tell v. Wilsender Berg, the sire of Berka v. Muhlenfeld.

Artus Sand and Bob v. Winterhauch are the grandsires of Hexe v.d. Lusshardt.

Rino Altenau-Prinz v. Trauteck & Rino Altenau-KS Michel v.d. goldenen Mark are the paternal and maternal great grandsires respectively of Wodan Peppenhoven.

Mars Altenau, through his son, Heidi v. Esterhof, is the paternal grandsire of Bob, Heidi, and KS Tasso v. Winterhauch. Flott Durbo Mannheimia is their maternal grandsire. KS Edelman Giftig is a triple great grandsire.

Heido Holstenperle-KS Claus v. Fuchspass & Bob v. Winterhauch-Mars v. Winterhauch are the paternal and maternal great grandsires respectively of Loni Sudwest.

Mars Altenau and Flott Durbo-Mannheimia are the paternal great grandsires of Cara Sudwest.—Her sire and dam are Heidi v. Winterhauch and Trudel Sudwest.

Panther v. Wittekind (KS & RS Bodo v.i. Radbach x-Senta v. Wittekind)

Atilla v. Choren (Treu Altenbach x-Herta Hofchwichelt)

Argo v. Samborn (Tiro v.d. goldenen Mark x-Heidi Harno)

Hestas Arminius (Rino Altenau x-Hestas Erna)

Lutjenburgerin-gennant Zilla (Widu v.d. goldenen Mark x-Vilga Gross Rode)

Adda Kingsheim (Artus Sand x-Pille Sand)

Widu v.d. goldenen Mark (a son of Edelman v.d. goldenen Mark) is the paternal and maternal grandsire of Trio, Heido, and Diana Holstenperle.

Best Pup of the Year made a champion later

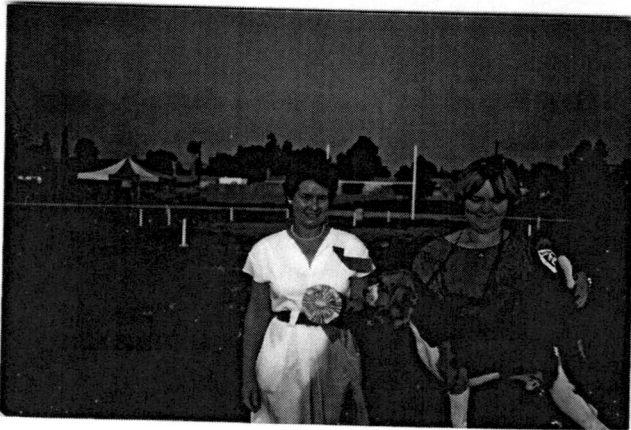

Subject: follow on history

Date: Saturday, 6 April 2013, 15:53

wo
at working still do working test field trials judged Scotland Ireland
and wales chosen for basc team and won clgame fair was secound
at clgame fair team and again fourth won the international weekend
with missdaisy for team for england won 50th anniversary weekend
working test deepthatch lovesong and second at 60th anniversary

SHOOTTING OVER VISZLASMR JIM FIELD HUNTING DOWN IN ARIZONA

HUNTING DOWN IN ARIZONA HALF AMILE FROM MEXICO WITH 2 OF BILL WYSSES VISZLAS/////

At Simi Valley Kennel Club Ruby Field Judge and
Karen Detterrich Bob group 4 with Paledin Sydney

first visit to judge in usa///

JUDGED AT SIMI VALLEYGSPS MY BEST OF BREEDWENT 4TH IN GROUP ENCLOSED GSP SOLID LIVER. THE DAY BEFORE I JUDGED PUP OF THE YEAR BAR 2 GROUPS NEXT DAY PUT UP OVERHALL WINNER DALMATION//// ENCLOSED PICTURES FROM PUP OF THE YEAR AND ENCLOSED THE MARKS OF MY JUDGING BY SOMEONE MARKING ME ONE TO SHOW SECRETARY ONE TO AKC AND ONE TO ME.///1988////

Kentisnorth Lark Jonguil son in U.S.A.

PARDAILLAN IMAGE OF DEEPTHATCH LOVELY DOG TO
OWN IN SHOW AND WORK WORKING TEST WINNER 2 C.C

DEEPTHATCH PARDAILLAN

Left hand side Mr Jim Field with Deepthatch Lovesong
and right hand side Fellicity Jafe with Deeptatch
Jezebel top winner but Lovesong took over

Lightning Source UK Ltd.
Milton Keynes UK
UKOW04n2013250215

246914UK00001B/13/P